# Contents

# Growth in Reading

Proceedings of the fifteenth annual course and conference
of the United Kingdom Reading Association
Nene College, Northampton, 1978

E

W ard Lock Educational

ISBN 0 7062 3862 1

First published 1979

SB11636. 76.50. 10 79

Set in 11 on 12 point Garamond by
Jubal Multiwrite Ltd, Lewisham SE13 7SN
and printed by Biddles of Guildford, Guildford, Surrey
for Ward Lock Educational
116 Baker Street, London W1M 2BB
A member of the Pentos Group
Made in Great Britain

# Foreword

The fifteenth annual course and conference of the United Kingdom Reading Association was held at Nene College, Northampton from 24–28 July 1978.

The Conference was concerned with the ways in which true growth and development in reading ability can be encouraged at all ages and stages. All the important theoretical and practical aspects of reading were considered in lecture, seminar and workshop sessions. This volume unfortunately can contain only a selection of the many excellent papers presented but on behalf of UKRA I wish to thank all contributors to the Conference programme for giving so freely of their time, energy and expertise in order to make the Conference such a valuable experience for the delegates attending.

Since the publication of the Bullock Report *A Language for Life* there has been a clear determination on the part of all concerned with the teaching of reading to raise the standards of literacy at all levels and it is hoped that this volume will help to encourage, and point the way towards, continuous growth in reading.

*Derek Thackray*
President 1977–78

# Part 1

# Growth in reading

# 1 Growth in reading

## Derek Thackray

The main purpose of my Presidential Address, which opens the Fifteenth Annual Course and Conference of the United Kingdom Reading Association, is to introduce the theme *Growth in Reading* and to set the scene for the programme of plenary, general, international and workshop sessions that are to follow this week. In following this purpose I plan to take a brief look at certain aspects of reading from the beginning stage upwards and so inevitably I will only be able to touch upon the aspects of reading I include, and many important aspects will not be mentioned. However, I have included most aspects of reading in the Conference Programme and during the week there will be an opportunity of studying topics of your choice in greater depth.

The title of the Conference was chosen to underline the generally accepted view that growth in reading, implying improvement in reading standards, reading materials, reading methods and knowledge about reading, is an important goal, and all participants have been asked to indicate how the development in their thinking about reading, or their research findings, can help us all towards this growth. Our final plenary session will focus on the way forward towards our goal.

Since the Bullock Report (DES 1975) the argument as to whether standards of reading in recent years have fallen or not has abated, but all concerned with reading agree that the reading skills of many children are not being developed and extended as they should, and that reading abilities of many school leavers are inadequate for the tasks expected of them. For example, we know that many secondary children do not have the book reading habit by the time they reach fourteen years of age; we know that a large proportion of school leavers do not reach a level of functional literacy; and we suspect that some two million adults are not functionally literate. Much needs to be done in our schools with regard to functional literacy but this is just one aspect of the problem: another important aspect concerns the readability levels of the day-to-day documents and leaflets put out by Government departments and professional organizations.

Williams (1976) reminds us that '60 per cent of our information is still communicated by reading' and points out that many of the important documents that all should be able to read and understand have readability levels beyond the capabilities of many of our school leavers: for example, the Highway Code needs a reading age of thirteen years; the income tax form fifteen years; the average hire purchase agreement too high to be calcualted. (The FOG Readability Graph was used for these calculations.) In the same context, more recently Barrow (1978) indicates that the first ten items compiled from categories of reading material rated most essential are dosage warnings, danger/warning signs, emergency procedures, traffic direction signs, official forms, job application forms, wage-slips, legal documents, first-aid instructions and the Highway Code. Readability levels again on the FOG Readability Graph for these items range from nine years to eighteen years. It is not surprising to learn of the opening of shops in the High Street staffed by voluntary workers for the express purpose of helping people to fill in their forms. This is one way of tackling this problem, but a more positive way is that of the Impact Trust in Liverpool, which works to produce the usual forms with lower readability levels.

Since the Great Debate and the Green Paper, much thought and writing has been centred on the curriculum in general, and literacy and numeracy in particular. Because of the thrust towards basic skills there is pressure to return to more formal, more highly-structured educational situations. Some movement in this direction could be beneficial for growth in reading, but there is the danger that too great a stress on the mechanical mastery of the basic skills might mean loss in understanding and application of these skills, and artistic, creative and scientific skills might be undervalued.

After the 1972 White Paper, the DES set up a nursery

research programme and at the same time the Social Science Research Council, the NFER and the Schools Council earmarked grants for pre-school research. This has meant the undertaking of a comprehensive study of nursery schools and playgroups, ironically at a time when the nursery sector has been subjected to severe spending cuts and we have tragic examples of new nursery schools and classes built and equipped but not manned.

With the newer projects has come a change in the style of research in the pre-school areas. Earlier researches, typified by the American Headstart project and more recently by NFER's project (Woodhead 1977) concerning compensatory education for disadvantaged children, used structured programmes designed to improve a narrow range of language and perceptual skills, and established the usual experimental and control groups to assess the efficacy of the programmes. For example, in the NFER project, teachers used a modified version of the Peabody Kit with groups of children for twenty minutes every day. At the end of the programme the experimental groups did better in various tests than the control group, but when the children were followed into their infant schools the advantages disappeared. These findings were typical of those in many of the Headstart programmes, but in recent months we have been invited to look again at experiments of this kind in the light of the effects in the long term rather than in the short term.

Despite the disappointing results just mentioned there is still a strong feeling that the traditional nursery school curriculum should be analysed with a view to improvement, and so the new-style nursery projects in hand are moving into the delicate area of nursery curriculum reform. Most of the research projects are starting out with observation, both of teachers and children. Research workers are trying to find out what happens in nursery schools and classes; what teachers' objectives are; what strategies they use; what materials they use; how the work is divided between teacher and nursery nurses; and what parental involvement there is. Again, many research workers are following up, by developing and using new materials and developing and using new strategies, and trying out changes in organization and curriculum that might make nursery schools more effective in developing the abilities of young children.

More and more, following the Plowden goal, we are taking parents into the educational partnership, but to do this effectively at the nursery level teachers have to sell parents their views that the child's nursery experiences *are* educational and persuade parents to reinforce them in appropriate ways. Tizzard, in an article in the *Times Educational Supplement* (March 1978) under the title 'Carry on communicating' points out from her research that there is often profound misunderstanding between teachers and parents regarding the value and purpose of nursery activities. Within the next year or two there should be a clear indication about the needs of parents and young children and the ways in which children's intelligence and abilities can be developed. It is to be hoped that resources will be diverted to pre-school children on a sufficiently large scale to put the knowledge to use and encourage growth in this vital area.

Moving on to the early stages of reading, we can take a brief look at reading readiness and early reading materials. With regard to reading readiness the Bullock Report (DES 1975) has finally laid the myth of waiting for children to be ready to read. No longer must teachers wait for readiness to occur – they must take positive measures to induce it. However, this change of emphasis – with more stress on learning and teaching and less on maturation and waiting – puts greater responsibility on the teacher and this must be realized and accepted. If reception-class teachers have actively to develop children's reading-readiness skills to the stage when they are ready for reading, then they must know the skills and abilities the children bring to the school situation, so some kind of early assessment of important reading-readiness abilities is necessary so the teacher knows which children need which kinds of pre-reading activities. For example, research has indicated quite clearly that many children come to school with adequate powers of visual discrimination for learning to read, and that where visual-discrimination training is needed then the matching of words and letters are the activities most valuable as they are closely related to the beginning-reading tasks. However, we find reception classes where nearly all the children are having visual-discrimination training and much of this involves the matching of shapes, pictures and other visual material unrelated to reading. So an early appraisal of the young child's reading-readiness skills and abilities will enable the teacher to provide more effective pre-reading programmes for her children, and is a vital part of the reception-class teacher's work.

To help the reception-class teacher in this task of appraising her children's skills and abilities a number of measures have been published, and a number produced by local authorities; and at the present time we have a wide selection of checklists, inventories and tests – some from birth, most from when the child enters school. An additional advantage of the appearance of checklists is that of reminding or informing teachers of all the important considerations making for readiness, but we must always remember firstly that checklists will be most valuable when devised by the teachers who are going to use them and, secondly, appropriate action must follow the completion of a checklist.

I mentioned earlier about parental involvement and before leaving the reading-readiness area it is interesting to note that the parents of Clark's (1976) *Young Fluent Readers* were all outstanding in the interest and pleasure they showed in their children's attainment and in the value they placed on education. In the children there was an unusual interest in, and awareness of, symbols, particularly language symbols, and an ability to retain and recall speech sequences and discriminate meanings.

With regard to which philosophy to follow at the beginning-reading stage, in recent years descriptions of the reading process have tended to stress the psycholinguistic or 'whole task' approach at the expense of the presentation of reading as a hierarchy of skills to be developed in some kind of sequential order. This change of emphasis has come about for at least three main reasons: firstly, because of the questioning by many writers of the importance attached to the ordering of skills in some kind of hierarchy; secondly, because of the questioning to the extent to which these skills when learned can be transferred to other situations; and thirdly, because the ideas of Smith (1971) and Goodman (1970) are now becoming well known and understood by teachers.

With regard to the criticism of the concept of a hierarchy of skills, a flavour of the arguments can be given by mentioning one or two researches. MacFarlane (1976) points out that we cannot assume transfer of one skill in literacy to another, and we cannot assume transfer to other real-life reading situations. Clark (1976) makes the point that the steps which are frequently regarded as sequential are so only because of the structure within which we *teach* reading rather than the pattern within which children *learn* to read. She points out the dangers of assuming that the way we teach is the way children learn. It would seem that taxonomies are models for understanding, not teaching; that development is not linear but that an ordering of patterns of needs, which differ from child to child, is probably more likely than one particular linear process. Evidence from Schools Council projects leads us to question a strict hierarchy of skills. Arnold (1977) states that the results of the measures in the *Extending Beginning Reading* project refutes this hierarchy, as children used *all* levels of language simultaneously in order to decode the words, and they tended to use their strengths which could not be the case in the sequential model of reading. Lunzer and Gardner (1978) in discussing findings from the *Effective Use of Reading* project suggest that comprehension is not a composite of many subskills but rather that comprehension is something unitary and rather than a skill it is an aptitude which relies on a skill. The question of transfer of skill was raised by some findings from this project: for example, knowing about study skills did not mean they would be put into practice.

Regarding this question of 'whole task' or skills hierarchy approach, in the United States the two schools of thought are tending to polarize and it is interesting that President MacGinitie in his Report to the Annual Delegates' Meeting of IRA in May 1977 felt a policy statement was necessary as an expression of the Board's belief that basic reading ability involves *much* more than decoding skills. He stated:

Word analysis skills, including phonics, are critical to learning to read. However IRA cannot support the position that reading instruction is defined primarily in terms of subskills. Effective instruction must account for word analysis as a means to the larger end goal of meaning and application.

I think this policy statement is one to which many teachers of reading in this country would subscribe. In the past there may have been too much emphasis on reading as a precise process involving exact detailed sequential perception and identification of letters and too little emphasis on reading as a psycholinguistic process involving the interaction of language and thought. But although reading for meaning is of paramount importance, the distinctive features of letters and words are needed to identify a word from a range of possibilities and for anticipation rather than guessing. Today's approach should be a balanced one, integrating these two philosophies with the development of all reading skills at every level but with differing degrees of emphasis on each skill as the child's reading ability develops.

With regard to reading materials, Roberts (1975) summarizes the weaknesses in the present-day reading schemes that were mentioned in the Bullock Report:

> Lack of any effective framework for the systematic development of word analysis and word identification; the lack of sequence and logical development in the text; the ill-thought-out use of illustrations, many of which distract rather than aid the child in his reading, and the paucity of ideas and their irrelevance to many children. However the discussion is so convoluted that the reader is left with a general idea that all is not well, but with no clearly enunciated picture of what should be done about it.

The Bullock Committee's definition of a good reading scheme is 'one which provides a sound basis for the development of all the reading skills in an integrated way'. To produce such a scheme is clearly a formidable task when one adds to the usual list of criteria parental roles, sex roles, cultural roles, attitudes to authority, and the extent to which the syntactic structures not only relate to the pattern of spoken language familiar to the child, but also develop the child's knowledge and use of more complex language structures. With the increasing difficulty of producing a good reading scheme and in face of mounting evidence that

14

more and more teachers are structuring and sequencing their own resources rather than following a ready-made solution from the publishers, it is often asked if here is a future for the reading scheme? It can be argued that there is still a place for the reading scheme, particularly in the early stages. Many teachers would agree that a sound beginning can be made using a reading scheme where the reading readiness and pre-reading activities develop the knowledge of the words, characters, concepts and skills that are going to feature in the first books of the reading scheme. In many schemes, some emphasis is placed on the controlled intake and adequate repetition of vocabulary, and the use of children's natural language structures, and therefore the use of books from *more* than one or two such schemes, undermines the value of these criteria. In the later stages teachers may never again rely completely on *one* scheme, but as books in a reading scheme have been graded carefully in so many ways they are suitable for interleaving with books in other schemes to produce a varied but structured reading programme.

When a child has completed a reading scheme or programme we begin considering extending reading and comments on the Schools Council project *Extending Beginning Reading* from seven to nine years would have been the obvious starting point, but at present the final research results have not yet been published and to the best of my knowledge not a great deal has been published along the way apart from articles appearing in our Conference Proceedings, written by Arnold (1977), Southgate (1976) and Southgate, Arnold and Johnson (1978). In personal communication Southgate mentioned important features of the research: firstly, the involvement of practising teachers and the valuable contribution they have made to the research work; and secondly, the nature of the research which has moved away from 'extensive' study – gaining a small amount of information about large numbers of children – to intensive study – the study of a small number of schools in depth, thereby gaining a great deal of information about fewer subjects. From published comments we can draw a few tentative pointers to some of the probable findings. There is some evidence that junior teachers look back to infant-school approaches rather than forward to the model of the skilled reader, and instructions and practice in phonic rules feature strongly in their teaching of reading. With regard to the phonic ability of the children in the sample it may well be found that a percentage of them were not familiar with the sounds of the common digraphs and other phonic rules.

It seems that many junior teachers are fairly good at estimating the level of reading ability of their children when comparisons are made with scores on the Word Recognition Tests. One statistically significant finding in this area was an overestimation of girls' and an underestimation of boys' level of reading ability compared with actual scores on the Schonell Word Reading Test. Again there seems to be some evidence that the assessment of reading progress from seven to nine years is carried out so informally and spasmodically that it is almost non-existent. Reading ages are usually gained from standardized Word Recognition Tests often administered annually by the headteacher at the request of the LEA, and there is little ongoing record keeping in the primary school. It would be interesting to look at the extent of the use of cumulative records in the primary school after another year or two, to see the effect of the Bullock Report's recommendations for language development and the systematic monitoring of children's progress.

There have also been a number of interesting findings concerning the levels of difficulty of the books which average children were reading in school; for example, as many as half the children in first and second year junior classes were reading, under their teachers' direction, books which they could profitably read on their own without any assistance. This kind of evidence will merit careful scrutiny when the Report is published.

Moving on to the middle years of schooling, most would agree that these are the years where growth in reading and language development is clearly needed. An analysis of the evidence, gained from surveys carried out mainly by the Bullock Committee and for the Schools Council projects indicates that secondary-school pupils generally do a great deal of listening and very little talking, do very little reading for pleasure, are confronted with books in the content areas which in the early stages are probably too hard for them to read and in the later stages too easy, do a great deal of transactional writing, have very few lessons in the reading of non-narrative tasks, have few lessons to teach them the necessary study skills to deal with the work demanded of them, read in tiny bursts which prevents the mastery of reading skills which are developed more through continuous reading and often are helped to avoid reading by teachers who paraphrase, simplify and use symbolic language. Although the picture looks rather bleak, comfort can be taken from the fact that any intervention is likely to improve reading and language skills and we must look for, and work for, growth in the secondary area.

The Schools Council Report on the *Effective Use of Reading* indicates some of the ways forward. Throughout the report the point is stressed that to get a child to learn by reading he must be motivated to read, must be interested in what he is reading and virtually know what is there to start with. Therefore, before the child reads, interest should be created, the concepts should be developed and the background discussed – then he will have a better chance of understanding what he reads. From the evidence the report presents, there must be a more careful matching between the capability of the reader and the readability of the text he is expected to read, and text here includes workcards which are often overlooked. However, when we know from research, for example the recent work of Stokes (1978), that not only do different readability formulae give different age levels for the same passage, but that when using one formula the age levels of passages from the same text vary widely, then the matching mentioned above presents a challenging task which only computers may help us to resolve.

The *Effective Use of Reading* project looked at the use and effect of certain reading materials and reading techniques, in particular the use of *SRA Laboratories* and group-discussion techniques such as group Cloze, group SQ3R, group sequencing, group prediction and group reading for different purposes. With regard to the use of *SRA Laboratories*, the investigation showed that, used systematically by a teacher conversant with the system, they contributed to the growth in reading ability of most average and above-average readers. Highly significant gains in reading comprehension were obtained, and these gains were sustained during a reasonable post-test period. With regard to the group-discussion techniques it was not possible to apply completely objective measures of assessment but in *one* study situation, children responded well, revealed the ability to think about their reading, and teachers noted an improvement in the quality of pupils' reflection on their reading, a feature the report stresses many times.

So with the publication of this important report we can study the ways in which we can best help pupils in the middle years to *read for learning*. The one danger is that some teachers may use these group techniques because they think it is now the thing to do, without fully understanding what the objectives are. If this were the case they could quickly become sterile exercises of the kind we have discarded in the past.

Looking in more general terms at secondary education we can consider the effects of the Bullock recommendations concerning language across the curriculum. It is encouraging to note that the Bullock Report is one report that has not been shelved. Most LEAs have taken some kind of action, such as calling meetings of headteachers and teachers to discuss its recommendations and how they can be implemented. One or two authorities, such as ILEA, have asked its schools to state in written form their individual language programmes and clear guidelines have been given to help schools in the preparation of the programmes. As a result of this kind of action there are now published language programmes, for example Hunter (1977), which can be studied by all interested. A number of organizations such as NUT, NATE and UKRA responded positively to the Bullock Report and, by publishing commentaries or guidelines, and by organizing lectures and conferences, they have tried to help their members to implement the recommendations.

The Schools Council has been active and continues to be active in this area and there are now under way a number of useful projects. The project *Language Across the Curriculum* stems directly from the Bullock Report, and is undertaking a series of case studies of schools trying to implement Bullock. The English Committee of the Schools Council has identified a number of possible research projects related to aspects of language across the curriculum, and the new three-year project *Reading for Learning in Secondary Schools (12–15)* directed by Lunzer and Gardner stems directly from their recently completed research.

Although a great deal of interesting work is going on aimed at translating into practical terms Bullock's central tenets that 'learning and the acquisition of language are interlocked' there is a danger that development may take the somewhat more narrow view that language development relates mainly to materials, activities, syllabuses, lesson sequences and forms of organization. The recent working paper produced by Her Majesty's Inspectorate under the title *Curriculum 11–16* (DES 1977), and particularly the one on language, is a timely document to encourage us to keep in mind a much broader view of language and language teaching. This is not a document that can easily be summarized, but one or two comments from the section on language might give the flavour of the thinking. The paper argues the case for a linguistic education, much of the responsibility for which lies in the school as a community. It comments:

> Pupils aged 11–16 need help in understanding the relevant features of many kinds of language that touch people's lives – their grammars, certainly, but also the reasons for their grammars which lie in the context of their use – in the nature and purpose of the task, the nature of the 'audience', the relationship of the speaker and writer with the audience, and the 'match' between language and context. The subject matter of English will be the study and production of language in variety, and the discovery of similarity, difference and pattern. The English teacher will so contrive matters that his pupils will extend their understanding and control of varieties of language while reading and writing about experiences and subjects which interest them.

And now a brief look at remedial education and the Adult Literacy Scheme. The Bullock Report pointed out that 69 per cent of the teachers teaching remedial groups are part-timers, many of whom have no recent experience of teaching reading and no inservice training to prepare them. There is no reason to think this situation has changed since the Report and all concerned with teaching in this area consider the situation unsatisfactory. Help should be given at the outset of the difficulty rather than after the child has fallen behind, and this help should be given by experienced qualified full-time teachers on a one-to-one basis. Bearing in mind these criteria it can be understood why the NUT are unhappy about schemes involving the use of sixth-form pupils as substitute teachers of reading for remedial children in lower forms. It is encouraging to note that more and more LEAS are developing screening procedures to establish those children who are at risk with regard to reading and other aspects of development, and the emphasis in remedial work is moving towards the preventative aspects of the work instead of seeing it as a rescue operation for those retarded in basic subjects. Remedial education should be concerned with prevention, investigation and treatment of learning problems from whatever cause, which hinders normal educational development.

The other encouraging development in this area is the change in the nature of the work of the remedial teachers. Remedial services are becoming reading services; remedial teachers are becoming reading advisers, working in all kinds of schools, giving advice and information to staff on all aspects of reading and setting up programmes at different levels and with groups of differing abilities. With limited resources this must be the way ahead as everything eventually depends on the diagnostic skill of the classroom teacher who, in this way, can be helped to play a more effective part in helping children with difficulties.

The Adult Literacy campaign has been remarkably successful since its inception in April 1975. In 1973, 5,000 adults were thought to be receiving literacy tuition. Just before the Adult Literacy Resource Agency wound up its work recently the DES put the number at *100,000*, and between 200 and 300 students are still coming forward each week. The thousands of volunteer teachers gained as much from the experiment as the people they taught, and all agree that in spite of some difficulties the BBC played a key role. It is interesting to note the new BBC project which started in Autumn 1977 aimed at teaching Asians, especially women, to speak English is being organized on similar lines. Kedney (1978) points out the difficulties in playing the numbers game with regard to how many adult illiterates there are, but certainly most careful research workers would accept a level of about one million and of course much higher figures are regularly quoted.

The Adult Literacy Unit has now taken over ALRA's work with a much smaller budget. But the Adult Literacy Unit is scheduled to finish its life in two years' time, when it is hoped the newly formed Advisory Council for Adult and Continuing Education will have plans for the continuation of adult literacy tuition but in the wider context of adult education generally. The Adult Literacy campaign has been a success story and it is vital that, in the broader context of a strategy for adult basic education, the adult illiterates now coming forward in growing numbers are not failed. We must press for LEAs to make continuing provision because as Devereux (1978), ALRA's former director, points out, the one outstanding failure of the campaign is not winning for LEAs a specific literacy grant.

With regard to the assessment and testing of reading ability there is little doubt that many schools and authorities are now actively interested in testing and in a recent survey reported in the *Times Educational Supplement* (October 1977) under the title 'What Do Teachers Think?' a majority of teachers in England and Wales were in favour of regular national tests for all children. At least ten LEAs have now established some sort of authority-wide testing programme and others are discovering what ought to be done. The Bullock Committee was dissatisfied with the established series of national monitoring exercises of reading ability and felt most tests used were inadequate as 'what they measure is a narrow aspect of silent reading comprehension'. There is no new evidence to suggest LEAs are using better kinds of tests and there is evidence to suggest the silent reading comprehension-type test is still the one most frequently used. It is for this reason that one looks hopefully towards the monitoring of language project at the NFER sponsored by the Assessment of Performance Unit which forms an important part of the Government's plan for assessment of national performance.

The initial task of the language monitoring team is to develop materials for regular surveys. Proposals for the assessment of reading and writing have been developed over two years, emphasizing the various uses of language skills across the school curriculum. Once the test materials have been developed they will form a bank of questions. Subsets of these will be given to relatively small samples of eleven and fifteen year olds in a succession of surveys. Over a period of time this approach will provide more and more accurate indications of national trends and this will be with a wider array of assessment criteria than could be applied in a single survey or to a single pupil. The first survey is scheduled for 1979 and is expected to involve a maximum of 15,000 children in each age group.

In the course of these surveys a programme of continuous development and updating of tests will be carried out, and in this way materials and techniques which cease to be relevant because of changes in curriculum, teaching methods or patterns of language, can be discarded and replaced by more appropriate, but statistically equivalent, ones.

The working group has already identified a number of tasks suitable for assessment at ages eleven and fifteen both for *writing*, for example responses to pictures, auto-biographical narrative, fiction, and for *reading*, for example to obtain information, to gain overall impression, to follow detailed instruction. But identifying tasks is not the same as assessing them, and it is the NFER team that is exercised as to how to measure some of these tasks. The team will also have to devise methods of assessment that will hold good as between different assessors and assessors in different years, and standardize the conditions under which work is carried out and data collected. Both analytical marking, where assessors are concerned with the occurrence of specific features, and impression marking, where the overall quality of a piece of work is judged, will be used. Impression marking is always fraught with difficulty, as a list of criteria will have to be established. Once the materials are available schools and LEAs should be encouraged to use them, even when not in the sample, as they must be weaned away from the one or two word recognition tests, and the one or two silent reading tests of comprehension which still seem to predominate in our schools.

To conclude my address I would like to say a few words about our Association, as all here are members, and Associations like ours concerned with literacy play an important part in the thrust towards Growth in Reading. My involvement in the work of the National Executive and its six committees, my visits throughout the year to Local Councils, my visit as your representative to the IRA Convention in Houston in May, and my many contacts with individual members of the Association have convinced me, in no uncertain terms, that in spite of some of its inefficiencies, UKRA is an organization which is well respected, very active and which is having a steadily growing influence on education in general and in the teaching of reading and language in particular. During my year of office I have been impressed, not only by the valuable work of Local Councils in helping their members to increase their knowledge about reading, but also by the efforts many of our members are making, on an individual basis. They are working to improve the quality of reading instruction in the classroom, of reading materials of all kinds at all levels, of reading tests and assessment procedures, of teacher-training programmes, of TV and radio programmes, of research study and ideas about reading. These individual members are obviously working for their various institutions but nevertheless are also working for the Association in that their work is aimed at improving standards of literacy at all levels.

We are now an Association of nearly fifteen years' standing and with the establishment of the Permanent Secretariat, we have reached a new stage in our growth. I am proud and privileged to be your President at this time and I hope that each one of you in some small way is also proud to belong to an Association that is dedicated to such a worthwhile cause. May I thank you all for your continuing support and work for the Association, and may I sincerely wish you all a very happy and rewarding week.

## References

ARNOLD, H. (1977) 'Teachers' perception of their pupils' reading ability' in J. Gilliland (Ed) *Reading: Research and Classroom Practice* Ward Lock Educational

BARROW, W. (1978) 'What adults read – implications for literacy' in D. Moyle (Ed) *Perspectives on Adult Literacy* UKRA

CLARK, M. M. (1976) *Young Fluent Readers* Heinemann Educational

DES (1975) *A Language for Life* (Bullock Report) HMSO

DES (1977) *Curriculum 11–16* HMSO

DEVEREUX, W. A. (1978) 'The work of the adult literacy resource agency' in D. Moyle (Ed) *Perspectives on Adult Literacy* UKRA

GOODMAN, K. S. (1970) 'Reading: a psycholinguistic guessing game' in H. Singer and R. B. Ruddell (Eds) *Theoretical Models and Processes of Reading* Newark, Delaware: International Reading Association

HUNTER, E. (1977) *Reading Skills: A Systematic Approach* Council for Educational Technology

KEDNEY, R. J. (1978) 'Adult literacy and the numbers game' in D. Moyle (Ed) *Perspectives on Adult Literacy* UKRA

LUNZER, E. A. and GARDNER, K. (Eds) (1978) *The Effective Use of Reading* Heinemann Educational

MACFARLANE, T. (1976) Reading skills: automatic transfer up a hierarchy *Reading* 10, 3, 12–19

ROBERTS, G. (1975) Early reading *Reading* 9, 2, 14–23

SMITH, F. (1971) *Understanding Reading* New York: Holt, Rinehart and Winston

SOUTHGATE, V. (1976) 'Extending beginning reading' in A. Cashdan (Ed) *The Content of Reading* Ward Lock Educational

SOUTHGATE, V., ARNOLD, H. and JOHNSON, S. (1978) 'The use of teachers' and children's time in *Extending Beginning Reading*' in E. Hunter-Grundin and H.V. Grundin (Eds) *Reading: Implementing the Bullock Report* Ward Lock Educational

STOKES, A. (1978) The reliability of readability formula *Journal of Research in Reading* 1, 1, 21–34

TIZZARD, M. (1978) Carry on communicating *Times Educational Supplement* (March)

WILLIAMS, A. (1976) *Reading and the Consumer* Hodder and Stoughton

WOODHEAD, M. (Ed) (1977) *An Experiment in Nursery Education* NFER

# Part 2

# Issues and problems

# 2 Reading, grammar and the line

## David Crystal

There are now several subjects with 'linguistics' as part of their titles which promise to make a contribution to our understanding of the nature of reading. Psycholinguistics is perhaps the most widely known, focusing as it does on the processes underlying the production and comprehension of language. Sociolinguistics is perhaps less widely known in this field, but has considerable potential in its concern to specify the functions of language in relation to different social situations. As a third example, there is neuro-linguistics, where recent attention has been increasingly directed towards the investigation of language disorders. Because of their interdisciplinary orientation, such approaches are likely to be able to provide models of reading that are more explanatory than any single subject, such as linguistics or psychology, alone. Nonetheless, my aims in the present paper are restricted to aspects of linguistic study as such. My justification is that, despite the attraction of model-building at an interdisciplinary level, a great deal of elementary spadework of a purely descriptive kind needs to be done and this in the first instance needs to be considered on its own terms. A theory is only as valid as the data it accounts for and it is a matter of concern that much of the data of reading still remains undescribed. Indeed, in several cases, it is unclear whether we would agree as to what the nature of the data should be; and there would certainly be disagreement over the terminological means we should choose in order to describe it.

As a linguist, then, I do not see it as my job to construct a model of the reading process, but I am anxious that when people try to do so they pay proper attention to the need to describe the linguistic elements of such a model precisely and comprehensively. Linguistic study has two obvious roles in relation to reading. First, it is needed in order to specify the nature of the input to the reader. This will include a description of the text to be read, as well as of the nature of the language available in the reader which he can bring to bear on the task (his prior language acquisition, in the case of the child). Second, it is needed to specify the nature of the reader's output, in descriptions of the process of reading aloud, of his writing, or of his derived linguistic behaviour (such as his responses to a comprehension task). In each of these areas, the need for precise descriptions is still paramount. It is still often difficult to compare pieces of research because the nature of the linguistic variables has been insufficiently specified. For instance, let it be agreed that one should 'read for meaning'; but what is the nature of the units of meaning out of which a text is constructed? Let it be agreed that a measure of readability will include a test of comprehension of some kind; but again, what are the units in the text which lead to a particular judgment being made? There are several such questions.

To illustrate this point, it is not necessary to go into great detail within branches of linguistic enquiry, but simply to concentrate on the major distinctions which need to be made. By using no more than the old three-level model of language (reviewed in Crystal (1976) for instance) a great deal can be said. This model sees language as comprising: meaning (*semantics*), *grammar* (morphology and syntax), and mode of transmission (writing and speech, in particular, analysed in terms of graphology and phonology respectively). The questions which the reading analyst has to ask are how far these levels are useful in clarifying the structure of the input and output data referred to above, and whether one can establish any interesting correlations between them, in relation to the reader's response to his text. It is important to phrase the questions in terms of reading response. It will not necessarily be the case that the insights into the nature of spoken language gained by applying these levels wil be paralleled when they are applied to the written language. The latter must be studied afresh, in its own terms. (It is perhaps ironic that, after several decades of linguists arguing for the necessity to study speech without reference to the written language, one must now stress that studies of the written language must also be independent, without prejudging issues in terms of the study of speech.)

The need for comprehensiveness is referred to above. I have been unable to find any reasonably comprehensive account of what is involved, even at a descriptive level. As a starting point, let me take a recent statement of the way in which print is said to be organized. It is part of the discussion of levels of response to print in the original Open University course PE261 (Unit 5, p.9). They specify five main levels: (i) letter; (ii) letter cluster; (iii) word; (iv) sentence; (v) paragraph. These levels, it would seem, they see to be organized hierarchically, in that they increase in the amount of information they carry, and seem to be in a relationship of inclusion (a paragraph consists of sentences, which consist of words, and so on). Also 'other levels could be added, such as the phrase, the clause and the chapter or story'. Ultimately, of course, it will be necessary to try to define the nature of the differential behavioural responses which such a series presumes to relate to, but in the first instance it is more important to ask the question, How far is this set of units a coherent or comprehensive account of textual organization?

It takes little reflection to see that units are neither coherent nor comprehensive. To begin with, the units recognized above are based on different criteria. There is not a single hierarchy here at all, but bits of different hierarchies. Putting this another way, the nature of the 'information' varies from level to level, as can be seen by using the language model referred to above:

1    Letter and letter cluster: this is purely graphological progression (though some might argue that semantic analysis is directly applicable to some clusters, as in the suggestion of sound symbolism).

2    Word and sentence (clause, phrase, etc.): this is a series of grammatical distinctions, in the first instance; some semantic correspondences are involved, and some reference is needed to graphology for some of the units (word and sentence, using spacing and punctuation).

3    Paragraph, chapter, story, etc: this is a primarily graphological progression, with a major semantic

correspondence involved; much recent research has been devoted to the attempt to apply grammatical techniques also to the analysis of these larger stretches of language ('text' or 'discourse' analysis), but so far with limited success (see Sinclair and Coulthard 1975).

4   If the correlation with phonology is to be introduced, as several views of reading would insist, then we are faced with a varying interdependence – strong, in the case of letters and clusters; less strong, in the case of words and sentences; and almost absent elsewhere. The point is taken up below.

Several textbooks operate with a notion of organizational levels similar to the above, though often lacking in detail. 'Letter/word/sentence' is a sufficient sequence for many writers. But it is doubtful whether this kind of selection is very meaningful or coherent, if more than a single continuum is involved, and thus more than one type of response pattern expected. On the other hand, the notion of 'levels of organization' seems to be an intuitively important one to be able to salvage, as it is one way in which the concept of 'reading response' might be made more specific. Let us then see what happens if the linguistic criteria above are applied systematically. All four dimensions will be relevant – graphological, phonological, semantic and grammatical. It will make sense to begin with the graphological, and relate other dimensions to this one, in view of my earlier comment about studying writing in its own terms; I shall pause to discuss only those notions which have been particularly neglected or which are particularly controversial.

Under the heading of graphology, it is possible to distinguish fourteen levels of textual organization, all intuitively recognizable. There may be others that I have failed to notice:

1   feature of letter (allograph)
2   letter (grapheme)
3   letter cluster
4   graphic syllable (as represented conventionally, in dictionaries etc.)

5   graphic word (i.e. the letter-sequence surrounded by white space)
6   word cluster (as demarcated using punctuation, or some other typographical highlighting convention, such as bold face)
7   line (the most neglected of all graphological units – see below)
8   line cluster (again, as typographically demarcated, as when a series of lines are printed in italics, or indented)
9   paragraph
10  paragraph cluster (as typographically demarcated, as when a series of paragraphs is set off in a set of instructions; *cf.* Wright 1977)
11  layout (for present purposes, this term is given a restricted sense, referring only to the distinction between text *v.* non-text on a page)
12  page
13  page cluster (as typographically demarcated, as in a section, chapter, etc.)
14  text (book, magazine, etc.).

If we now take these fourteen units and attempt to correlate them with the other linguistic levels, some interesting differences and similarities suggest themselves:

1   letter feature: in phonology this correlates with the notion of distinctive feature of sound; no equivalent in grammar or semantics;
2   letter: in phonology, correlates with the phoneme; no systemic equivalent in grammar or semantics (an occasional correspondence exists, as when an individual letter or letter cluster signals a grammatical morpheme, as in 'adding an *s*' for plural);
3   letter cluster: in phonology, correlates with the phoneme clusters as described by the language's phonotactic roles; no systemic equivalent in grammar (but *cf.* (2) above) and semantics (with the possible exception of sound symbolism);
4   graphic syllable: correlates partly with the phonological syllable; no equivalent in grammar and semantics;
5   graphic word: correlates only partly with the phono-

logical word, defined in terms of stress, structure, etc., partly equivalent to the notion of grammatical word, and with the semantic action of letters on the many definitions of the 'word' (see Robins 1970 and Lyons 1968);

6  word cluster: correlates partly with some prosodic features, such as extra loudness and pause; no regular correlation with grammar; presumably a statable relationship with semantics, e.g. the expression of important or summarizing information (no attempt will be made in this paper to categorize the types of semantic information realized by the formal distinctions represented – the general label 'information' will be used solely as a reminder that this level is relevant);

7  line: no phonological correlation (except in relation to the metrical line in poetry, see Crystal 1971); no equivalent in grammar or semantics;

8  line cluster: a possible but unclear phonological correlation; no obvious correlation with grammar (other than in certain very general features, such as consistent tense reference – a point which applies to all higher-order stretches of language); presumably correlates with a statable information structure in semantics;

9  paragraph: no phonological correlation (apart from in a few styles, such as newsreading, where prosodic features often mark units of text); no predictable grammatical correlation; some suggestion of a statable informational structure in semantics;

10  paragraph cluster: no phonological or grammatical correlation; presumably a statable correlation with informational structure in semantics;

11–14  layout, page, page cluster and text: as (10).


A schematic representation of this information (see Figure 1) brings to light some interesting features:

(a)  Factors 1–4 demonstrate a regular correspondence between graphology and phonology only,

(b)  Factors 8–14 demonstrate a regular correspondence

Figure 1  Schematic relationship between graphological features of text and other linguistic levels

| | Graphology | Phonology | Grammar | Semantics |
|---|---|---|---|---|
| 1 | feature | feature | – | – |
| 2 | letter | phoneme | – | – |
| 3 | letter cluster | phoneme cluster | – | – |
| 4 | graphic syllable | syllable | – | – |
| 5 | graphic word | phonic word | word | lexeme |
| 6 | word cluster | some prosodic features | sentence analysis | information |
| 7 | line | – | – | – |
| 8 | line cluster | – | – | information |
| 9 | paragraph | – | – | information |
| 10 | paragraph cluster | – | – | information |
| 11 | layout | – | – | information |
| 12 | page | – | – | information |
| 13 | page cluster | – | – | information |
| 14 | text | – | – | information |

between graphology and semantics only,

(c) Factors 5 and 6 are central to this schema, in that these are the only factors where there is some kind of statable correlation between levels; grammar seems to have a pivotal role in interrelating graphology to prosody and semantics. Moreover, when one considers the sub-divisions within grammar, in the light of this correlation with graphology, one reason for the centrality of the notion of sentence becomes clear; this is the only notion which is in principle capable of being used at each graphological level. It may be coterminous with a letter (e.g. an alphabet book label), a letter cluster (e.g. *ssss* of a snake), a syllable (e.g. *John*), or a word (same example); a word cluster (e.g. . . . . *any more to say*, *THIS MUST STOP, I say again* . . . ); a line or line cluster (examples are obvious); a paragraph (may consist of a single sentence), as may a paragraph cluster (as in some instructional language, where the main clause is outside a set of subordinate clauses set off as paragraphs); layout (as when a diagram is part of a sentence, as in many scientific texts – see again Wright 1977), and page. It is, I suppose, possible in principle to have a larger unit coterminous with a sentence – even a text? – though admittedly this is somewhat unlikely! Given the typographical ubiquity of the sentence, its traditional definition in punctuational terms evidently leaves much to be desired.

(d) The remaining factor, 7, the line, is unique. It stands out in that it is the only factor which has no statable correlation with any other level. It also seems to be a particularly significant boundary, from the point of view of phonology: above this, there is some degree of correlation with phonology; below this point there is none. This suggests that the line may have a particularly important role to play in interrelating the two main views of reading, the 'synthetic' approach of letters → words → sentences etc., and the 'analytic' approach (of text → paragraphs → sentences etc.). It certainly makes the lack of reference to the line, in the accounts of reading organizational levels above very surprising. Perhaps this is because the line is so ambivalent; its very ambivalence suggests it may be a fruitful area for experimentation into readability.

Indeed, several studies have been made concerning the role of lines in readability (usually measured in terms of speed of reading plus some kind of comprehension check). What suggests itself immediately is that if lines as conventionally represented (i.e. with justified right-hand margins) have no apparent linguistic purpose then they must be an unfortunate distraction in learning to read, imposing boundaries where there are none, and taking up valuable visible processing time (often painfully apparent, while a child searches for the beginning of a new line, trying at the same time to retain the old). [There are of course many arguments based on aesthetic and economic considerations, which would have to be taken into account in any total appreciation of the notion of the line. The linguistic implications, however, can be discussed without reference to these factors, whose relevance to our understanding of readability is in any case obscure.] One might try to do without lines, in a sense, by producing texts which could be of great horizontal length (as has been attempted). More practically, one might attempt to turn the notion of line to linguistic advantage, and this is where most work has so far been done, largely by a further application of Miller's fruitful notion of 'chunking' of text as an aid to memory, recall, etc. The obvious suggestion, again, is to leave the lines unjustified, and to make a line correlatable with some linguistic unit. The big question is, Which?

Research into line justification and readability has so far had mixed results, suggesting that in some respects the question is not a particularly fruitful one; but from the point of view of reading acquisition there is a great deal of potential still in this field of research. The main conclusion of Zachrisson (1965), Fabrizio *et al* (1967), Cromer (1970) and others is that for a mature reader, whether a line is justified or not, and whether amount of space between words varies or not, makes little or no difference. Hartley and Burnhill (1971), for instance, examined whether some methods of setting unjustified text were more efficient than others, and found no significant results between making syntactic divisions or not for their informants (first-year students). They concluded that unjustified text can be quite markedly manipulated without affecting reading speed or comprehension. Likewise, Carver (1970) modified line endings and spacing, and produced five different unjustified formats to see whether there was any evidence of a facilitating effect due to chunking. In his mature readers, however, there was no evidence that efficiency is improved.

Hartley and Burnhill specifically excluded slow readers, people with learning problems and children from these results, and indeed there is some evidence in these studies to suggest that poor readers do find some kinds of justified lines more difficult. Carver (1970), for example, found that this was so only for relatively short line length (about seven words); when line length was twelve words, this was no longer a disadvantage. He interpreted this to mean that spacing was the most relevant factor (space differentials would be less in the twelve-word line). Cromer (1970) grouped words into constituent phrases in sentences by extending the amount of space at phrase boundaries. He too found comprehension of this kind of text superior in poor readers. Other indications of the potential of chunking were provided in varying experimental settings by Graf and Torrey (1966) and North and Jenkins (1951).

In all of this, however, little attention has been paid to the linguistic nature of the chunks of unjustified text, as defined grammatically. There has been a preoccupation with quantitative indices – with line length, in particular, and with spacing size. This is not to deny the importance of length and spacing in line readability; unpredictable spacing, for example, is a disadvantage, as Burt (1959) and others have shown. But there is a great deal more to it than this. Some attempt has been made to classify lines qualitatively. North and Jenkins (1951) operate with the vague notion of 'thought unit' along with punctuation. Graf and Torrey (1966) approach the question grammatically, however, as do Klare *et al* (1957) who attempt to set up a series of guidelines as to where line boundaries should come. They use three common rules for all their text samples:

1    existing punctuation should be followed;
2    never break a thought unit (*sic*) at the right-hand margin;

3    technical terms of more than one word are not to be broken.

In addition, a break is always permitted:

4    between Predicator and Object;
5    between loosely attached prepositional phrases;
     and sometimes (depending on the length of the unit):
6    between Subject and Predicator;
7    between Subject/Object single words and the adjoining structure;
8    between main and subordinate clauses.

In addition:

9    noun and verb modifiers, if short, go with the words they modify.

It is plain that these are only some of the significant possibilities. An ongoing project to produce some material for remedial readers at lower secondary level, in which I am involved, is attempting to come out with a more orderly and comprehensive set of guidelines (Crystal and Foster 1979), but to make it so, a more complete analysis in terms of grammatical levels is essential. In brief, at least the following distinctions must be recognized. Primacy is given to the notion of the *clause* within the *sentence*, and other grammatical notions are related to these. A sentence is viewed as an item in a sequence using sentence *connectors* of various kinds. Within the sentence, the notion of clause is analysed in terms of *elements* of structure (Subject, Verb, Object and Adverbial, in particular). The concept of *phrase* is important, in order to describe the various things that can happen grammatically within each element of clause structure. Phrases are seen as composite of *words*, and word-structure is handled in terms of *morphemes*. Within these terms, then, the working principle is that the line, as far as possible, should be coterminous with the clause. As this is the unit with which the prosodic system of the language most readily seems to correlate (see Crystal (1975), ch. 1), an interesting possible mutual reinforcement is suggested, in the case of reading aloud. Decisions about the placement

36

of line-endings are then made with reference to the types of subordinate clause, the complexity of elements of clause structure, and the complexity of phrase structure(particular reference here being made to the amount of pre- and post-modification such phrases contain). This series of decisions has some quite specific consequences, such as that a line should never end in a Determiner, or a preposition, and some interesting hypotheses about readability are generated, which we hope shortly to begin investigating experimentally. It is already plain, however, that studies of textual organization in relation to reading response must begin to consider systematically the interrelationships existing between grammar and the line; and in this area I do not doubt that linguistic analysis will be able to make a quite specific contribution.

## References

BURT, C. (1959) *A Psychological Study of Typography* Cambridge University Press

CARVER, R. P. (1970) Effect of 'chunked' typography on reading rate and comprehension *Journal of Applied Psychology* 54, 288–96

CROMER, W. (1970) The difference model: a new explanation for some reading difficulties *Journal of Educational Psychology* 61, 471–83

CRYSTAL, D. (1971) Intonation and metrical theory *Transactions of the Philological Society*; reprinted in D. Crystal (1975), ch. 7

CRYSTAL, D. (1975) *The English Tone of Voice* Edward Arnold

CRYSTAL, D (1976) *Child Language, Learning and Linguistics* Edward Arnold

CRYSTAL, D and FOSTER, J. L. (1979) *Databank* Edward Arnold

GRAF, R. and TORREY, J. W. (1966) Perception of phrase structure in written language *Proceedings of the 74th Annual Convention of the American Psychological Association* 83–4 (summary)

GREGORY, M. and POULTON, E. C. (1970) Even versus uneven right-hand margins and the rate of comprehension in reading *Ergonomics* 13, 427–34

HARTLEY, J. and BURNHILL, P. (1971) Experiments with unjustified text *Visual Language* 5, 265–78

FABRIZIO, R., KAPLAN, J. and TEAL, C. (1967) Readability as a function of right-hand margins *Journal of Typographical Research* 1, 90–95

KLARE, G. R., NICHOLS, W. H. and SHUFORD, E. H. (1957) The relationship of typographic arrangement to the learning of technical training material *Journal of Applied Psychology* 41, 41–5

LYONS, J. (1968) *An Introduction to Theoretical Linguistics* Cambridge University Press

NORTH, A. J. and JENKINS, L. B. (1951) Reading speed and comprehension as a function of typography *Journal of Applied Psychology* 35, 225–8

ROBINS, R. H. (1970) (2nd ed.) *General Linguistics: an Introductory Survey* Longman

SINCLAIR, J. and COULTHARD, M. (1975) *Towards an Analysis of Discourse* Oxford University Press

WRIGHT, P. (1977) Presenting technical information: a survey of research findings *Instructional Science* 6, 93–134

ZACHRISSON, B. (1965) *Legibility of Printed Texts* Stockholm: Almqvist and Wiksell

# 3 Towards a defined objective: cybernetics and soul-making

## Angela Ridsdale

We live in an age of computers – technology has taken our language by the throat and rattled it into whole new arrangements of syntax and expression. Under its influence our new 'operant systems' have turned teachers into 'facilitators' or 'resource personnel' who use 'perspective insight' to construct 'specific performance objectives' that take a 'treatment model' and offer 'professional input' of 'structured learning experiences' keeping in mind 'receiver variables' so that by 'interaction analysis' certain desired 'outcomes of attitudinal teaching' are attained. If you can detect the meaning concealed in that jungle of jargon you will be in a position to appreciate the incursions of the dread linguistic octopus's tentacles into even our literature making the Ten Commandments read something like this:

> I am the Lord your God: polarize your religious potential on me, unitwise. Do not initiate any concrete image, nor the structural representation of any concept above or below the heaven–earth interface, or in the natural resources of the environment. Have no interaction with them. For I, your Authoritarian, operate our holistic human input, and extrapolate the backlash trend of the paternalists on an ongoing basis through three and four generation gaps of them that display Authoritarian rejection symptoms; and exhibit warm feelings of acceptance towards them that have empathy with me and relate

with my outputs; and I remediate them . . . and so on.

It is a truism to say that the outstanding malaise of this century is alienation and that the inexorable onward march of the machine has brought increasing depersonalization of man. It is salutary to reflect that man himself is not only the victim of the process, but also its agent and willing accomplice. In the news recently was a man who wished to change legally his quite normal name to Mr 1069. He had considerable trouble obtaining a driver's licence and getting utility companies to accept his unique numerical self-designation. Finally a County Court judge rejected his request and ruled that 'Dehumanization is widespread. To allow the use of a number instead of a name would only provide additional nourishment upon which the illness of the dehumanization is able to feed and grow.' A confirmation of the Orwellian vision of 1984 with a vengeance! Yet, despite gloomy prognostications of disaster the future continues to become the present at an exponentially accelerating rate of change and the language of cybernetics becomes the voice of prophecy. The American magazine *Time* (1978) recently investigated the possibilities and probabilities of the so-called 'miracle chip' – the new microtechnology that, a quarter of an inch square, represents a quantum leap in the technology of mankind, a development that over the past few years has acquired the force and significance associated with the development of hand tools or the discovery of the steam engine. There is a fear, amongst scientists and non-scientists alike, of intellectual inadequacy, of powerlessness before the magic of the electronic merlins and of their potential for use as formidable weapons; they can become subverters of society through their very versatility and ubiquity. Human dependence on computers has in many cases become irreversible and in that dependence resides a frightening vulnerability. Social critics are concerned that a democratization of computers, made possible by the miracle chip, will make them as common as television sets are today and may eventually cause human intellectual powers to atrophy. There is danger too, in fast-expanding computer data banks with their concentration of information about people and governments and in the possibilities of access to those repositories. All who respect the sanctity of personality view with foreboding the existence of computerized details of their private affairs becoming available without their consent to anybody other than those to whom they have been obliged to reveal them. Yet, ironically, the new micro-technology, with all its threat to the human person, offers it new possibilities. The Industrial Revolution had the effect of reducing variations, of standardizing and stereotyping life in processes of mass-production routines. Microtechnology, with its nearly infinite capacities and adaptability, tends on the contrary towards individualization: with computers, it is claimed, people can design their lives far more in line with their own preferences. They can work at terminals at home instead of in offices, educate themselves in a variety of subjects at precisely the speed they wish, shop electronically with the widest possible discretion. The computer, it seems, may only appear to be a dehumanizing factor and the opposite may in fact be true. It may lead the consumer society away from the mass-produced homogeneity of the assembly line to that ultimate in individuality, the custom-made object.

What will this mean for us as educators? Californian author Robert Albrecht, a pioneer of electronic education estimates that:

> In schools, computers will be more common than carousel slide projectors, movie projectors and tape recorders. They'll be used from the moment school opens, through recess, through lunch period and on as far into the day as the principal will keep the school open.

Already, across the USA thousands of computer terminals are offering intellectual challenges to students from pre-school to college level. In Illinois, at the University of Illinois Champaign-Urbana campus, a system known as PLATO (Programmed Logic for Automatic Teaching Operations) helps teach some 150 subjects. The student sits in a booth in which he can conduct a Socratic dialogue with the computer via a typewriter keyboard. Its proteges praise PLATO for its 'kindness' and 'personal attention'. But it is interesting that amongst its 150 subjects taught, from Swahili to rocketry, the PLATO system does not teach PLATO – it does not lend itself to the philosophical speculation that enables students to learn that which is not programmable logically, that cannot be quantitatively measured or prescriptively presented. Yet the search for a meaning in life remains the paramount concern for us all as human beings, a search that begins when our existence dies and ends only with our physical extinction.

It is undeniable that computer-assisted instruction can be seen to have many advantages over more orthodox teacher-based methods. It allows for truly individualized learning beginning with the child's present level of achievement and is paced for his level of response. It is not dependent upon the competence, energy or resourcefulness of any one teacher nor in competition with the simultaneous and divergent demands of other learners. In many respects it might be seen to meet many of the criteria Bloom (1976) offers for defining quality of instruction. In an effort to define quality of instruction as it relates to managing learning, Bloom uses as a model the tutor attempting to teach something to a single student. The student is actively involved through participation (either overt or covert) in the learning process; the tutor supplies the learner with reinforcement, and provides a feedback/corrective system. In the present furore over standards of literacy, Bloom's theory of mastery learning is gaining many adherents. His book *Human Characteristics and School Learning* offers ideas that must be considered revolutionary. For example, Bloom holds that it is possible for 95 per cent of our students to learn all that the school has to teach, all at or near the mastery level. He sees only 1–3 per cent at either end who do not fit the pattern he outlines. Bloom's research has convinced him that most students become very similar with regard to learning ability, rate of learning and motivation for further learning when provided with favourable learning conditions. Under such conditions there are no 'good learners' and 'poor learners', 'fast learners' and 'slow learners'. However, his research demonstrates also that when students are provided with unfavourable learning conditions they become more dissimilar in learning ability, rate of learning and motivation for further learning. He claims that the latter is unfortunately exactly what the schools provide today. There is not time here to discuss in detail all the features of his proposition. Briefly, he theorizes that variations in learning and the level of learning of students are determined by the students' learning history and the quality of instruction they receive. School achievement is viewed as a quantitative variable. Mastery learning depends upon the notion that most students can attain a high level of learning capability if instruction is approached sensitively and systematically; if students are helped when and where they have learning difficulties; if they are given sufficient time to achieve mastery and if there is some clear criterion of what constitutes mastery. Also essential for mastery learning is the development of units of analysis. A learning unit must be manageable and analysable. Such a unit should be large enough to have elements and parts that form a separate whole. Bloom believes that such a learning task should take between one and ten hours for the student to learn, that it should contain a variety of ideas, procedures or behaviours to be learned over a relatively short time, and that it should fit well into existing courses and curricula.

Bloom offers his theory in regard to proposed changes in management and structure, the school and its curriculum, arguing that schools will need to be very specific about their educational objectives. This is a value-neutral theory. He does not specify goals nor take any position as to what learning is desirable. That is the first and probably the most difficult task of the school. Instead he uses his theory to predict what will happen under particular conditions, to explain why things happen as they do, and to state what will occur if particular student characteristics and instructional conditions are changed in specific ways.

For us, concerned with the development of literacy in

the child, Bloom raises several challenging questions. Is there a necessary core of common learnings? He suggests that verbal ability, the ability to read with comprehension are so important for school learners that particular care must be taken to ensure that learners possess these cognitive entry behaviours. There is in fact the need for a common core of skills to be developed to give the child access to further learning. Since children, however, vary so greatly in their levels of performance in cognitive and psychomotor tasks, effective assessment techniques need to be employed to identify each child's beginning level. The prescription phase may be even more critical. In order to prescribe the best learning activities for a child and to select the most effective and efficient teaching strategies for him, it is necessary to know very specifically how that particular child learns best. At present, schools seem to take but scant cognizance of the way individuals process information and the child's preferred mode of thinking, perceiving, remembering, communicating, relating to others and problem solving. It seems imperative that techniques be developed to help classroom teachers assess cognitive styles.

The 'miracle chip' microcomputer may well point the way to a solution to these problems if it can be used to offer learners both diagnostic and prescriptive help in mastering the basic skills of literacy. This is not to deny the role of the teacher but rather to re-emphasize the humanistic nature of true teaching. Much of the initial learning of any skill depends upon practice and the motivation for over-learning to make automatic the basis for the next learning to occur. Computer assistance can be seen to free teachers from much of this routine work, offering variety and flexibility of approaches with individualized pacing to meet the learner's needs during this phase of learning. Assured of systematic and individualized instruction in fundamental skills, the teacher is better able to offer the children what the computer cannot – the meeting of two or more human minds engaged upon the same common search for answers to the same, common questions: Who am I? Why am I here? What should I do? For it is not in the *how* of reading, but rather in the *why* and the *what* that true literacy develops. The acquisition of the skill of reading becomes devalued and even meaningless when what one has learned to read adds nothing of importance to life.

Bettelheim (1976) in *The Uses of Enchantment* makes a powerful and persuasive case for the fairy tale as the stuff upon which to nourish the growth of the child in self-understanding and awareness and hence to a satisfying relationship with others. He claims (p. 5):

> ... nothing can be as enriching and satisfying to child and adult alike as the folk fairy tale. True, on an overt level fairy tales teach little about the specific conditions of life in modern mass society: these tales were created long before it came into being. But more can be learned from them about the inner problems of human beings, and of the right solutions to their predicaments in any society, than from any other type of story within the child's comprehension.

Bettelheim goes on to claim that because the child's life is so often bewildering to him he needs to be helped to make some coherent sense out of the turmoil of his feelings, to be able to create order in his life based on an inner order he has developed. He needs a moral education which, subtly and by implication only, conveys to him the advantages of moral behaviour, not through abstract ethical concepts but through that which seems tangibly right and therefore meaningful to him.

The title of this Conference 'Growth in Reading' seems particularly apt for a period in the twentieth century when society seems bent on destroying itself, when confusion over conflicting sets of values and modes of behaviour is producing children who appear not only confused but stunted or even crippled in their moral growth. Growth in Reading means far more than mastery of the basic skills of literacy or even sophistication in their higher application. It refers also to Growth Through Reading, the coming to full personhood of the reader in and through the experiences reading has to offer. Although Bettelheim addresses himself in particular to the opportunities that folk fairy tales give the reader to recognize an existential dilemma and to come to grips with the problem and its solution in its most eventual, accessible form, much of what he has to say is applicable to all true literature. It is particularly essential that teachers realize this and use their resources and efforts consciously to contribute to the total growth of their children. To believe that growth in reading can occur simply by continuing practice after initial decoding is mastered is as foolish as to believe that running on the spot will carry a runner over the course. Programmed instruction, computer assisted or otherwise, is valuable for its own systematic sake but also because it liberates the teacher to share, to talk, to question, to read with and to the reader. It is interesting to observe the zeal with which teachers of very young children pursue the task of developing in their charges both an adequate sight vocabulary and strategies for decoding and to observe the corresponding shift of emphasis in teachers of older primary-school children. This is so not only with so-called 'silent reading' or 'comprehension activities' but is evident even with many otherwise competent teachers in their approach to the material in hand.

Once the child is introduced to literature there too often occurs a kind of false delicacy on the teacher's part – an unwillingness to intrude upon what is considered as holy ground or to come between the child and the author. Teaching literature in the primary school is looked upon as an invasion of the child's privacy. Somehow the child's responses are sacred and must be inviolate. This romantic illusion is very prevalent but is quite divorced from fact.

Literature, above all forms of creative expression, is the very stuff from which the web of living is woven. It must of necessity be personal to the reader since it demands both an intellectual and an emotional response. But to say it is solely a personal response is to ignore the possibilities for growth through reading as a shared activity. By recounting personal reactions and inviting the contribution of others the reader not only enriches his response to language but does so through language. If language is the means by which we learn, the method we employ to order experience, our tool for structuring reality, then the sharing of experience becomes critical to the proper development of the child both as reader and as responder.

Together, all who share can grow – indeed, must grow, by the experience in their perception of the characters and of the conflicts of the book in their realization; the making real, of its delight and wonder, its sorrow and ugliness. This growth is growth in humanity. The reader is aware not only of his own involvement with the book and its challenges but, by sharing this awareness, has a far more heightened sensitivity to the universality of such experiences. Adults normally regard the child as separated in some way from first-hand knowledge of the human condition. If this is true, then his vicarious experience of it through the mass media, and in particular television, is of tremendous importance.

The child glued to the TV set very quickly becomes familiar with crime, war, poverty, injustice, suffering and violence; and familiarity breeds contempt. Very soon the anaesthetic takes effect and how are adults, concerned with the growth of the child's moral awareness and sensibility, to help him set in perspective the seemingly all-too-real world of the cathode tube and the less assertive, lower-keyed universe which he inhabits day by day? There is ample evidence to document the role television plays in legitimizing violence and normalizing the unacceptable for children whose frame of reference is so peculiarly vulnerable to warping. However, it is the solitary nature of television viewing that is of concern here. The one-way traffic with the box allows of no interchange, no sharing, no interaction. Language cannot flourish and develop when conditions like today's astronomic levels of child TV viewing inhibit even minimum response.

Literature can go part of the way both in counteracting the numbing of sensibility and distorting of values that TV seems to produce and in giving the child opportunities to share through language his perceptions of his world and so learn to articulate them and to shape them nearer a reality than that the box presents.

In *The Republic* Plato, who was concerned with the development of the wisest and most noble feature in man to its fullest stature – the process of soul-making, revealed his belief in what intellectual experiences made for true humanity. He believed that through myth his children would grow to wholeness, to integration of personality, to wise and happy citizenship in the ideal society. Possibly Plato was the first philosopher to illustrate with such clarity the possibilities of Growth in Reading.

## References

BETTELHEIM, B. (1976) *The Uses of Enchantment* Thames and Hudson

BLOOM, B. S. (1976) *The Human Characteristics and School Learning* New York: McGraw-Hill

# 4 Dispelling myths and examining strategies in teaching non-standard dialect speakers to read

## Sara G. Zimet

Winston Churchill's profound comment that Americans and Britons are separated by a common language appears to me to be an apt beginning for my talk today. What Churchill did not say is perhaps even more important than what he did say – that many Americans and Britons also believe that American Standard English is, in fact, a sloppy, substandard form of English Standard English (Shuy and Williams 1973). I must admit that I was one of those who shared that viewpoint – that is, until I became acquainted with the research evidence provided by anthropologists and linguists. I now know, despite the teasing of a few of my close English friends, that American Standard English is not just a funny way of speaking your dialect. Both our languages are rule-governed, predictable – with regularities and exceptions – and capable of expressing any common experience within our own cultures. It is not a matter of one language being superior to the other. The major factor is that both languages represent an effective basis for communication and conceptualization and both are equally liable to poor, good, better, and best use.

Well, you can just imagine how this information changed my view of myself. One day I felt linguistically inferior and deficient, and the next day I felt linguistically competent, articulate, equal and proud.

This feeling of euphoria lasted only momentarily, however. Suddenly I realized that what was true for my dialect and yours also held true for all other dialects. It came as quite a shock for me to recognize – indeed actually to acknowledge – that I had actively contributed to a linguistic hierarchy or pecking order. English Standard English was at the top, the vernaculars spoken by White and Non-White poverty groups at the bottom and many other Non-Standard Dialects fell somewhere in-between. This belief in the inferiority of non-standard forms of English was possibly a carry-over from the theory of racial inferiority which I had long ago rejected and discarded. Thus, it was not too surprising, in this chronology of my growing awareness, that I found myself in agreement with a group of well-meaning psychologists and educators in the USA who advanced a theory of environmental impoverishment. Promoting this theory was an attempt to provide a strong argument against the re-emergence of the old racial inferiority explanation for the high incidence of academic failure among these economically-depressed groups. In retrospect, however, I came to understand that this ethnocentric, middle-class perspective on environmental immutability was almost as harmful in its effects as the theory of biologically-determined unmodifiability. Out of this deprivation theory grew the myths of verbal and linguistic deficiency – myths that I would like to dispel today.

First I would like to present the components of these myths and discuss the scientific evidence repudiating them. Then I plan to identify the various ways they are per-petuated in society at large and in the schoolroom in particular. And finally, in keeping with the theme of this Conference, 'Growth in Reading', I would like to review briefly the literature which examines various approaches to teaching reading to Non-Standard Dialect speakers. I hope that in the discussion following my presentation, you will raise the issues which concern you and share the teaching strategies that you have found useful and useless.

Exactly what are the myths of verbal and linguistic deficiency?

*Myth Number 1*
People of the lower classes, both Non-White and White, have no legitimate language at all. What little speech they use is filled with grammatical errors and incomplete sentences.

## Myth Number 2

These people do not know the names of common objects, cannot form concepts and do not use language to convey logical thoughts. In fact, their speech is primarily a form of emotional expression. It is primitive, simple, and childlike, not merely a substandard version of Standard English but rather the expression of the primitive mentality of the savage mind.

## Myth Number 3

They receive little verbal stimulation as children and hear very little well-formed language throughout their daily lives within their ghetto communities. In effect, language as a means of communication and interaction is not used or valued.

## Myth Number 4

The end-result of this language impoverishment is poor performance in all academic areas in the school and social and economic failure in the community at large.

What is the scientific evidence that repudiates these myths? These myths are based on limited observations and interviews between an adult and child in formal and threatening situations occurring in the classroom or while the child is being tested. The children are in a situation where anything they say can literally be held against them. The primary response to this evaluative and judgmental situation is an unconscious or conscious inhibition of verbalization sometimes referred to as disfluence. However, when the interview or test situation is changed – made more like a party by including the child's best friend, providing snack food, reducing the height difference between the adult interviewer and child, and introducing topics of conversation that are of genuine interest to the child – the monosyllabic speakers of Myth Number 1 are transformed into verbally-productive people with increased volume and style, who have so much to say that they keep interrupting one another (Labov 1972). Thus, a warning signal is sounded for all educators. They must recognize that what the child says may reflect how he or she thinks, but what the child doesn't say does not reflect that she or he is not thinking, or is thinking poorly or is not able to think at all (Anastasiow 1971), all components of Myth Number 2.

From the above discussion it would appear that the social situation is the most powerful determinant of verbal behaviour for these children. If adults wish to find out what children can do with language, then they must enter into the right kind of social relationship with them (Labov 1972).

People who conclude that the grammar of Non-Standard Dialect speakers is filled with errors as stated in Myth Number 1, do not themselves understand the rules of grammar and are not familiar with the linguistic structure of dialects. For example, in the case of the expression 'they mine', in Black American vernacular, the absence of the present copula and the conjoining of subject and predicate complement without a verb, is not evidence of a childlike, primitive grammar and the absence of logic. Rather, it is a legitimate grammatical structure, and one which occurs in the standard form of languages such as Russian, Hungarian and Arabic (Labov 1972).

The fact of the matter is, as I had stated earlier, all linguists are in agreement that Non-Standard English Dialects are highly coherent, logical and structured language systems which vary to some extent from each other and from Standard English in grammar and vocabulary. These differences are not deficiencies. All dialects are equal to one another. The differences between them may be great enough to impede communication but not prevent it (Goodman 1973). Dialect differences emerge among people separated by history, geography, social class, age and interest. For example, here in England you have dialects from the West Country, Scotland, London, Birmingham, Liverpool and from your West Indian and Asian communities. In the USA we have distinct urban and rural speech communities made up of Hispanos, Native American Indians, Blacks, Appalachians, Pennsylvania Dutch, and Texans, to name just a few. And no communication problems exist within these dialect communities in England and America. In effect, these dialect variations are perfectly valid alternatives to Standard English and should not be demeaned, dismissed or destroyed.

William Labov, a well-known linguist in the USA and field investigator of Non-Standard language use, debunks Myths Numbers 2 and 3. He reports that Black poverty children in ghetto areas are 'bathed in verbal stimulation from morning to night . . . (with) many speech events which depend upon the competitive exhibition of verbal skills . . . (events) in which the individual gains status through his use of language' (1972, p. 62). An example of such an activity may be found in different Black communities throughout the USA under the various names of 'Sounding', 'Signifying', or 'Playing the Dozens'. This activity requires strict adherence to rules of ritual insults and includes a whole variety of rhyming couplets. It is essentially a contest of verbal skill and quickness of thought, and is subject to active audience approval for replies which are fast, colourful and appropriate, and disapproval for those that are not (Labov 1972). The play-party game, a folk song-dance combination, is part of the rich oral language tradition of the Appalachian Whites. The rhyming verse described in *Borstal Boy* by Brendan Behan may be an equivalent example of the skilful use of language by a Non-Standard Dialect-speaking group here in England. Not only do we have evidence of high verbal production and valuing of verbal behaviour, but we are apprised of the cognitive skills required in these activities and completely ignored by Myth Number 2.

In summing up what I have said so far, in Labov's words (1972, pp. 59–60) it appears that:

> The concept of verbal (and linguistic) deprivation has no basis in social reality; in fact black children in urban ghettos receive a great deal of verbal stimulation, hear more well-formed sentences than middle-class children, and participate fully in a highly verbal culture; they have the same basic vocabulary, possess the same capacity for conceptual learning, and use the same logic as anyone else who learns to speak and understand English.

What appears to be true of urban Blacks is also said to hold true for other Non-White and White Non-Standard Dialect speakers (Goodman 1973).

How, then, can we justify the existence of Myth Number 4 – that educational, economic and social failure is due to the so-called language impoverishment of the lower-class, different dialect-speaking child?

We do know that in the USA segregated ethnic groups

perform more poorly in school than any other group (Johnson 1975). I suspect that the equivalent is true here in England as well for self-segregated ethnic groups. By tracing the educational failure of the child to his or her personal characteristics – specifically to the language he or she uses – we take the focus of responsibility for this failure away from the school and place it on the 'deficient' child, the 'deficient' family, and the 'deficient' community. Since, according to the linguists, there is no reason to believe that the language is deficient then there is no reason to believe that any non-standard vernacular is in itself an obstacle to learning. Nor can we hold to the position that the standard language is the only medium in which teaching and learning can take place. This is not to say that everyone should not have the right to learn the standard language and culture in reading and writing and speaking. What is being said is that *this acquisition should be the end-result of the educational process, not the beginning of it.*

I had promised to help identify those issues in our society and in the school curriculum which help to perpetuate the myths of verbal and linguistic inferiority. It may help to gain some perspective on this issue by briefly examining why we have a standard language and how language becomes the standard one for any nation.

Without attempting to make this an exhaustive list I would like to suggest that a standard language helps to unite a diverse group under one flag; helps to facilitate the socialization process; helps to create a cohesive community of people by increasing the opportunity for communication between them; and helps to facilitate commerce.

Since all languages such as English are, in fact, a family of related dialects (Goodman 1973), who, then, determines which language and/or dialect shall prevail in commerce, education and the mass media? Just as you may have guessed, it is a political decision made by the most powerful and prestigious in a country. For example, during the reign of Philip XII of Spain, everyone was expected to speak with a lisp just as the King did. This same pronunciation prevails today. Here in Great Britain, Standard English is still sometimes referred to as the King's or Queen's English. In colonized African countries it was the victor, not the majority, who determined which language would be the 'norm'. In the new, emerging African nations, dialect decisions are still being made by the most powerful.

The powerful and the rich of society determine what is acceptable and standard in all aspects of social behaviour. The enforcement of that decision may be by direct or more subtle means of pressure, involving political, economic and social consequences as reward or punishment.

What inevitably appears to happen in competitive, class-oriented societies such as ours is a process of social stratification with the powerful and rich at the top – the 'good' people who speak the 'best' language, and the poor and powerless at the bottom – the 'bad' people who speak the 'worst' language and who are culturally disadvantaged, deprived and deficient. The degree that a person's speech differs from the standard one will determine his or her place in the dominant society's hierarchy.

What I have said, then, is that dialects vary in the social prestige which they carry and this variation is a reflection of the social status of the people who use them. Low-status people speak low-status language and high-status people speak high-status language *because that is the status the general society assigns to all aspects of their culture.* Those who struggle for upward social mobility must rid themselves of the stigmatizing lower-class dialect as a basic first step in that climb.

This, then, is the prevailing attitude which pervades our society. Many of our educators – school teachers and administrators – just like the rest of the population, have internalized this social-class value system. It should be of no surprise, therefore, to learn that research in the USA has indicated that teachers' attitudes towards minority group members and towards non-standard dialects are generally negative (Guskin 1968; Labov 1969; Coates 1972; Blodgett and Cooper 1973; Ford 1974; Crowl and MacGinitie 1974).

For example, my husband and I studied teachers' social perception of dominant and minority group members (Zimet and Zimet, 1978). We found, as had other investigators (Coates 1972), that teachers had not attributed any attractive personality characteristics to this group as they had to members of the dominant culture. In further support of the negative views held by society, the teachers reported very low achievement expectations and very high expectations for hostile and rebellious behaviours. Teachers also have been reported to react negatively towards students who speak a different dialect than the standard one, even those teachers who had been dialect speakers themselves. In fact one researcher found that teachers unconsciously used forms which they themselves ·stigmatized in the speech of others (Labov 1969). For example, Black English-speaking students were rated as lower-class, belligerent, delinquent, less intelligent and less able to do well academically than Standard-English-speaking students, when the work evaluated was identical in content (Blodgett and Cooper 1973 ; Ford 1974; Crowl and MacGinitie 1974).

This same negative attitude is reflected in curriculum decisions which forbid the use of Non-Standard English in the classroom. It is not to be spoken; it is not to be seen in print; for all intents and purposes, it does not and should not exist. In fact, the major effort of education in the USA has been to eliminate Non-Standard English usage and to force children into performing in a linguistic system other than their primary one. The absence of multi-ethnic curriculum materials also reinforces the schools' attitude of rejecting the child's language and culture (Zimet 1976).

The educational ramifications of this all-pervasive negative attitude is twofold: (1) it influences educators' expectations, assessments and interventions; and (2) it forms the basis of how these individuals view themselves and their culture.

This policy of exclusion has been justified because it is believed that such an intervention in the sociocultural development of the poor will make them more ready for the majority culture and all the economic advantages of the middle class. Instead of producing the desired effects, these efforts have increased the distance between these children and the school. There is a distrust and a dislike for school experiences which have demeaned and ignored their culture. There is little to wonder about when we take note of the low self-esteem and the high drop-out rate among these children.

One does wonder, however, why the goal of economic opportunity for all must carry with it the price of a multicultural society. The school should be designed to serve a multicultural society and to prepare children for full participation in that society.

Linguists tell us that language is a form of social behaviour and we have no business interfering with a people's social relationship to their own community (McDavid 1969). 'One uses the language which helps to preserve one's life, which helps to make one feel at peace in the world and which screens out the greatest amount of chaos' (Creswell 1969, p. 71). Rejecting that part of a people's life – their language, and one of their most intimate possessions – has serious psychological ramifications that should not be dealt with lightly. Any programme aimed at helping people to break out of the cycle of poverty should be both linguistically and humanly sound.

As far back as 1953, the United Nations Educational, Social and Cultural Organization, known as UNESCO, made the following recommendations:

> It is axiomatic that the best medium for teaching a child is his mother tongue. Psychologically, it is the system of meaningful signs that in his mind works automatically for expression and understanding. Sociologically it is a means of identification among the members of the community to which he belongs. Educationally, he learns more quickly through it than through an unfamiliar medium.

The way to teach new forms or patterns of language is not to eliminate the old forms but to build upon them (Creswell 1969). In effect, our goal should be bidialectalism. Becoming bidialectal, however, has been recognized as more difficult than becoming bilingual. The interference between two closely related dialects such as Non-Standard and Standard English is far greater than between two completely different languages. We know that human beings do not hear or see every sound or sight in the world. Their senses are highly selective and they hear and see only what they have learned in the process of acquiring their primary language. If certain grammatical concepts do not exist in their dialect, it is likely that they are unaware of the sound segments that signify these concepts. People, therefore, must be trained intensively to hear the significant sound segments in a word, particularly those representing grammatical concepts, so that they might penetrate their consciousness (Lin 1969). This might be done by an inductive technique in which pupils compare their own speech patterns with the patterns of the standard language then isolate the differences, and practise the use of these patterns as a part of 'role playing' in a second language – not as a replacement of their first language.

Although speaking and writing correctly in another dialect is very difficult, it would appear that most urban dwellers are able to understand the speech of a person who does not speak their particular dialect. In fact, several studies have demonstrated that when children who speak Non-Standard English read Standard English and vice versa, they code shift (Ames, Rosen and Olson 1971; Rosen and Ames 1972; Weber 1973; Hall and Turner 1974; Kachuck 1975; Lamberg and McCaleb 1977). In other words, they translate the material into its equivalent in their own dialect. Children who change the sentence to conform to their language are demonstrating an active intelligence (Anastasiow 1971). It would appear, then, that the so-called errors in oral reading comprehension tests are not errors at all but instead a dialect-shift, demonstrating, in fact, a high level of comprehension. Thus, teachers are alerted to modify their scoring procedures when using formal and informal oral reading measures. In order for teachers to make these judgments, they need to know their pupil's dialect (Harber and Beatty 1978).

A very strong case has been made for using the Language Experience Approach in teaching dialect-speaking children to read (Hildreth 1964; Hall 1974; Serwer 1969; Stockler 1971). This method builds upon the use of reading materials created by writing down children's spoken language. It accepts and recognizes that what children have to say and how they say it is important. Not only is this approach consistent with the UNESCO recommendations, but it fits in with what we know about the process of learning to read. Before children can read, they need to learn that their speech sounds can be represented by print and the print they are asked to read is meaningful to them (Anastasiow 1971). We also know that words children use in their own speech are easier for them to read in print than words they do not use

(Hildreth 1964). Since the myths of linguistic deficiency and inferiority have been debunked, we also know that the elements for success in learning to read are present. These children possess a rich oral language tradition and are linguistically active within their own communities.

In keeping with this approach, Baratz (1969) found very strong evidence for the use of curriculum materials written in Black English. Some attempts have been made in the USA to study the effectiveness of reading texts produced by major publishing companies that were written in the dialect of the children using them. But these books met with a great deal of community resistance and had to be withdrawn (Harber and Beatty 1978). In retrospect, it is obvious that such a reaction would occur without appropriate communication with parents and other significant members of the communities in which they were introduced. The alternative, that of preparing dialect renderings of conventional materials, might also meet with resistance unless efforts were made beforehand to educate the community. Then it might be possible to involve community members as well as the children in preparing these materials.

Not only do we need to educate everyone about the validity of dialects, but we need to capitalize on the strengths we know exist in these children. We need to start them at their current level of ability, respect them and their language, apply teaching strategies that are appropriate to the situation, and make realistic expectations of the children. Should we be disposed to make these major curriculum adjustments, we should not expect that changes in the children will be immediate. Time may be needed for the child's and parent's distrust of school experiences to be overcome before any appreciable changes will come about.

The myths of racial inferiority and linguistic deficiency have been dispelled. There are some useful guidelines to follow in teaching children whose language is different from the standard. What is needed is the will to overcome our own negative attitudes towards Non-Standard English dialects and apply what we have learned so that children will no longer be the victims of our biases.

# References

AMES, W. S., ROSEN, C. L. and OLSON, A. V. (1971) 'The effects of non-standard dialect on the oral reading behaviour of fourth grade Black children' in C. Braun (Ed) *Language, Reading, and the Communication Process* Newark, Delaware: International Reading Association

ANASTASIOW, N. (1971) *Oral Language: Expression of Thought* Newark, Delaware: International Reading Association

BARATZ, J. C. (1969) 'Teaching reading in an urban Negro school system' in J. C. Baratz and R. W. Shuy (Eds) *Teaching Black Children to Read* Newark, Delaware: International Reading Association

BLODGETT, E. G. and COOPER, E. B. (1973) Attitudes of elementary teachers toward Black dialect *Journal of Communication Disorders* 6, 121–33

COATES, B. (1972) White adult behaviour toward Black and White children *Child Development* 43, 143–54

CRESWELL, T. J. (1969) 'The twenty billion dollar misunderstanding' in R. W. Shuy (Ed) *Social Dialects and Language Learning* Champaign, Illinois: National Council of Teachers of English

CROWL, T. K. and MACGINITIE, W. H. (1974) The influence of students' speech characteristics on teachers' evaluations of oral answers *Journal of Educational Psychology* 66, 304–8

FORD, J. F. (1974) Language attitude studies: a review of selected research *Florida FL Reporter* Spring/Fall, 53–4, 100

GOODMAN, K. (1973) 'Up-tight ain't right' in *Issues in Children's Books* New York: R. R. Bowker Company

GUSKIN, J. (1968) *Negro Dialect: Effects on Teachers' Perception of Ability and Personality* (unpublished paper) Lansing, Michigan: University of Michigan

HALL, M. A. (1974) *The Language Experience Approach for the Culturally Disadvantaged* Newark, Delaware: International Reading Association

HALL, V. C. and TURNER, R. R. (1974) The validity of the 'different language explanation' for poor scholastic performance by Black students *Review of Educational Research* 44, 69–81

HARBER, J. R. and BEATTY, J. N. (1978) *Reading and the Black English Speaking Child: an Annotated Bibliography* Newark, Delaware: International Reading Association

HILDRETH, G. (1964) Linguistic factors in early reading instruction *The Reading Teacher* 18, 172–8

JOHNSON, S. S. (1975) *Update on Education* (A Digest of the National Assessment of Educational Progress) Denver, Colorado: Education Commission of the States

KACHUK, B. L. (1975) Dialect in the language of inner-city children *Elementary School Journal* 76, 105–12

LABOV, W. (1965) 'Stages in the acquisition of Standard English' in R. W. Shuy (Ed) *Social Dialects and Language Learning* Champaign, Illinois: National Council of Teachers of English

LABOV, W. (1972) Article in *The Atlantic Monthly*

LAMBERG, W. J. and MCCALEB, J. L. (1977) Performance by prospective teachers in distinguishing dialect features and mis-cues unrelated to dialect *Journal of Reading* 20, 581–4

LIN, S. C. (1969) 'Pattern practice in a freshman English program' in R. W. Shuy (Ed) *Social Dialects and Language Learning* Champaign, Illinois: National Council of Teachers of English

MCDAVID, R. I. (1969) 'Social dialects: cause or symptoms of social maladjustment' in R. W. Shuy (Ed) *Social Dialects and Language Learning* Champaign, Illinois: National Council of Teachers of English

ROSEN, C. L. and AMES, W. S. (1972) 'Influence of non-standard dialect on the oral reading behaviour of fourth grade Black children under two stimuli conditions' in J. A. Figurel (Ed) *Better Reading in Urban Schools* Newark, Delaware: International Reading Association

SERWER, B. L. (1969) Linguistic support for a method of teaching beginning reading to Black children *Reading Research Quarterly* 4, 449–67

SHUY, R. and WILLIAMS, F. (1973) 'Stereotyped attitudes of selected English dialect communities – in R. W. Shuy and R. W. Fasold (Eds) *Language Attitudes: Current Trends and Prospects* Washington, D.C: Georgetown University Press

STOCKLER, D. S. (1971) *Responses to the Language Experience Approach by Black, Culturally Different, Inner-City Student Experiencing Reading Disability in Grades Five and Eleven* (unpublished doctoral dissertation) Bloomington, Indiana: Indiana University

WEBER, R. (1973) 'Dialect differences in oral reading: an analysis of errors' in J. L. Laffey and R. Shuy (Eds) *Language Differences: Do They Interfere?* Newark, Delaware: International Reading Association

ZIMET, C. N. and ZIMET, S. G. (1978) Educators view people: ethnic group stereotyping *Journal of Community Psychology* 6, 189–93

ZIMET, S. G. (1976) *Print and Prejudice* Hodder and Stoughton

# Part 3

# Early reading

# 5 Opportunities for developing language and reading in early childhood

## Gwen Bray

There was never a time when more concern was shown regarding children's progress, and Government-sponsored committees of inquiry have been initiated, to make available the expertise of men and women of outstanding service and responsibility in their professional lives. These committees have provided a statement of opinion and information relevant to the rearing and educating of young children in our present-day society. Their findings are available for all to read in two reports written within a decade. The first, entitled *Children and Their Primary School* (DES 1967), was produced under the chairmanship of Lady Bridget Plowden, whilst the second, *Fit for the Future*, was the report of the committee on Child Health Services under the chairmanship of Emeritus Professor S. D. M. Court. This idea of unity of purpose between health, care and education is a relatively new concept, but as a paediatrician reported ten years ago:

> Preventive money spent on improving provision for this age group (pre-school) is valid. It would substantially reduce later expenditure on straightening out people who have grown up inadequate, delinquent or emotionally stunted because of the bad effects of their formative years.

Those responsible for the formative years will appreciate the quotation taken from the writing of the late Katherine Mansfield, and will apply it to individual children: 'I want to be all that I am capable of becoming.' Dr Mia Kellmer

Pringle, Director of the National Children's Bureau defined the role of teachers as 'innovators and bridge builders' in the community or neighbourhood schools, with parents as partners in the interests of their children. This shared responsibility may be accepted as attitudes gradually change.

The rapid rate of development in the variety of pre-school provision within the private and public sectors has accelerated the progress of many pre-school children. The social opportunities in meeting an ever-widening circle of interested adults, to visit new places and buildings, to have varied opportunities and space to play, and above all to be with grown-ups who will talk and listen, cannot fail to encourage and stimulate the youngest children. The 'starting points' of compulsory schooling need to be adapted accordingly to the requirements of these more sophisticated children. Their opportunities must be progressive rather than repetitive. These obvious changes are implicit in the very descriptive name of Early Childhood, compared with the word 'Infant' from the Latin 'infaus' meaning without language.

What of the homes? There are countless variations, and the importance of recognizing individual differences and attitudes cannot be overestimated. There are those children who grow up without ever having a chance to use their potential intellectual capacity. They live in homes where the vision is limited and where they do not receive enough stimulation, and so do not have the opportunity to learn through the various kinds of play with educational toys. Let us consider a typical stable, happy home where the child has interested parents, who can spend time providing social opportunities and wide experiences. Relatives may live nearby, the child has toys and space to play, books to look at and grown-ups with leisure to read stories to him. This child's speech will be a reflection of what he hears at home, and his vocabulary will be determined by his parents' interests. His further language experience comes with children of similar age and development who he meets in the Nursery or play group. The contrast is the atypical home of the unsupported parent, where there may be stress and anxiety, and little time or understanding of the need for intellectual stimulation. In the first example the child will enjoy the extension of learning possibilities, when he comes to school; whilst the child from the second home will require a compensating environment and the understanding of supportive and encouraging adults.

The teaching in most primary schools is geared to the educational and social needs of the area, and is concerned with developing the basic skills of communication. There is a wide variation of age range; for example, there can be Nursery provision from 3½ years, in a separate unit, or it may be an Infant School from 5–7 years, or Junior Mixed and Infant School from 5–11 years, or the reorganized Primary School 5–9 or 5–8 years. There is an even wider variation in the ethos of these schools due to the interaction of the head-teacher and staff. Children are introduced to areas which are meaningful within subjects, and as Professor M.A.K. Halliday has said, 'The new maths, the new science and all the other things that are new are making much higher demands on the children's language ability than what went before them.' It is by reading that we all have enlarged our vocabulary from early childhood onwards and children commence school eager to read and write and talk. Obviously they need to learn how to listen, and school should be the place where they can expect to find an adult who will have much that is interesting for them to hear. The balance of time to give opportunities for talking and listening has to be considered by teachers when structuring a programme. The formal and informal exchange of speech between teachers and children is essential to their success, for continual instruction bewilders many children as it outruns their experience and concentration.

There can be no doubt that the third report with relevance to the primary school is *A Language for Life* (DES 1975) produced under the chairmanship of Sir Alan Bullock, Vice-Chancellor of the University of Oxford, which has helped many teachers to clarify their thoughts on developing language and reading skills. The chapters on 'Attitudes and Standards', 'Language in the Early Years', and 'The Reading Process' are an excellent source of reference for those concerned with the youngest children. Many headteachers have reconsidered their programmes or schemes of work, to ensure progression in initial literacy, and have revitalized their resources. Whilst there should be an agreed expectation of performance in reading skills, with the necessary books and equipment available, what is required to meet the wide variation of ability amongst the children?

The use of space within schools has changed considerably as buildings have become more informal and domestic in character and are more likely to foster good personal relationships and a greater involvement in the life of the school. A wide variety of equipment and materials, including more books, has led to new needs for display and storage. Areas of interest which are frequently developed in halls and classrooms are a motivating force for enquiry. Books are seen to be in evidence for topical events or curriculum needs and are always accessible. Class libraries and book corners are essential to enable children to make choices from books suited to their age and stage. No doubt, with the falling rolls within primary schools, space may be made available for a school library, equipped with suitable furniture, a wide choice of books and audio-visual aids – the hub of the school where reading becomes an enjoyable and vital activity.

In order to encourage the creative use of words, the children need to hear exciting stories, truthful descriptions, to follow sequences of events, to predict and recall, to take part in simple dramatization and role playing. Children not only need to listen to each other, by using tape recorders, but to the many radio and TV programmes suited to their needs with ideas for follow-up work. The school policy on the teaching of the mechanical skills of decoding, and the use of reading schemes and supplementary materials, has to be carefully structured to meet the needs of children, as they will vary in the degree of interest that they show and their urge to learn will be strengthened or weakened by the attitudes of parents and teachers. It may be possible to involve parents following the ideas the 'Family Reading Groups' pioneered in the former East Riding of Yorkshire by Colin Wigglesworth, who is now Headmaster of Norton County Primary School, North Yorkshire, but was at that time Headmaster of Penhurst Primary School, East Yorkshire. The late Mrs Eve Astbury, the County Children's Librarian, cooperated with headteachers in the area to give parents an insight into children's attitudes concerning fiction, and to reading as an activity to participate in at home. In the past few years Cecilia and Tony Obrist have been instrumental in developing this idea in North Bedfordshire and other parts of the country.

The organization of classes within schools which were formerly classified by chronological age can be varied to include partial vertical groups, or full vertical grouping in early childhood. Each class containing children from five to seven years of age, remaining throughout this stage in the care of the same teacher. It is prevalent in some parts of the country, which have schools developing outstanding work amongst their youngest children. It is claimed that the teacher gains a far more intimate knowledge of her children and that there is no regression occurring due to change of class. Whatever the organization, it is vital to have an orderly workshop arrangement with detailed record keeping, to ensure progression in reading skills. Dr Derek Thackray's Reading Readiness Profiles have helped many teachers to ascertain where individual children need compensatory programmes.

Most teachers have their own individual ways of grouping children when teaching reading skills, and of recording their progress. In so doing, the following children are likely to be identified:

1 children who are articulate, can read fluently, with interest, understanding and enjoyment;
2 children who can read fluently, but their level of comprehension is doubtful and they are unable to recall what they have read;
3 those who have grasped the mechanics of reading, but remain hesitant, and need constant practice and encouragement;
4 those who have made a start and may be able to use a variety of apparatus, but require help in word-attack skills.

It is obvious that great efforts are made by teachers of young children, and similar efforts are required to ensure continuity and the extension of early reading skills.

There have been at least seven Schools Council projects which have included the development of language and reading skills as part of their main theme. The information compiled is of particular relevance to the class teacher, as the trial materials have been used in schools all over the country. Schools which have taken part in these pilot studies will have given critical appraisals of the materials to be published to the Director of the relevant Project who will have considered these when revising the materials for publication. These are the projects which are of special interest to teachers of children in early childhood and in the primary school:

|  | *Director* |
| --- | --- |
| *Linguistics and English Teaching* | Professor M. A. K. Halliday (1970) |
| Project Organizer (*Breakthrough to Literacy*) | David McKay |
| *Pre-School Language Project* | Dr. J. Tough (1971–2) |
| *English for Immigrant Children* (Infant Section) | Miss J. Derrick (1966–71) |
| *Children as Readers* (Colin Wigglesworth) | Jeremy Mulford (1970) |
| *Communication Skills in Early Childhood* | Dr. J. Tough (1973–6) |
| *Extending Beginning Reading* | V. Southgate Booth and Helen Arnold (1973–6) |
| *The Effective Use of Reading* | Professor K. A. Lunzer and W. K. Gardner (1973–6) |

The climate of schools is usually evident to parents and other visitors by the ease and courtesy with which they are received. If good personal relationships exist between staff and children, there is a lack of tension in communication, and children will be encouraged to talk to some purpose. The time spent by teachers in attending inservice courses, conferences or on specialized visits can only enhance an awareness in their teaching, and new ideas can be discussed on their return to school. A wealth of such courses is available in universities, colleges and teachers' centres concerned with the theory and practice of the teaching of reading and related skills. Authors of reading schemes often come to teachers' centres to talk about the thinking behind the production of their scheme. Reading centres have developed in various areas, where displays of the full range of new materials can be examined. The commercial pressures in the provision of books is obvious, and the more informed a teacher can be, the more selective he or she becomes.

There is a world of difference between focusing on the academic issues in the continuing debate on reading, and being caught up in the turbulent demands of young children in the classroom. The time spent in wider reading is a personal matter; often those who seem the busiest read the most. It is an absorbing interest for some to follow the development in learning theory, in linguistics, psychology and sociology, though the language of research is often obscure and can be contradictory between the different disciplines. The learning theorists such as Skinner believe that language is acquired largely through reward or reinforcement of verbal responses, whilst others emphasize the role of imitation in the development of language. Psycholinguists studying the development of syntax and semantics have been influenced by the theory of Noam Chomsky – that children have a language acquisition device that enables them to process language, to construct rules and to understand appropriate grammatical speech.

It is not surprising that those who are concerned with the stage of early childhood never cease to wonder at the infinite variety of knowledge concerning theory and practice that is required. It has been mostly a woman's world, and one can only pay tribute to the practitioners.

## References

DES (1967) *Children and their Primary Schools* (Plowden Report) HMSO
DES (1975) *A Language for Life* (Bullock Report) HMSO
HALLIDAY, M. A. K. (1970) 'Foreword' in D. MacKay, B. Thompson and P. Schaub *Breakthrough to Literacy: Teacher's Manual* Longman for the Schools Council

# 6   Do teachers make a difference?

## Bridie Raban

The Bullock Report (1975) reasserts the importance of the teacher, pointing out that debates about methods and materials are peripheral to the central issues of teaching children to read:

> There is no one method, medium, device or philosophy that holds the key to the process of learning to read. (6.1)

> The quality of learning is fashioned in the day-to-day atmosphere of the classroom through the knowledge, intuitions and skill of individual teachers. (Introduction)

Whilst these assertions appear to be intuitively appropriate, they are not unequivocally matched by the evidence from research carried out to date. For instance, the conclusions of *The Roots of Reading* (Cane and Smithers 1971) state that successful schools are characterized by systematic and planned series of exercises and activities, reading teaching begins as soon as the children enter school, and firm but friendly teacher control is exercised over the children's learning. But the results of this study and others have been seriously questioned (Gray 1975; 1976; 1977). Qualitative differences between teachers and how these relate to their pupils' progress in learning to read remain apparently easy to define in theory, but less than possible to quantify in practice. To study this more elusive aspect of the teaching of reading was one of the aims of the Bristol research project 'Children Learning to Read' (SSRC Grant No. HR 3797/1) in which observations were made in eighteen infant schools during 1975-7 (Wells and Raban 1978).

The project was set up to investigate the interaction between the relative emphasis and timing in the strategies employed by their teachers in the initial stages of learning to read. A substantial part of the data collected took the form of cumulative records of each child's progress in reading and writing based on regular observations of their encounters with reading material in teacher-directed and other activities. The sample consisted of twenty children for whom longitudinal records of language development from three-and-a-quarter years had already been obtained as part of the study of 'Language development in pre-school children' (Wells 1974). A second sample of children was selected from the children who entered the same classes at the same time to act as a 'control' group. The target number was five peers for each child in the original sample, with an equal number of boys and girls in the complete sample. The final sample of peers (Sample B) consisted of ninety-one children: forty-five girls and forty-six boys. The children in Sample B were tested and assessed in exactly the same way as those in the original sample (Sample A), although no classroom observations were made of these children, neither was any information obtained from parents about their pre-school experience.

A substantial part of the data collected on the twenty Sample A children took the form of individual records of amount of time spent on different activities during the course of a complete morning. Observations were made once a month over the first two years of schooling and individual profiles were constructed based on the summed information over the whole two-year period and for each of the first and second years separately. Additional information was collected by means of the administration of interview schedules to the Head and class teacher of each child and summary measure of the school catchment area was obtained in two ways: headteacher assessment and DES Social Priority Area ratings.

Assessment of the children's attainment was made on entry to school and at the end of the first and second years. Standardized tests were used on all these occasions, supplemented at the end of the second year by information supplied by the class teacher in the form of responses on an assessment schedule. Further information about the parent's contribution to the children's oral and written language development, both before and during their two years at school, was obtained through interview schedules and by reference to transcripts of audio recordings of spontaneous interaction, made at three-monthly intervals during the two years before school entry. (For further details *cf.* Wells and Raban 1978).

Scores on all these measures were first submitted to correlational analysis. Regression analyses were then performed on subsets of the data with attainment in reading at seven years of age as the dependent variable. The major and consistent finding from these analyses was that variation between children in their academic readiness and know-ledge about literacy on entry to school accounted for the greater part of the explained variance in reading attainment at age seven; characteristics of schools as learning environments and the distribution of time across activities in the classroom together accounted for a very much smaller part of the variance.

The general finding from a further analysis of variance was that, in the majority of cases, the within-school differences were greater than the between-school differences, thus suggesting that the schools as learning environments were more similar than the children who entered them. An alternative way of interpreting this finding is that attainment in reading is more strongly related to individual differences between children than to differences in learning environ-ments provided by the schools. Similar results have been obtained in other studies of school achievement (e.g. Douglas 1966; Manchester Survey in the Plowden Report 1967) and these have frequently been interpreted as showing that schools account for little of the variation in the educational achievement of pupils. However, it is clearly not the case that schools contribute nothing to children's learning, rather it is the case that schools do not significantly change the overall rank order of children which is established right at the very beginning by the very wide variation in their level of attainment on entry to school.

Although schooling may not significantly alter relative levels of attainment in the population as a whole there is no doubt that particular individuals make greater or lesser progress than their attainment on entry to school would predict. If this were not so there would be perfect correlation between attainment on entry and at age seven or any later point in time, and this clearly is not the case. In order to investigate further the possible relationship between this variation in progress and aspects of the school environment, a further analysis was carried out which took deviation from predicted attainment at age seven as the dependent variable.

The children's knowledge of literacy at age five was established as a composite score of the Concepts about Print and Letter Identification tests (Clay 1972), whilst their reading score at age seven was the result of factor analysing all the measures of attainment in reading obtained after two years in the infant school:

Tests of Word Recognition (Carver 1970)
Analysis of Reading Ability (Neale 1966)
Teacher Assessment Schedule (Raban 1978; also Raban and Moon 1978)

The regression line of reading factor scores upon knowledge of literacy scores was then calculated. These two sets of scores were found to be highly correlated, $r=0.793$ ($p<.001$). Given this result, progress was then defined in terms of deviation from the score that would be predicted from knowledge of literacy at age five on the basis of the regression line. The children were grouped into over-achievers and under-achievers on the basis of their relationship to this line.

It was hypothesized that those children whose classroom experience included more learning-to-read activities would make greater progress with their reading during their first two years at school than would have been predicted from their knowledge of literacy scores alone.

However, in order to establish that the individual children's progress scores were a function of the general classroom experience provided by their teachers rather than of their individual style of interaction with the teacher concerned, similar regressions were calculated for each of the groups of children (Sample A child + Sample B) who shared the same teacher, or teachers, through the two years of the investigation (N = 70). An analysis of co-variance was computed for these data as a means of statistically testing for differences of reading factor scores at age seven between these groups of children while allowing for the initial differences between the groups in their knowledge of literacy scores at age five.

| source of variance | sum of squares | df | mean sq. | F |
|---|---|---|---|---|
| Between groups | 3.431 | 5 | 0.685 | 2.430 |
| Within groups | 7.328 | 26 | 0.282 | |
| Total | 10.76 | | | (p <.1 level) |

The results of this analysis indicate a positive trend, although not statistically significant, in the direction that teachers do influence the progress of children in their class, this being a stronger claim than their influence on an individual child which was discussed above. If this is the case, what are the parameters that differentiate between teachers?

During the classroom observations, which have been described above, it was the individual Sample A child on each occasion that provided the focus of attention (Raban *et al* 1976). Time spent on different curricular activities, to the nearest quarter of a minute, was recorded, with all 'off-task' time being noted and extracted from the final totals. Particular attention was paid to any interactions with the teacher and, since the amount of individual attention a child received from the teacher could be assumed as an important factor to consider, the observer timed these occurrences in seconds. In addition prose notes were made of what happened during these interactions.

There appeared to be three main reasons for the teacher to talk to a child: firstly, to organize and direct his activities; secondly, to sustain a social relationship, with little or no reference to the task in hand; and thirdly, to give individual instruction as she prepared a child for a task or went over the activity with him, either during its progress or when it had been completed. This latter form of teacher-child interaction was coded on the observation sheets with subscripts: $p$ for preparation, and $f$ for feedback or recapitulation. The reason for this detail of coding was that, during the early observations, a marked difference was observed between those teachers who offered praise and encouragement for work completed, and those who took opportunities to add to this positive reinforcement by going over the children's work with them, discussing it in detail. Busy teachers may, without realizing it, find themselves dealing only with the products of children's activities, saying, for example, 'Very

Table 1

| | Time with teacher (Literacy) in minutes | | Deviation from predicted scores | |
|---|---|---|---|---|
| | Tp | Tf | | |
| Over- | – | 38.23 | 15.92 | |
| achievers | 0.45 | 34.07 | 19 | |
| $N_1$=11 | 1.95 | 32.38 | 13.29 | |
| | 2.08 | 37.12 | 11.29 | |
| | 2.82 | 14.27 | 12 | X Tp,r=0.099 non sig |
| | 3.8 | 44.65 | 13.23 | |
| | 4.08 | 45.73 | 17.13 | X Tf,r=0.184 non sig |
| | 5.73 | 52.83 | 13.15 | |
| | – | 49.2 | 12.4 | |
| | 1.58 | 16.25 | 12.54 | |
| | 9.02 | 33.12 | 14.21 | |
| | $\bar{X}_1$ 2.86 | $\bar{X}_1$ 36.17  r=.118 | $\bar{Y}_1$ 14.02 | |
| | $S_1$ 2.59 | $S_1$ 11.76 | $S_1$ 2.37 | |
| Under- | – | 21.48 | 5.13 | |
| achievers | 2.18 | 5.23 | 3.23 | |
| $N_2$=9 | 1.38 | 11.43 | 4.58 | X Tp,r=0.288 non sig |
| | 9.93 | 65.33 | 4.13 | |
| | – | 20.12 | 9.09 | X Tf,r=0.293 non sig |
| | 0.58 | 24.65 | 5.23 | |
| | 0.18 | 38.22 | 0.47 | |
| | — | 7.35 | 4.15 | |
| | 8.75 | 73.15 | 9.72 | |
| | $\bar{X}_2$ 2.56 | $\bar{X}_2$ 29.66 | $\bar{Y}_2$ 5.08 | |
| | $S_2$ 2.56 | $S_2$ 23.2  r=.847  p<.01 | S 2.84 | |
| | $\bar{X}$ 2.73 | $\bar{X}$ 33.24 | $\bar{Y}$ 9.99 | |
| | S 3.14 | S 18.13 | S 5.21 | |

$Tp_1$ x $Tp_2$    t=0.092 non sig
$Tf_1$ x $Tf_2$    t=1.43   non sig

good, John. Now go and put your book away and drink your milk.' We hypothesized, however, that those teachers who attended to the processes that children went through in the production of the finished artefact, whether it be a line or page of writing, a sum, or a collage picture, will ultimately be doing more for their children's mastery of the necessary skills.

Table 1 displays the Tp and Tf times together with the progress scores, as defined above, for each child.

Surprisingly, no significant positive relationship was found between time spent with the teacher receiving either preparation for, or feedback on, a reading task and progress with reading during the two-year period of the investigation. Whilst these data were normally distributed (Geary's test: D'Agostino 1970) linearity was sought in an effort to test out the further hypothesis that teachers spent most time with the fastest and with the slowest children. A curvi-linear display was not found; indeed the points fell in random pattern, giving rise to the conclusion that there is no relationship whatsoever between time spent with the teacher, for whatever purpose, and progress in reading after two years in the infant school.

There is a significant positive relationship between Tp and Tf time for the under-achieving group which may be related to an idiosyncracy of the coding scheme. Tf included all the time which a child spent reading aloud to the teacher as it was considered that teacher feedback was an appropriate coding for this experience from the child's point of view, given that difficult words were prompted and words read correctly were listened to without comment. Obviously if the child could read at all, then he experienced this level of Tf more frequently than those other children who could not, and whilst the difference between the means for the two groups with respect to Tp and Tf separately are unrelated (t non-significant), the relationship between Tp and Tf for each group is unrelated for the over-achievers and highly significantly related for the under-achievers ($p<.01$ level). This may well be related to the over-inflated Tf score for those children who read aloud to their teacher more often, that is, from early on in their school career, as opposed to those who were reading aloud for less time overall.

It might be expected that dichotomizing the total sample

into over- and under-achieving groups could have a cancelling-out effect, one group on the other. Therefore, a further chi-square analysis was computed for extremes of the two groups, but no statistically significant differences were found, supporting the earlier conclusion that there is no ascertainable relationship between teacher-time and progress scores.

Teacher–pupil contact is a classroom process variable which remains elusive to define operationally and the Bristol study has not solved any of the problems which it poses. Garner and Bing (1973) pointed out some of the inequalities in teacher–pupil contact which they observed for 179 first-year junior pupils, with active, bright, personable pupils receiving high levels of contact, along with the 'naughty' pupils. It is not surprising, therefore, that quantity of teacher-time is ultimately unrelated to the progress scores of the children. Boydell (1974) attempted, as we did, to capture more of the quality of teacher–pupil contact, again in junior classrooms, and concluded that most time was spent with individual pupils at the level of supervision with relatively little time being spent on the substantive content of pupils' work. Even when this latter category was attended to, as exemplified by the codings Tp and Tf, it was not possible to demonstrate a statistically significant relationship between these quantitative/qualitative variables and the progress scores of the pupils.

Further analysis was made of the time spent on literary activities in the belief that those children who experienced more opportunities for reading and reading-related activities would make more progress during their first two years in the infant school (Gray and Satterly 1978). Table 2 displays these data and also the statistically non-significant interrelationships of these two measures for these groups. Clearly, time scores alone give no indication of the quality of the learning experience for individual children and it is, therefore, not surprising to find, once again, little direct relationship, for as Garner (1972) has pointed out:

> It seems reasonable to comment that this variable is analogous to the process of leading the horse to water. Although the child may not learn when he 'reaches' the task, it is obvious that he cannot possibly learn if he does not get to the task. (p.39)

Table 2 Time spent on learning to read x progress scores

| | Time in minutes: Year 1 and 2 | Deviation from predicted score | |
|---|---|---|---|
| Over-achievers | 139 | 15.92 | |
| $N_1=11$ | 107.75 | 19 | |
| | 64.75 | 13.39 | |
| | 202.25 | 11.29 | |
| | 208.75 | 12 | |
| | 153 | 13.23 | |
| | 277.75 | 17.13 | |
| | 302.75 | 13.15 | |
| | 189.75 | 12.4 | |
| | 323.25 | 12.54 | |
| | 175 | 14.21 | |
| | $\tilde{X}_1$ 194.91 | $\tilde{Y}_1$ 14.02 | |
| | $S_1$ 80.66 | $S_1$ 2.37 | r=0.258 non sig |
| Under- | 186.5 | 5.13 | |
| achievers | 33.5 | 3.23 | |
| $N_2=9$ | 148.25 | 4.58 | |
| | 226.5 | 4.13 | |
| | 143.25 | 9.09 | |
| | 209.75 | 5.23 | |
| | 89 | 0.47 | |
| | 69.75 | 4.15 | |
| | 146 | 9.72 | |
| | $\tilde{X}_2$ 139.17 | $\tilde{Y}_2$ 5.08 | |
| | $S_2$ 64.71 | $S_2$ 2.84 | r=0.317 non sig |
| Total | $\tilde{X}$ 169.83 | $\tilde{Y}$ 9.99 | r=0.318 non sig |
| | S 77.44 | S 5.21 | |
| | t=0.91 non sig | t=7.69 | p<.0001 |

The chi-square analysis of scores for extremes of the over- and under-achieving groups was also calculated for these data, once again supporting the conclusion reached above.

The actual time spent on learning-to-read activities is shown in Tables 4 and 5. These more specific activities included familiar distinctions:

*RG: Reading Games* designed to develop the child's sight vocabulary, using word cards and picture/word cards in a variety of tasks.

*RA: Reading Activities* – these activities drew the child's attention to the structure of words and included all phonic work.

*RC: Reading Comprehension* usually characterized by the child writing the answers to questions after reading a text or drawing pictures which accurately represented a sentence written by the teacher.

Table 3    Time spent on learning-to-read activities – Year 1

*Over-achieving group*    N=11

|  | RG | RA | RC | Total |
|---|---|---|---|---|
| Ann | 13.5 | | | 13.5 |
| Susan | 13.25 | | | 13.25 |
| Janet | 7.5 | 2.25 | | 9.75 |
| Kathleen | 22.75 | 5.75 | | 28.5 |
| Elizabeth | 65.25 | | | 65.25 |
| Allan | 3.75 | 27.25 | | 31 |
| Derek | 24 | 100.5 | | 124.5 |
| Judy | | 0.75 | | 0.75 |
| John | | 8 | | 8 |
| James | 20 | 21.75 | | 41.75 |
| Wendy | 5.25 | 28.25 | 4.25 | 37.75 |
| Total | 175.25 | 194.5 | 4.25 | 374 minutes |

$\tilde{X}$=34
S=33.59

*Under-achieving group*    N=9

|  | RG | RA | RC | Total |
|---|---|---|---|---|
| Paul | 42.25 | | | 42.25 |
| George | | | | |
| Mary | 17.5 | | | 17.5 |
| Jane | 52.5 | | | 52.5 |
| Peter | 16.25 | | | 16.25 |
| Andrew | 22.75 | | | 22.75 |
| Sandra | 4.5 | | | 4.5 |
| Philip | 11.75 | | | 11.75 |
| David | | | | |
| Total | 167.25 | | | 167.25 minutes |

$\tilde{X}$=20.94
S=16.88

Cumulative time across 7 x 3 hr observations taken monthly.

Inspection of these tables reveals distinctions between the two groups of children who were considered to be over-achieving and under-achieving at age seven. In Year 1 the over-achieving group scored in all three columns whilst the

**Table 4    Time spent on learning-to-read activities – Year 2**

*Over-achieving Group*    N=11

|  | RG | RA | RC | Total |
|---|---|---|---|---|
| Ann |  | 11.75 | 3.25 | 15 |
| Susan |  | 10.75 | 15.75 | 26.5 |
| Janet |  | 11.5 | 23 | 34.5 |
| Kathleen |  | 55 | 26 | 81 |
| Elizabeth |  | 26 | 13 | 39 |
| Allan |  | 54.25 |  | 54.25 |
| Derek |  | 31.5 |  | 31.5 |
| Judy |  |  |  |  |
| John |  | 14.25 | 64.75 | 79 |
| James | 21.25 | 70.5 |  | 91.5 |
| Wendy |  | 20.5 | 44.5 | 65 |
| Total | 21.25 | 306 | 190.25 | 517.5 minutes |

$$\tilde{X}=47.05$$
$$S=28.08$$

*Under-achieving Group*    N=9

|  | RG | RA | RC | Total |
|---|---|---|---|---|
| Paul | 5.5 |  |  | 5.5 |
| George | 14.5 |  |  | 14.5 |
| Mary | 51.5 | 31.5 |  | 83 |
| Jane | 1.75 | 44.25 |  | 46 |
| Peter | 0.5 |  |  | 0.5 |
| Andrew |  |  |  |  |
| Sandra |  | 4.25 | 11.25 | 15.5 |
| Philip | 5 | 7.5 |  | 12.5 |
| David | 26 | 10 |  | 36 |
| Total | 104.75 | 97.5 | 11.25 | 112.5 minutes |

$$\tilde{X}=23.72$$
$$S=25.55$$

Cumulative time across 7 x 3 hr observations taken monthly.

under-achieving group received RG alone, this group entering the three columns by the second year. Mean scores of the total time spent on the learning-to-read activities is markedly different for the two groups, with the over-achieving group receiving consistently more time overall.

Tests of statistical significance were applied to the mean scores of each group (Year 1 and 2) with respect to the time spent on learning-to-read activities:

pooled variance formula  t  = 5.94 (p<.001 level)
Mann Whitney U test     U = 26    (p<.05 level)

Given that the data could not be assumed to be normally distributed (*cf.* standard deviations), the U value alone indicates a statistically significant difference between the two groups, pointing to the conclusion that there is a positive relationship between time spent on learning-to-read activities during the first two years of schooling and achievement in reading which is more than would have been expected from their knowledge of literacy scores at age five. Although a statistically non-significant correlation ($r=0.329$) was found between these time measures and progress scores, the relationship is still in a positive direction.

Data collected from these Bristol classrooms suggests that those teachers who adopted a varied approach to learning-to-read activities, including both synthetic and analytic methods from the early stages, provided their children with greater opportunities for progress. Those teachers who filled in time at the end of the morning with a word card game (Paul), or who left children alone for too long with materials they did not understand (Jane), or who felt their children were not yet ready for learning-to-read activities at all (George and David) appear to have failed to give their children a firm basis on which to build later progress. Teachers of the children in the over-achieving group mainly spent time with their pupils whilst activities were carried out, with other children in the class being occupied in a variety of alternative activities; they provided a range of different kinds of activities (Derek) and did not wait for 'readiness' to be exhibited by the child – they anticipated it. Judy, who apparently received a small amount of learning-to-read activities, experienced an idiosyncratic learning-to-read programme which laid great emphasis on children writing their own stories for reading and much of her learning-to-read experience was not coded in a way which could be captured by the RG–RA–RC framework.

John and Sandra shared the same class teacher throughout the two-year period of the investigation and it is, therefore, surprising that they appear in different groups. From the time scores it is indicated that John experienced more learning-to-read activities, possibly implying that Sandra would have done better if she had been involved in these more, but she was a shy, withdrawn girl, who exemplifies the case of an able child who, whilst making progress, under-achieved perhaps because she did not draw the teacher's attention to herself, and did not get included in the specific learning activities of the classroom (*cf*. Garner and Bing *op. cit.*). Ann and Susan also shared the same teacher and it is interesting, in contrast, to notice that their experience of learning-to-read activities is similar with respect to time spent, implying perhaps that their teacher was more orderly in her record keeping, ensuring the equal experience of her children rather than leaving this to chance.

## Summary

The statistical analysis of the time-based data alone was unsuccessful in establishing clear relationships between classroom variables related to reading activities and the progress in reading which the children made during their first two years in school. The sample size is too small for general statements to be made, but the indications are that consideration of time spent by pupils does not reveal the differences between classrooms with respect to the differential progress made by individual pupils. How much time teachers devote to their pupils, and pupils devote to learning-to-read activities, seem rather less significant than what they do in the time and, more importantly, the way in which the interaction and the task is shared by the teacher with each pupil. Whilst it is the case that the statistical evidence does indicate, although not conclusively, differences between teachers in their effect on the progress scores of their pupils, the exact parameters of these differences do not emerge without additional case-study accounts of individual children's classroom experiences. Further work is in progress (Wells 1978) in which both video and audio recordings in infant classrooms are being collected as a means of capturing more precise information with respect to the differences between teachers. Whilst other studies report such differences with confidence, it is implied from the results of this investigation that differences between teachers are more subtle than any that have so far been systematically studied. It is also suggested from these finding that the traditional statistical model of analysis is perhaps not the most appropriate for use with data collected in the field of classroom research.

# References

BOYDELL, D. (1974) Teacher-pupil contact in junior classrooms *British Journal of Educational Psychology* 44, 313–18

CANE, B. and SMITHERS, J. (1971) *The Roots of Reading* NFER

CARVER, C. (1970) *Word Recognition Test* Hodder and Stoughton

CLAY, M. M. (1972) *The Early Detection of Reading Difficulties: a diagnostic survey* Heinemann

D'AGOSTINO, R. B. (1970) Simple compact portable test of normality: Geary's test revisited *Psychological Bulletin* 74, 2, 138–40

DES (1967) *Children and Their Primary Schools* (Plowden Report) HMSO

DES (1975) *A Language for Life* (Bullock Report) HMSO

DOUGLAS, J. W. B. (1966) *The Home and the School* MacGibbon and Kee

GARNER, J. (1972) Some aspects of behaviour in infant school classrooms *Research in Education* 7, 28–47

GARNER, J. and BING, M. (1973) Inequalities of teacher-pupil contacts *British Journal of Educational Psychology* 43, 234-43

GRAY, J. (1975) The Roots of Reading: a critical re-analysis *Research in Education* 14, 33–47

GRAY, J. (1976) 'Good teaching and reading progress: a critical review' in A. Cashdan (Ed) *The Content of Reading* Ward Lock Educational

GRAY, J. (1977) Teacher competence in reading tuition *Educational Research* 19, No. 2, 113–21

GRAY, J. and SATTERLY, D. (1978) Time to learn? *Educational Research* 20, 2, 137–42

NEALE, M.D. (1960) *Analysis of Reading Ability* Macmillan

RABAN, B., WELLS, G. and NASH, T. (1976) Observing children learning to read *Research Intelligence* 3, 1, 36–7

RABAN, B. (1978) 'Teacher Assessment Schedule' in *Children Learning to Read* Final Report to SSRC.

Also parts to appear in:

RABAN, B. and MOON, C. (1978) *Books and learning to Read* School Library Association

WELLS, G. (1974) Language development in pre-school children *Journal of Child Language* 1, 1, 158–62

WELLS, G. (1978) Talking with children: the complementary roles of parents and teachers *English in Education* 12, 2, 15–38


Further papers related to this topic (with reference to junior schools):

SOUTHGATE, V., ARNOLD, H. and JOHNSON, S. (1978) 'The use of teachers' and children's time in *Extending Beginning Reading*' in E. Hunter-Grundin and H. U. Grundin (Eds) *Reading: Implementing the Bullock Report* Ward Lock Educational

MORRIS, J. M. (1978) 'Children's reading achievement in relation to their teachers' attributes' in E. Hunter-Grundin and H. U. Grundin (Eds) *Reading: Implementing the Bullock Report* Ward Lock Educational

# 7 Why put the cart before the horse?

## Douglas Pidgeon

It is the intention of this paper to provide a theoretical justification for a basic hypothesis which is being tested in a new Programme for teaching beginners to read. The Programme, which also includes some novel practical considerations that are discussed elsewhere (Pidgeon 1978), is now undergoing developmental and evaluative trials. There are two points to be made clear at the outset. First, that the Programme deals basically with beginning reading, including what many might describe as pre-reading activities, except that the view is taken here that there is no clear distinction between pre-reading and reading – the former being considered as an essential part of the latter. Second, the concern is with ensuring that children learn *how* to read and not just with teaching them *to* read.

To provide a background to the hypothesis to be developed, it is clearly necessary to discuss briefly the early stages of beginning reading. Before attempting this task, however, it might be helpful to examine how the process of reading is usually viewed. At a very general level, for example, few would disagree that reading is obtaining meaning from printed words. As Barron (1978) has pointed out, however, 'there has been very little research, at least until recently, about whether fluent readers always obtain access to the lexical meanings of printed words by first decoding them into sound, or whether the visual pattern of the word provides sufficient information for meaning access'. He gives an extensive review of the relevant literature and concludes, perhaps not surprisingly, that both play a part. The graphemic representation alone will provide access to the meanings of individual printed words, although a phonetic recoding is necessary as 'a means of

holding printed words in memory until they are understood'
(*ibid.*).

So much for the fluent reader, but what about the beginner? Is a knowledge of 'phonics' necessary in the very early stages in order to hold printed words in the memory, or can a store of whole words be built up first, without access to sound? There is no intention of resurrecting here the 'phonics' versus 'whole word' controversy, for it would seem that both are needed if any degree of fluency is to be attained. As the Bullock Report (DES 1975) sums it up:

> Competence in phonics is essential both for attacking unfamiliar words and for fluent reading. The question, then, is not whether or not to teach phonics; of this there can be no doubt. The question is how and when to do it.

The advice proffered by the Bullock Committee was not exactly precise but clearly tended towards the initial building up of a sight vocabulary based on the language experience approach. Its own survey did reveal, however, that approximately 97 per cent of reading teachers used both phonics and 'look and say' with *six* year olds, but no information was obtained on how or when they used each approach. It might be noted here that apparently only 35 per cent of teachers used pre-reading exercises, although what these were was not fully described.

Sound, it would seem, plays an important part in learning to read, although it should be understood that it is not a necessary requisite. The totally deaf can be taught to read without access to sound although the task is difficult and the degree of success is not very high (Conrad 1977), and there are some ideographic or logographic languages like Chinese or the Japanese Kanji where the main association is a direct one between character and meaning. The great drawback with such languages, as with the deaf learning an alphabetic script such as English, is that there is a limit to the number of associations which can be formed without any phonemic help. There is no doubt that the evolution of alphabetic writing was a major step forward for mankind. Having to learn, say, some 3,000 associations between different printed words and their meanings would be quite a task for some children, but even so they could only be classed as very backward readers since the comprehension vocabulary of even six to nine year old children is around 9,000 words (Berdiansky *et al* 1969), and usually increases rapidly.

It would follow from what has just been said that, unless a beginner masters the phonemic principles fairly early in learning to read, a course could be set for failure – a view which is supported by the research evidence summarized by Chall (1967) and by the analysis of 'sight word' learning by Groff (1974). The steps taken by most teachers of reading are worth examining a little more closely. A few, it would seem, start directly with 'phonics', but most build up a small sight vocabulary first, mainly because reading is for meaning and meaning resides in whole words not letters. The tendency these days is to use the child's own words through some adaptation of the language experience approach. This would seem to have much to commend it since no teacher would want to present a word for reading the meaning of which is unknown to a child. By the same token, however, the teacher developing 'phonics' should not present, say, the letter *k* and expect the child to learn that it makes a /k/ sound which is equally unknown. And this is *not* a matter of an inability to discriminate sounds. As Downing has recently said, '(A child) may articulate perfectly, showing a clear distinction between phonemes such as /f/ and /k/, without knowing what he is doing' (Downing 1977).

An attempt has been made in Model 1 to represent diagrammatically the usual approaches by which a child learns to extract meaning from the printed word.

Briefly, the first column shows the usual route by which a beginner builds up a sight vocabulary. The main column in Route 2 lists the steps which have to be acquired if phonemic principles are to be employed in arriving at the meaning of a hitherto unknown word, while the boxes to the right illustrate what is necessary if these steps are to be understood. Route 3 is the direct route, once a word is known and available for direct access from a child's internal lexicon. A point to be stressed, of course, is that a large store of 'sight words' does not, of itself, make a fluent reader. The analysis by Barron (*ibid.*) showed that a complete understanding of the middle 'phonic route' is also essential. Any failure here not only results in a limitation of known 'sight words', but it also influences the ability to understand what is being read.

**Model 1**

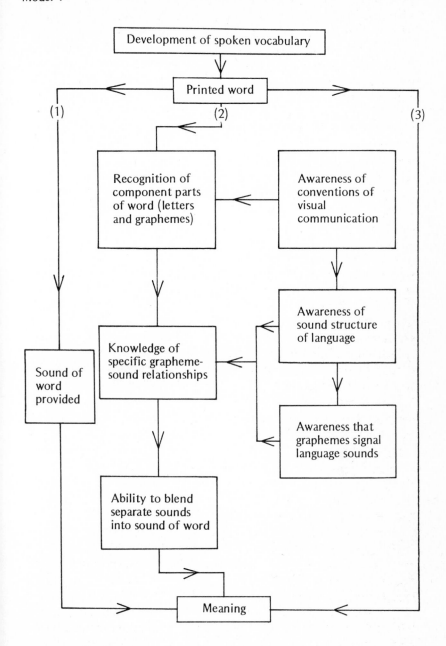

Learning to read by Route 2 is both more complex and difficult than by Route 1, and hence it can easily be appreciated that those who find decoding a problem through lack of understanding of phonemic principles, or for any other reason, revert to the simpler technique of relying on building up a direct 'sight vocabulary', and thus never really master the process of fluent reading.

Route 1 then, typifies the whole word approach: the child is presented with a printed word and in some way is informed of its spoken form, with which meaning is associated. With repetition and practice the direct association is learned and committed to memory so that the meaning comes directly from the visual presentation and the word added to the child's internal lexicon, available through Route 3. In order to take advantage of the phonemic properties of an alphabetic script, of course, Route 2 is followed at some point. This involves first being able to recognize the component parts of the presented word – basically the graphemes, which may be either single letters or combinations of letters – an activity usually going under the name of visual discrimination. It should be noted that, at this stage, the learner must also develop an awareness of the accepted conventions of viewing print, such as the appropriate orientation of letters, visual seriation and left-to-right and top-to-bottom eye movements. A child should in fact be fully operational in the use of these conventions before even Route 1 is followed otherwise reversals in writing may easily occur.

The next stage is to learn the specific grapheme-sound relationships appropriate to the English language. These can be – and often are – learned parrot-fashion. It should be noted, however, that if there is to be any understanding of how this aspect of the reading process works so that further progress can be made, then it is clearly necessary that the learner (a) should have reached the level of the symbolic function, or, in other words, understands that marks on paper (i.e. letters or graphemes) can represent or signify different sounds, and (b) should have developed an awareness of the sound structure of spoken language.

The first of these points relates learning to read to Piaget's stages of cognitive development, an area which, according to Waller (1977) has tended to be rather neglected. The idea that before attempts to teach reading are made, more time should be spent encouraging the development of the appropriate thought processes required in reading and getting children to learn what reading is all about has been put forward by Furth and Wachs (1974), Waller (1977), and Kirkland (1978) amongst others. Unfortunately, a number of children who have not developed the symbolic function nevertheless form letter-sound relationships and *appear* to be making progress in reading. But if they do not know that a printed letter or word can exist in its own right and at the same time signify something else – a sound or meaning – then any time spent trying to teach them to read is probably wasted.

The second point, it is maintained, is equally crucial. If children are to master the reading process they must, at the very least, understand that a relationship exists between the spoken and written forms of their language. But there are many children undergoing reading instruction who do not appreciate this relationship. Rozin, Bressman and Taft (1973), demonstrated, for example, that there were some second graders in the USA who could not recognize a relation between sound length and print length, in letters, of various words. It would seem clear that, for many children, how their spoken language works is as much a mystery as how reading works. As Downing (1977) has put it, ' . . . it is the normal state of affairs for the young child to be skilled in speaking without knowing what he is doing or how he does it'. He also adds, however, 'But in developing literacy skills he has to become aware of his own language behaviour if he is to understand how written language operates' (*ibid.*). This would seem a basic point. How can children employ phonemic principles in decoding a new word not already in their internal lexicon if they have no clear understanding of how their spoken language works? Elkonin, the Russian psychologist, who has worked extensively in this area, has concluded, 'Hence it follows inevitably that the first problem to be solved *before* teaching literacy is to reveal to the child the sound structure of spoken words: not only the basic sound units of language but also how language is constructed from them.' (Elkonin 1973)

Returning to Model 1, therefore, it is argued that unless the beginner has a basic awareness of the points made in the boxes on the far right, and in particular understands how his spoken language works, there will be a failure to understand how phonemic principles operate. Although some associations between letters and sounds may become established, no efficient working of Route 2 will be possible. After a hard struggle, a tentative pathway down the centre boxes will be formed but it will provide minimal help. Incidentally, the final step in this Route can cause a stumbling block for many beginners; even knowing the composite sounds in an unknown word does not lead to meaning unless the ability to combine or blend them into a total word sound can be accomplished.

To avoid any misunderstanding, it should be made clear that the problems associated with understanding phonemic principles do not apply to all children. Many develop an awareness of these basic constituents of the reading process before they even get to school, largely because they will have been read to extensively in their early pre-school years and much attention will have been paid to their language development. Possibly it is to such children as this that the Bullock Report refers when it states that 'over a period of time children learn to make intuitive generalizations about phoneme-grapheme relationships. Even if there is no explicit teaching of phonics many children will still work out phonic relationships for themselves' (DES 1975, pp. 87–8).

Unfortunately, as many teachers will testify, such a statement does not apply by any means to all children. Surveys, such as that by Start and Wells (1972), have demonstrated that up to 25 per cent of school leavers are backward readers, being at least two years retarded. The hypothesis being considered here is that many of these failed to grasp some of the basic essentials of understanding the reading process and as a result simply continued to acquire a few more additions to their 'sight vocabularies', using essentially logographic principles. Of course, some phonic associations might have been learned, but there would have been a tendency to stick on the infamous plateau where reading becomes a chore and the expectation of failure itself prevents any further positive progress. Gleitman and Rozin (1973) discuss this situation and say:

Despite phonics instruction, some children seem to

have acquired merely a sight vocabulary of some whole words after tedious years of schooling... experience suggests that this problem may persist to adulthood. Some children end up...with a vocabulary of at best a few thousand words. But this is exactly what we would expect as the outcome of learning a logographic system: there is a slow accretion of items and, in the absence of overriding motivation, a diminishing return as the number of items increases.

The main point to note in reviewing Model 1 is that, in learning to read, the general movement is from sight to sound. There might seem nothing surprising about this since, after all, reading is a visual activity. Certainly this view has been advocated in nearly all textbooks on reading. The first of the four major aspects of Gray's famous conceptual framework for the total reading act was the perception of words (Gray 1960). Most other workers, whether advocating code emphasis (phonic) methods or meaning emphasis (whole word) approaches seem to take it for granted that, apart from certain pre-reading activities such as language development and visual and auditory discrimination, the actual task of learning to read starts with visual presentation of letters, words or sentences. This applies also to those who have attempted descriptions of the stages of learning to read. The first two of Gibson's three stages leading to fluency are 'learning to differentiate graphic symbols' and 'learning to decode letters to sounds' (Gibson 1965).

At this point, the reference to the horse and cart in the title of this paper should become clear. If sound plays such an important part in producing fluent readers of an alphabetic script, why is it relegated to second place where lack of understanding can apparently cause problems? Why is a start made to teach reading by moving from sight to sound instead of from sound to sight? After all, it is a sound educational principle to progress always from the known to the unknown and not to make a leap into the dark which is what happens for many children who are asked to learn, for example, that the letter *c*, that is a hitherto unknown squiggle on paper, signals (sometimes) /kuh/, an equally unknown sound. But if printed letters and words are the cart, the horse is not just spoken language – it is an understanding of the sound structure of that language. Using children's own language, especially if it is presented to them in print to copy, misses the point. It may be a valuable help for those fortunate enough to come from good linguistic backgrounds, but it is questionable whether those who lack an understanding of how their spoken language works are gaining much more than a little motor control and possibly adding a few words to their 'sight vocabularies'. Certainly, the teacher cannot be sure that there is any understanding of symbolic functioning or that such pupils have any real idea what learning is meant to be taking place.

What has been suggested by Elkonin and Downing and is the theme of this paper is that a pupil should possess an awareness of the sound structure of spoken language and appreciate that the unit sounds of language can be represented on paper *before* any attempt is made to introduce reading *per se*, that is, before the pupil is required to learn word-meaning or grapheme-sound associations. This idea is not entirely new, of course. It was suggested, for example, by Van Allen (1959); and Carroll (1970), in his list of eight requirements for successful reading, places 'The child must learn to dissect *spoken* words into component sounds' second only to 'The child must know the language he is going to learn to read'. Yet little work has been carried out, outside Russia, to test the general hypothesis.

An attempt to illustrate this alternative pathway to learning for beginners is given in Model 2.

The equivalent of Route 1 in the first Model – the direct acquisition of a sight vocabulary – is missing entirely and is replaced by Row 1 comprising a series of steps through which children gain a basic understanding of what reading is all about. An internal lexicon is built up as an aid to fluent reading, but only *after* an understanding of phonemic principles has been established. Row 2, which follows on only after Row 1 has been successfully completed, reads from right to left and involves the learning of specific sound-grapheme relationships, but always in the context of meaningful words. In effect, the spoken word, whose sound structure is known and understood at this stage, is mapped onto the printed word, the specific relationships being learned during the process. Route 2 in Row 3 illustrates how

94

**Model 2**

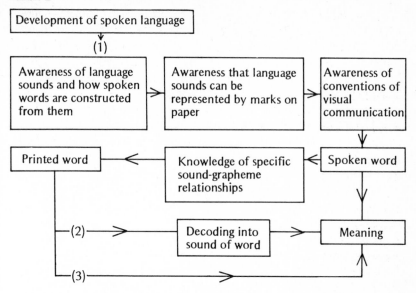

unknown words are subsequently decoded, and is equivalent to Route 2 of Model 1 except that there is one fundamental difference: the learner is not operating in the dark but has a clear awareness of how the process works before the exercise is attempted. Route 3, of course, provides direct access to meaning from the usual presentation of a word. For fluent readers, as for beginners, Routes 2 and 3 operate together.

The major benefit to be obtained from Model 2 is the fact that the teacher can be assured at the outset that the beginner is first going to obtain an understanding of what reading is all about. This is certainly not true of many normal beginners as Reid (1966), Downing (1969 and 1970) and Francis (1973) have demonstrated. The possibility, therefore, that many children are reading via Route 3 alone and hence are only *appearing* to make progress in reading is thus removed. Put another way, a foundation, solid enough to support full fluency in reading, is built up first, *before* any attempt is made to teach reading *per se*. This contrasts with the usual practice, typified in Model 1, in which, apart from the odd 35 per cent who are given pre-reading activities mostly in visual and auditory discrimination which cause problems for only about 1 per cent of beginners, most children are introduced directly to some form of reading, and the necessary understanding which comprises the basic foundation is only supplied later – often too late.

There are, of course, some objections to this approach. Progress in learning to read is judged by many teachers and also, one must add, by many parents, by the actual ability to read, usually measured by a pupil's passage through a set of reading books, if not by a test of some kind. While movement through Model 2 may be quite rapid for those children with adequate pre-school language experiences, the same cannot be said for other slower learners lacking suitable linguistic backgrounds. The temptation to skip too quickly through the important early stages in order to get pupils reading (especially if pressure from parents is substantial) can be quite strong, although to do so could lead to a lack of understanding and become a forerunner of future failure. A lesson to be learned from the first year's developmental trials of the new Programme is the need for teachers to affirm their professionalism and resist the temptations offered by the easy way out.

Another objection is that it could be claimed that many reception-class children of four and a half to five years of age are incapable of distinguishing the phoneme as a unit of speech sound and therefore cannot grasp the sound structure of language. This view is propounded by Gleitman and Rozin (1973) who advocate the use of a syllabary to teach early reading, and they quote a study by Liberman *et al* (1972) in support. However, this does not negate the general principle set out here but, to the extent that it is true, a child's passage through the early stages of Model 2 may be that much the slower. It must be pointed out in defence that understanding the phonic principle in the traditional approach also requires the same learning and if it does not occur then the learner may revert to acquiring a direct sight vocabulary alone with all the limitations this involves.

One further objection revolves around the difficulty of coping with the mismatch which occurs between the spoken and written forms of the English language. If the sound structure cannot be matched to its graphic representation in

96

a way that is meaningful and acceptable to the learner, what is the point of starting by teaching sound structure? In reply it may be said that this problem is capable of solution though it lies outside the scope of this paper. It should, of course, be added that it is not unique to the approach put forward here, but exists even if the direction of learning is from sight to sound.

It is too early to report any quantitative results from the present study – the evaluation proper only starts in September 1978. The work carried out during this last developmental year, however, gives every reason to believe that, using the materials developed for the purpose, progress through the learning stages of Model 2 can be satisfactorily achieved to the eventual benefit of both pupils and teachers.

# References

BARRON, R. W. (1978) 'Access to the meanings of printed words: some implications for reading and learning to read' in F. B. Murray (Ed) *The Recognition of Words* Newark, Delaware: International Reading Association

BERDIANSKY, B., CRONNELL, B. and KOCHLER, J. (1969) *Spelling – Sound Relations and Primary Form – Class Descriptions of Speech – Comprehension Vocabularies of 6–9 Year Olds* South-West Regional Laboratory for Educational Research and Development, Technical Report No. 15, cited in DES *A Language for Life* HMSO

CARROLL, J. B. (1976) 'The nature of the reading process' in H. Singer and R. B. Ruddell (Eds) *Theoretical Models and Processes of Reading* Newark, Delaware: International Reading Association

CHALL, J. (1967) *Learning to Read:The Great Debate* McGraw-Hill

CONRAD, R. (1977) The reading ability of deaf school leavers *British Journal of Educational Psychology* 47, 2, 138–48

DES (1975) *A Language for Life* (The Bullock Report) HMSO

DOWNING, J. (1969) How children think about reading *The Reading Teacher* 23, 217–30

DOWNING, J. (1970) Children's concepts of language in learning to read *Educational Research* 12, 105–12

DOWNING, J. (1977) Linguistics for infants *Reading* XI, 2, 36–45

ELKONIN, D. B. (1973) 'Reading in the USSR' in J. Downing (Ed) *Comparative Reading* New York: Macmillan

FRANCIS, H. (1973) Children's experience of reading and notions of units of language *British Journal of Educational Psychology* 43, 1, 17–23

FURTH, H. G. and WACHS, H. (1974) *Thinking Goes to School: Piaget's Theory in Practice* New York: Oxford University Press

GIBSON, E. J. (1965) Learning to Read *Science* 148, 1066–72

GLEITMAN, L. R. and ROZIN, P. (1973) Teaching reading by use of syllabary *Reading Research Quarterly* VIII, 4, 447–83

GRAY, W. S. (1960) 'The major aspects of reading' *Sequential Development of Reading Abilities* Supplementary Monographs No. 90, Chicago, University of Chicago Press. Cited in A. Melnik and J. Merritt (Eds) *The Reading Curriculum* (1972) Open University Press

GROFF, P. (1974) The topsy-turvy world of 'sight' words *The Reading Teacher* 27, 572–8

KIRKLAND, E. R. (1978) A Piagetian interpretation of beginning reading instruction *The Reading Teacher* 31, 5, 497–503

LIBERMAN, I. Y., SHANKWEILER, D., CARTER, B. and FISHER, W. F. (1972) *Reading and the Awareness of Linguistic Segments* University of Connecticut (mimeo). Cited in 'Teaching reading by use of a syllabary' *Reading Research Quarterly* VIII, 447–83

PIDGEON, D. A. (1978) A logical reading programme for beginners *Primary Education Review* 4, 19–21

REID, J. F. (1966) Learning to think about reading *Educational Research* 9, 56–62

ROZIN, P, BRESSMAN, B. and TAFT, M. (1973) 'Do children understand the basic relationship between speech and writing?' The MOW-Motorcycle Test. University of Pennsylvania (mimeographed). Cited in 'Teaching reading by use of a syllabary' *Reading Research Quarterly* VIII, 447–83

START, K. B. and WELLS, B. K. (1972) *The Trend of Reading Standards* NFER

VAN ALLEN, R. (1959) 'Concept development of young children in reading instruction' in M. P. Douglas (Ed) *Claremont Reading Conference*, 24th Yearbook. Claremont Graduate School Curriculum Laboratory

WALLER, T. G. (1977) *Think First, Read Later* Newark, Delaware: International Reading Association

# 8   New phonics for old

## Joyce Morris

During their early school years most children build up a stock of sight words. But their growth in reading is impeded and can be permanently stunted if, at the same time, they do not begin to develop the word-analysis skills, including phonics, which are necessary for independent reading.

The nature of the task with regard to reading English is particularly difficult mainly because of the nature of traditional orthography and its relationship to the phonological system. In consequence, even clever children can fail to develop these skills without systematic instruction from expert teachers using appropriate materials.

The literature contains many examples of such children. A case in point is a bright boy of ten who, in a diagnostic interview with Clymer (1968), was asked, 'Why do you think you have trouble reading?' To which the boy replied without hesitation, 'Oh, I read all right, it's just the words that bother me.' As Clymer points out, this child had a 'fairly good stock of sight words and an excellent technique for gaining general significance from his reading, but he had no word analysis skills'. His concept of reading was 'getting the gist of the author's message', and it prevented him from 'seeing clearly his shortcomings as an effective reader'.

### 1 Slogans
Unfortunately, everyone would not agree, or even be aware, that such a boy should be given systematic instruction to develop word-analysis skills, i.e. the skills used in analysing an unfamiliar word for clues to its sound and meaning. Or, indeed, some of the strategies for accurate word identification known as 'word-attack' skills, and which

include the use of configuration, phonic, structural and contextual clues. This is partly because 'reading for meaning' is a battle cry once again and 'reading to get the gist of the author's message' is doing just that.

Another perennially popular slogan which can prevent young children being taught to decode words is 'reading for meaning from the beginning'. Yet another is 'children learn to read by reading' and the fallacious 'reading is a natural process'.

Such slogans are dangerously naive, and their widespread use stems largely from the fact that teachers and others concerned professionally with reading are generally busy people. A slogan certainly saves time in explaining where one stands, particularly with regard to controversial issues. Nevertheless, to my knowledge, all those mentioned have caused teachers to feel somewhat 'reactionary', especially when using phonic methods and materials.

## 2 Theories and their implications

Even more potentially harmful to children's reading growth are theories of reading with names which sound scientific inasmuch as they incorporate such terms as 'psycho-linguistic', 'substrata-factor' and so on. Again this is partly because teacher-trainers, who advocate the practical application of this or that theory, usually have not sufficient time to study with the accurate intensity of a scholar. Consequently, important aspects of reading theories are neglected and even omitted when discussed with student and practising teachers, or in publications prepared for their use.

What must be stressed here is that research has revealed more of the complexities of the reading process since Robinson (1968) summed up the position ten years ago for the National Society for the Study of Education. At that time she wrote:

Major effort in the past has been given to methods and procedures for teaching reading, with considerably less attention being given to how children learn or to the process of learning to read. Whild fragments of information are emerging, not enough is yet known to develop a descriptive model of the reading process.

Today, as will be seen from the large IRA publication called *Theoretical Models and Processes of Reading* (Singer and Ruddell 1976), although further advances in knowledge have been made, we are still a long way from having a definitive model of the reading process. What is more, some researchers such as Robinson (1977) now think that there is no such entity as *the* reading process. Hence, our hope for the future lies in having definitive models for different reading processes according to purpose.

Be that as it may, research in the theoretical field must go on for the sake of teachers and children because, in the words of the eminent psychologist Kurt Lewin: 'What is most practical is a good theory.' Meanwhile, it is important that all concerned with children's reading growth should examine very carefully those theories which lend support to the popular slogans previously mentioned, and, hence, tend to be opposed to systematic instruction to develop the skills which previous research has shown to be essential. In other words, the phonic and other word-analysis skills which are *critical* to learning to read according to a recent policy statement of the International Reading Association (1977).

In the space available, it is not possible to examine all pertinent theories or, indeed, any of them in scholarly detail. However, attention is focused on the theories of Kenneth Goodman and Frank Smith because they are the most publicized in Britain and, therefore, could have the most influence on British teachers.

*Goodman's model of the reading process*
At last year's conference, we heard from Goodman that 'reading is a psycholinguistic guessing game' and not, as common sense would have it, a precise process involving exact, detailed, sequential perception and identification of letters, words, spelling patterns and large language units. In his writings he repeats the same thing, and also states (Goodman 1976):

> This is not to say that those who have worked diligently in the field of reading are not aware that reading is more than precise, sequential identification. But, the commonsense notion, though not adequate, continues to permeate thinking about reading.

101

In the same paper, he then offers a replacement for the commonsense notion by stating:

Reading is a selective process. It involves partial use of available minimal language cues selected from perceptual input on the basis of the reader's expectation. As this partial information is processed, tentative decisions are made to be confirmed, rejected or refined as reading progresses.

Of course, the problem with this definition is that it does not apply to all kinds of reading. Reading has to be a precise process in many circumstances of life in a literate society. Moreover, teachers might well ask Goodman how one acquires text sampling ability in the first place. In other words, what does his theory mean in terms of classroom practice? Here Goodman (1972) tends to evade the issue by saying that, as yet, there is no articulated *theory* of reading instruction, but he will present some of the essentials. In doing so, he categorically states, 'There is *no possible sequencing of skills* in reading instruction since all systems must be used interdependently in the reading process even in the first attempts at learning to read.' He also declares, 'Fractionating language for instructional purposes into words and word parts destroys its essential nature.' Consequently he feels that 'materials designed and prepared to facilitate learning to read are perhaps a contradiction in terms, since such materials are likely to distort and fragment language.'

One wonders what American teachers make of all this, especially if they use the Scott Foresman Reading Systems and also note that Goodman is a co-author. It is also difficult to see how publishers, in any country, could produce materials to meet his eighth and last essential requirement which states, 'Materials for reading instruction must involve natural language; they must be highly predictable on the basis of the learner's language; and they must involve meaning within the learner's grasp; that is, they must be related to the reader's linguistic competence and his experience.'

Clearly, teachers who try to put Goodman's theories into practice are in for a difficult time. They must abandon hope of finding precisely the right materials at least for the foreseeable future. Amongst other things, they must also refrain from giving systematic instruction in word-analysis skills, including phonics, because this would entail fractionating language and sequencing skills. As for their pupils, research suggests that they might become expert guessers, but certainly not expert readers unless motivated and able to learn to read by themselves.

Undoubtedly, Goodman has already made a significant contribution to our thinking about the reading process. It is a pity, however, that some teacher-trainers seem to have fallen in love with his model without examining its imperfections. It is also regrettable that, in their own writings, they tend to ignore research which indicates intrinsic flaws at a deeper level. For instance, the research of Walker (1977) indicates that, although principles of cue sampling and meaning reconstruction apply to both listening and reading, greater precision is required for reading comprehension. Studies of children during their first years of reading instruction respectively by Weber (1970), Biemeller (1970) and Clay (1972) show that, contrary to Goodman's thesis (1976) and that of Frank Smith (1971), the use of contextual information does not typically differentiate between good and poor readers. Whereas, the errors (or 'miscues' in Goodman's terminology) of good readers indicate that they made more use of orthographic information. This also applies to older children according to research reported by Kolers (1975) and by Allington and Strange (1977). In short, there is a considerable amount of evidence, to which only a few references have been made, which suggests that it is probably as well to remember that a good reader need not guess; the poor reader has to and, usually, will continue to do so until given effective instruction to develop accuracy in word recognition.

*Smith's rules for reading teachers*
Turning now to the theories of Frank Smith, we find that they have much in common with those of Goodman. This is perhaps not surprising because both are concerned to define 'reading' and, hence, they study primarily what readers do or don't do, rather than studying how children learn to read from the very beginning.

103

Smith's writings tend to be an amalgam of his own ideas and those of others of like mind. *Understanding Reading* (Smith 1971) is the title of his first book to reach Britain. In the preface, he says it was written 'to stimulate the layman rather than satisfy the scholar', and, not being a teacher of children, he 'would not presume to assert that a particular instructional method is superior to any other'. It seems churlish, therefore, to point out that he does not substantiate his principal claim that, contrary to the mainstream of expert opinion, meaning comes first in reading and not the decoding of print to sound and thence to meaning. In other words, Smith claims that print is directly converted to meaning by the reader. It also seems niggardly to ask for proof of his contention that children cannot be taught the skills necessary for accurate word recognition. Acording to him, they must acquire this ability through their own experience of looking for significant differences in the visual configuration to eliminate alternatives.

As editor of a second book *Psycholinguistics and Reading*, Smith (1973) presents and debates what he claims are three radical 'insights' supported by contemporary linguistics and cognitive psychology. These are:

1    Only a small part of the information necessary for reading comprehension comes from the printed page.
2    Comprehension must precede the identification of individual words.
3    Reading is not decoding to spoken language.

Considering the radical nature of these so-called 'insights', it is not surprising that the book attracted attention from scholars. The linguist Shuy (1973) reviewed it critically and commented, 'Smith seems to feel that decoding is used by the *bad guys*', i.e. all who do not belong to the group of contributing authors. He suggests that this may be a justifiable over-reaction against teaching which never gets beyond the decoding stage. He also doubts that one of the major claims of the book, that decoding is unnecessary, has been adequately made.

Shuy does not recommend the book to the average teacher, and perhaps his advice should be heeded insofar as, to my knowledge, even outstanding teachers have been unsettled by its content; in particular a chapter by Smith sardonically entitled 'Twelve easy ways to make learning to read difficult, and one difficult way to make it easy'. He summarizes the text in a list headed 'Twelve rules for reading teachers', the effect of which is to deride practices which are essential for children's growth in reading. For example, the practice of trying an alternative method if the one being used is unsatisfactory, and the practice of identifying and giving special attention to problem readers as soon as possible. The text itself contains untruths and partial truths passed off as total veracity For instance, Smith declares, 'All proficient readers have acquired an implicit knowledge of how to read, but this knowledge has been developed through the practice of reading, not through anything that is taught at school.' He sums this up in the words of a previosuly mentioned slogan, 'Children learn to read by reading'. He then goes on to say that a prominent aspect of what he calls the 'reading by rules' fallacy is the notion that reading ability depends on a knowledge of spelling-to-sound correspondences. This is eventually summed up as the 'phonics fallacy'. He then proceeds to set up and demolish a series of strawmen and, in doing so, reveals that, in no way, could he support the use of phonic methods and materials or, indeed, any other form of systematic instruction to promote the accurate recognition of words. According to Smith, 'In order to read one must guess, not recklessly but on an informed basis. Informed guessing means by making the best use of non-visual information, of what one already knows.'

At the end of all this, teachers might well ask, 'But how can we help children to read as so many obviously need our help?' To which, Smith would reply, 'Learning to read is a problem for the child to solve. Glance back at all my twelve easy rules and you will see that none of them is really concerned with what the child is doing.' Therefore, what you must do is, 'Respond to what the child is trying to do.' In other words, follow the only rule that makes reading easy for the learner, be a good intuitive teacher, sensitive to 'the unspoken intellectual demands of a child, encouraging and responding to his hypothesis testing'.

### 3 Phonics reconsidered

It may seem strange to have spent so much of my allotted space on theories which offer such little practical help to teachers. However, it was important to do so because they are opposed to systematic instruction for developing accuracy in word recognition and, as the most publicized theories from across the Atlantic, they are potentially harmful to classroom practice in the UK if taken at face value. Furthermore, they do not make teachers explicitly aware of differences between the older, more traditional phonics, and what might be termed the 'new' phonics based on up-to-date linguistic knowledge.

*Old phonics*

In my view, this lack of explicit awareness is a basic cause of the continuing heated debate about phonics which I have had cause to be very aware of since 1958. For, in that year, the first issue of *Educational Research* contained an article (Morris 1958) I had been asked to write on what research then had to say about 'The place and value of phonic methods' in teaching children to read. As the editor expected, the topic was so controversial that it helped to attract the widespread attention necessary to make the new journal a viable proposition for the National Foundation for Educational Research where I was responsible for reading research.

Reading that article of twenty years ago, it is clear that the term 'phonic' had many meanings even in those days. To add to the confusion, phonic methods were generally classified as *synthetic* although analysis was involved therein. This was because they incorporated the principle of building up words from their constituent elements, and types of blending to form words. The older generation of teachers tended to use a letter-by-letter approach in which, for example, the word CAT was attacked as KUH-A-TT. But, in the 'modern' phonic teaching of the 1950s, it was usual to find children being taught to divide simple words into initial consonants and phonograms. Thus, the word SAND would be divided into S-AND, and then by combining the phonogram with different preceding and following letters a word family was built up, for example band, hand, land and so on. Training in the recognition of common syllables, and in analysing long words by syllables was also a recognized part of phonic instruction.

Besides these so-called 'synthetic' phonic methods, there was available to teachers at that time a different kind of phonic approach pioneered and researched by Daniels and Diack (1956). This is the now well-known 'phonic-word' method which, with certain provisos, gets a seal of approval in the Bullock Report (DES 1975) because it encourages children to learn phoneme-grapheme relationships in the context of whole-word recognition.

*New phonics*

What research had to say about phonics by 1958 was very much the same as the conclusions reported from research in the period to the present day. For instance, phonic instruction is undoubtedly of value in teaching children to read, but it must be regarded as only one way of developing word recognition ability and as a means to a larger goal of meaning and application.

This is in accord with the policy statement of IRA (1977) previously mentioned, and with the literature published for teachers on inservice reading courses, notably those of the Open University. It accords too with the findings of a national survey carried out for the Bullock Committee. These indicated that, nowadays, teachers of six-year-olds adopt an eclectic approach to the teaching of reading. They also revealed that 97 per cent of the teachers said they used phonic methods which focus attention on letter sounds, digraphs and diphthongs. Moreover, approximately 70 per cent of these teachers gave, in addition, phonic training based on syllables.

The teachers in this recent survey were not asked to give more specific details of the phonic methods and materials they used. Nor, it would seem, were any of them interviewed or observed giving phonic instruction. This is a pity because information is needed about what teachers actually mean and do with regard to phonics, and how it agrees with what, in effect, they *say* they do when ticking boxes on a postal questionnaire. It is important too to know in what way, and to what extent, the phonic instruction given could be termed 'systematic'. In short, much detailed information is required for the Government's proposed expansion of inservice training so that, more than ever before, the content of reading courses reflects and meets the needs of teachers responsible for children's reading growth.

Meanwhile, personal experience as a contributor to, and an examiner of, inservice courses for reading teachers suggests that it would be useful in future to distinguish between the older, more 'traditional' phonics, and what might be termed the 'new' phonics based on up-to-date linguistic knowledge. At first, it seemed better to give the latter a new name altogether. But it did not work even with teachers taking an advanced diploma in reading, insofar as they have persisted in using the term 'phonics' to cover all methods and materials which help the learner to relate sound and symbol.

Briefly, 'new' phonics is based on linguistically defensible information derived from research into the English language; in other words, on good descriptions of the sound and spelling systems of English and their relationship. Whereas, traditional or 'old' phonics developed before such descriptions started to become available in the 1960s.

In practical terms this means that, just as the continuing controversy about phonics has resulted in vital deficiencies in most basal reading schemes, with notable exceptions, the continuing use of 'old' phonics has resulted in errors and confusing differences in reading materials generally, both with regard to content and sequence of phonic provision. Naturally, teachers wonder why materials differ in this way. But it is not usually until they have had opportunities for further study, that they are aware that, without linguistically defensible information, the authors of most materials have proceeded to highlight particular sound-symbol relationships on an *ad hoc* basis. For instance, such authors naturally know that children have to learn to recognize words containing consonant digraphs, but the order in which they highlight words containing *sh*, *ch*, *th* etc. is usually a matter of personal preference from their own classroom experience.

This is not to say that the contributions of such authors are without value. On the contrary, many generations of children have learned to read and to spell using materials which are not as soundly based as they should be from a linguistic standpoint. What is more, through them, teachers have demonstrated that systematic phonic instruction is essential, contrary to what the theories of Goodman and Smith suggest. Even so, now that advances in linguistic knowledge have made improvements possible, would it not be a good idea for teachers to examine their materials more closely, and consider what type of phonics they incorporate? Would it not be best for children's growth in reading if they and, indeed, all professionally concerned considered the gains to be made from substituting 'new phonics for old'? I certainly think so. What is more, 'new phonics for old' is a slogan to which, in practical fashion, I can and am lending my support.

## References

ALLINGTON, R. L. and STRANGE, M (1977) Effects of grapheme substitutions in connected text upon reading behaviors *Visible Language* 11, 3, 285–97

BIEMELLER, A. (1970) The development and use of graphic and contextual information as children learn to read *Reading Research Quarterly* 6, 1, 75–96

CLAY, M. (1972) *Reading: The Patterning of Complex Behaviour* Heinemann Educational Australia

CLYMER, T. (1968) 'What is "Reading"?: some current concepts' in H. M. Robinson (Ed) *Innovation and Change in Reading Instruction* Chicago: University of Chicago Press

DANIELS, J. C. and DIACK, H. (1956) *Progress in Reading* University of Nottingham Institute of Education

DES (1975) *A Language for Life* (The Bullock Report) HMSO

GOODMAN, K. S. (1972) 'The reading process: theory and practice' in R. E. Hodges and E. H. Rudorf (Eds) *Language and Learning to Read: What Teachers should Know About Language* Boston: Houghton Mifflin

GOODMAN, K. S. (1976) 'Reading: a psycholinguistic guessing game' in H. Singer and R. B. Ruddell (Eds) *Theoretical Models and Processes of Reading* Newark, Delaware: International Reading Association

INTERNATIONAL READING ASSOCIATION (1977) *Annual Report 1976–7*

KOLERS, P. (1975) Pattern-analyzing disability in poor readers *Developmental Psychology* 11, 282–90

MORRIS, J. M. (1958) Teaching children to read: the place and value of the phonics *Educational Research* 1, 1, 38–49

ROBINSON, H. A. (1977) 'Comprehension: an elusive concept' in

J. Gilliland (Ed) *Reading: Research and Classroom Practice* Ward Lock Educational

ROBINSON, H. M. (1968) 'The next decade' in H. M. Robinson (Ed) *Innovation and Change in Reading Instruction* Chicago: University of Chicago Press

SHUY, R. (1973) A review of *Psycholinguistics and Reading* by Frank Smith *Journal of Reading 17, 1, 69–70*

SINGER, H. and RUDDELL, R. B. (Eds) (1976) *Theoretical Models and Processes of Reading* Newark, Delaware: International Reading Association

SMITH, F. (1971) *Underatanding Reading* New York: Holt, Rinehart and Winston

SMITH, F. (1973) *Psycholinguistics and Reading* New York: Holt, Rinehart and Winston

WALKER, L. (1977) Comprehension of writing and spontaneous speech *Visible Language* 11, 1, 37–51

WEBER, R. (1970) A linguistic analysis of first-grade reading errors *Reading Research Quarterly* 5, 3, 427–51

# 9 'Mapping', speech segmentation and phonics

## Elizabeth Goodacre

In acquiring language, children must learn the importance of the 'bits' of language, and with the help of adults they start to do so very early. They 'map' meaning on to the speech they hear around them, until they are able to isolate the meaningful 'bits' out of the stream of sound with which they are surrounded. They do this by mapping what they know about objects, events and relations on to words, word endings and word order.

There appear to be two assumptions underlying this process of making sense of speech (Clark and Clark 1977). They are that language is communication and that it makes sense in context. In the early stages of oral language development adults do much to help children make sense of what they hear, so that long before children come to school and learn to read, they have been receiving 'lessons' which are likely to influence the way in which they later acquire reading skills.

What adults say to children provides them with information about the structure and function of language, and parents or parent substitutes provide conversation, mapping, and segmentation 'lessons'. In this paper I wish to explore the way in which this previous language experience may be related to reading progress.

### Conversation lessons and 'reading'

Children soon realize that conversation involves communication and this type of talk involves, for instance, taking turns. They pick up such things as the difference in intonation and vocabulary when talking to different people according to their status and relationship with the speaker: for example, you learn that you talk to Granny in a different way to how you address your baby sister.

In similar fashion, they learn from adults what counts as 'reading', and from an early age they make observations about what adults may be doing when they 'read'. Hadley (1970) asked five year olds what their parents did when they read, and found that the children's answers could be divided into responses which varied from evidence primarily based on observation to inference about what might be happening: for example, 'they sit down'; 'they don't *do* anything'; 'they read newspapers in their heads – you can see their lips moving'. Hadley reported that in somes cases it was nearly a year before the younger children in the age group reached the more sophisticated descriptions. One would suspect that parents who read to their children may find themselves talking to their children about what happens when they 'read'. Certainly pointing to words and relating the content of pictures to words in the text must help. Also, in the close intimacy of the reading situation, the child can observe the adult's eye movements and how they turn the pages and refer to the text.

In the early stages of speech development, adults make sure that children know that they are being addressed by such attention-getters as saying the child's name, and attention-holders such as varying the pitch of their voice. These devices are signals that the utterance is intended for that child alone. They encourage children to take turns in conversation by switching from listener to speaker role. They expand the child's utterance and they ask follow-up and prompt questions. Generally they seem to correct 'for truth value – that is, they make sure that the child uses the appropriate words for the situation, and correct for pronunciation' (Clark and Clark 1977). Detailed observation of teachers' 'hearing' of children at school might well show similar reasons for correction and interjections.

In teaching reading linguistic concepts occur which may be confusing to the young child. It has been suggested that concepts such as letter, sentence, sound (i.e. phoneme) are likely to be vague to the young reader and yet these concepts are used in the language of reading instruction as if children have a clear understanding of their meaning. This metalanguage or talk about language is probably developed

112

as children learn to read, particularly in the hearing situation when children read aloud to their teacher. There must be many opportunities in such situations for the teacher to clarify children's understanding of these concepts involved in the reading process. There is an increasing amount of research being carried out on children's ability to demonstrate their understanding of the terminology of reading instruction (Downing 1970, 1973–4; Holden and MacGinitie, 1972; Kingston *et al* 1972; Meltzer and Herse 1969; Mickish 1974).

## Mapping lessons
It seems that adults tend to pick out objects, actions and events that are immediately accessible to children for comment during conversations. They focus on the 'here and now' and this allows children to make full use of any contextual clues to what the word may mean. Shatz (1974), for instance, has reported the way in which indirect directives can be understood by contextual clues. The sentence 'can you shut the door?' can be obeyed because the listener knows the word *door* and makes use of his knowledge; i.e. that the door is open and that the speaker is glancing in that direction. The 'here and now' of the situation sets limitations and narrows the range of possibilities. It provides children with a way into the situation, a technique for making deductions and mapping meaning on to the language being used. In reading, particularly with the materials of the early stages, teacher and child both have access to the visual cues of the illustrations. Tim, aged 5:3 years, reads, 'Have a look; come and look; Peter has a (pause)' – the book says 'look' – Tim reads 'fish' with the rising tone of interrogation. He has tried to map on to the printed word *look* the picture-clued, four-letter word *fish*. Miscues or substitutions can often be understood in relation to the child's efforts to 'read' the pictures and then on the basis of assumptions on this evidence, their mapping of meaning on to the printed text.

The dialogue between child and adult provides many opportunities for mapping. When an adult talks about the child's contribution to the conversation to the child, the adult provides the child with other words for different elements in the 'here and now'. Thus, if a child is talking

113

about the *pussy* in the garden the adult may use the words *cat*, *that old Tom*, or the 'brute from next door'; or actions associated with the cat's movements such as *slinking*, *springing*, *crouching*, thus developing the child's vocabulary in different conceptual domains. Probably the corrections adults make are important: 'no, that's a *donkey*, not a horsie – a nice old *donkey* – shall I hold you up so that you can see the old *donkey*' (emphasis on the new word). Observing a student at packing up time in a reception class the other day provided a good example of the way in which lack of communication leads to the adult modifying her speech. 'Collect your possessions' said the student to be greeted by blank stares of incomprehension. She tried again. 'Pick up your things.' Still some blank looks – final effort on the part of the student – desperate mimed gestures imitating the picking up of bags and satchels.

Correction and expatiation on the part of the adult are probably important as they help the child to be more precise in developing a feel for the appropriate or 'best' word. Transcripts of teachers' 'hearing' of children might provide evidence of the way in which the effective teacher uses the 'here and now' of the subject matter of the reading material to extend the children's vocabulary development, by relating the unfamiliar text word to a more familiar one in the child's spoken vocabulary, a word that the teacher knows he knows. The danger is that this instruction interrupts the child's efforts at comprehension of the totality of the text, and possibly teachers have to learn to 'choose their moment' for imparting this type of lexical and conceptual information.

### Segmentation lessons

Adults speaking to young children tend to speak slowly and to pause at the end of each utterance. The fact that they tend to use familiar frames such as 'Look at the . . . ', 'there's a . . . ', 'here's the . . . ' enables their young listeners to identify the new words. Adults also make use of repetition, repeating single words, phrases and sometimes whole sentences. Such repetitions help children to detect the various constituents of the utterance.

Marie Clay (1972) has discussed the difficulty young children are likely to have in locating word units in spoken language: 'The puzzle in finding a word is to "detach" that word from the whole utterance.' She suggests that, in reading, spaces help the child to segment the visual display of print, and pauses aid the reader to segment the flow of words. Using a test where the child has to slide two masking cards across a line of print to show the tester 'just one word'; 'just one letter'; and 'just the first letter of the word' she found that only 40–53 per cent of six year olds could pass these items after a year's schooling. She suggested that explanation might be in terms of confusion of concepts but also involved would be the child's ability at establishing part-identities within wholes. Directionality appeared to be established much earlier, 84 per cent of the group being able to synchronize their 'pointing' (using a finger to point to each word) with their word-by-word reading of the text.

Basic categories used in language tend to vary with the expertise or subculture of the people naming the objects in their environment. Language development studies suggest that terms which are easiest to acquire are those with dimensions which are perceptually salient. Such dimensions are most useful for adults to refer to, and hence tend to be maintained better and with greater accuracy. Possibly the problem with 'word' and 'letter' in comparison with directionality, is that the finger can point to each word and in Clay's phrase the child can 'finger flow along the line'. The segmentation of words may be more difficult because there is an absence of perceptually salient dimensions; i.e. how does the child pin down the 'bits' in the words.

The Russian researcher Elkonin (1973) has directed his research towards revealing to the child *before* reading instruction, the 'sound structure of spoken words'. He used three pieces of training which involved placing plastic tokens in a row of squares representing the number of sounds in a word, which seems one way in which an abstract concept can be given greater perceptual saliency.

Liberman (1973) compared the ability of children aged from four to six to segment spoken words into phonemes and into syllables. The child had to repeat a word or sound and to tap out the number of segments (phonemes or syllables) that he could distinguish. Four year olds could not segment into phonemes but about half of them could identify the number of syllables. Only 17 per cent of the five

115

year olds could segment phonemes, but, by the age of six, 70 per cent could identify the number of phonemes and 90 per cent tapped out the correct number of syllables. Stress is produced by making the vowel in a syllable louder, higher in pitch, or longer, so stress tends to be a property of the vowel centre of each syllable.It would be interesting to know whether it is children's developing use of stress and intonation as they read aloud with greater fluency which leads to this improvement in the identification of syllables. A phoneme is a phonological segment, a speech sound which can be classified by the way it is pronounced, the classification depending on the sound making a difference to meaning. It would seem possible that this would be the most difficult basic-level category of reading instruction for children to grasp conceptually.

Kavanagh (1972) reported that he had found that adults in a phonetics class who were not able easily to associate sounds and phonemes had been helped by *stretched speech* and also by immediate feedback. Transcripts of young readers made by the writer when they were reading aloud suggest that some children at the word-by-word stage tend to 'stretch' particular words, and possibly the funtion of this is to enable them to match more easily auditory with visual segments and is part of the overall mapping process in reading. They tend to 'point' with their voice – using stress and pause – to break up words into their constituent letter-cluster sounds, matching them with the visually focused letter forms. This would be one way in which the phoneme-grapheme match might be made perceptually salient for the beginning reader.

In speech development the learner goes about constructing his phonological system in terms of the oppositions he can make at each stage rather than in terms of particular speech sounds; i.e. contrast is an important element (Clark *et al* 1977). Writing about the phonological development of an eighteen month old child, Waterson (1971) suggested that the child perceives utterances as whole units, and in perceiving the phonetic features of utterance may not necessarily be aware of this sequential ordering. Similarly, in the early stages of reading, the child may be unable to process simultaneously the identification of phonemes (listening to the heightened elements of the

116

stretched word) and their matching to the visual symbols (graphemes) and their sequential ordering, so as to be able to synthesize and 'blend' the sounds into a familiar word. Certainly there has been little research as yet into the way in which children master the suprasegmental features of the phonological system (word stress, sentence stress and intonation contours) in relation to reading aloud and the effects of this on their ability to segment printed language. It seems quite likely that because of the abstract nature of phonological segmentation, some children are likely to get fixated at the stretched speech stage and not accomplish the speeding-up process commented on by Clay (1972):

> ... developmentally there is usually a gradual transition in good readers from finger pointing, to staccato reading, to light stress of word breaks and, finally, to phrasing. The fact is learners make this transition so rapidly that it may hardly be noticed. (page 71)

## Phonics

A common practice in this country is to draw children's attention to the phonemic similarities of words within their basic sight vocabulary, once they have a small basic recognition core of words. Alternatively children are taught single letter phonics and encouraged to 'blend' letters and their sounds to formulate familiar words. In both cases, the teacher is trying to make explicit knowledge about the phonological level of language, knowledge which both teacher and pupil share since they are able to communicate and comprehend each other's speech. The difficulty is that, by reason of their past experience of talk, children have learned to listen for meanings. As Huttenlocher (1964) and Karpova (1955) found, meaning units take priority in the child's analysis of speech. Sequences of words composing a meaningful utterance are difficult for the child to analyse into units such as the syllable and the phoneme. The sound of the word is more likely to elicit the imagery of its meaning than its sound composition. Venezsky *et al* (1972), testing Israeli children, reported that success on a rhyming task was found to correlate very significantly with scores on a test of reading achievement at the age of seven. Ability to recognize and produce rhyme may well be a useful indication of the ability to deal with speech sounds as *abstractions*. This type of evidence would suggest that teachers might do well to examine phonic games and materials and see the extent to which such apparatus will help children to proceed to the more abstract grasp of phonemic segmentation by reason of the perceptual saliency of the material's task: for example, words are divided into reliable phonological segments and children gain a conceptual grasp by motor operations or techniques which stress the 'cutting up and putting together' of the elements involved.

Certainly some phonological segmenting can be aided by the teacher using beginning letter blend and digraph prompts to help children decipher unknown words with the help of conceptual cues. This is all part of the teacher's function in the 'hearing' situation, as a helpful adult providing useful feedback. However, not all children may be clear about the reasons for their teacher hearing them read. A recent study carried out by the writer with the assistance of thirteen primary teachers provided the following types of answers from children aged 6:0–10:10 when they were asked to reply to the oral question, 'Why do teachers hear children read?':

*Incomprehension:* I don't know. I dunno. I can't think/say.
*Word emphasis:* Because they can learn words; to see how to pronounce and to see what word they know; because if they don't hear them read they wouldn't know the words; to learn more and more words; so you can get really good at reading; so I don't get the words wrong.
*Testing and grading:* To test how good they are; so that they know they can read; to see how well they can read; to put you on a book – high book – or a low book; I think teachers hear you read so that they can see what level you are so you can mix with others the same.
*Functional:* So children learn to read better so when people send letters they can read them; if they want to go anywhere they want to be able to read the signs; when they grow up they'll be able to read – I don't like reading; so when they are grown up they can read signatures and things; because if they go out on their own ... on a road ... and it said stop ... you might run out and then be killed; so that when children grow up

they read signs on roads.

## Implications

1    The extent to which perceptual saliency is involved in the basic categories of reading instruction may be an important factor in children's reading progress. Children acquire left-to-right direction by finger-flowing along the line and the 'word' by finger-pointing. How do they learn to segment words into smaller units? Does the imagery associated with content words interfere with the level of abstraction needed to think about the temporal and phonological aspects of language? What part do reading games and apparatus play in enabling children to cope with segmentation, to grasp the idea of segmentation by means of manipulation and the counting of 'sounds' in words?

2    If some children make use of 'stretched speech' to achieve phoneme-grapheme match, are they developing their knowledge of the phonological system of language as applied to the printed-written language? Evidence of their generalizations may be found in their spelling attempts, and Mason (1976) has carried out work which suggests that the kinds of errors made when learning to read reflect the child's level of reading competency – they tend to overgeneralize, particularly in regard to vowel sound patterns, rather like the overgeneralizations in regard to morphemic endings in language acquisition: for example, I catched my ball.

3    The generalizations of phonic teaching may be ineffective with some children because of the problems of transfer of learning; phonic information given in the 'here and now' of the 'hearing' situation or the classroom exchange may be a more practical approach.

4    The tenets of phonic instruction may be useful knowledge for the teacher but such information may have to be made perceptually salient for children according to their cognitive and linguistic stages of development. Sometimes phonics is taught as a useful tool for the decoding of written language. However, according to their experience of language use in the home, children are likely to vary in the strategies they

use in the task of speech and print matching, especially in regard to the use of the units of the syllable and the phonemes in the different words they learn to recognize.

5   Phonic teaching has some sociological and philosophical implications. Very often phonic instruction seems to be connected with a part-whole approach which seems at variance to what we know about children's experience of language and mapping of meaning on to it. Also, phonic teaching seems to be related to styles of communication and thinking in the classroom. The assumptions about language implicit in phonic teaching appear to be more closely related to the transmission than the interpretation view of language (Barnes 1973). If a teacher believes his or her main task is to transmit information, in this case about phonics, their pupils will probably not be ready to think and reason about reading until they have mastered a great deal of information by rote. The teacher at the other extreme, who emphasizes language as a means of interpretation, will probably help children to talk about their ideas and assumptions about reading, will credit them with the ability to make sense of experience for themselves, since knowledge for this type of teacher tends to be something which each learner must make for himself.

6   The results of a study by Mazurkiewiez (1977) on didactic versus discovery phonics instruction and effects on speech articulation suggest that reading instruction is used unconsciously to develop a standard pronunciation in particular groups: 'The results do not suggest that *a* Standard American pronunciation is being developed nationally as a result of a common standard pronunciation key used in phonic materials since the phonic key is interpreted by each other to match his/her idiolect which is a reflection of regional, local or social phonology.' The researcher concluded that children's speech characteristics are affected by phonic instruction in the dimension of a teacher's pronunciation.

Sociologists might well suggest that how children acquire their knowledge about the phonological level of their language and its relationship to the reading process has implications for both the role of the teacher and for the model of the reading process acquired at school by children.

# References

BARNES, D. (1973) *Language in the Classroom* Open University Press

CLARK, E. *et al* (1977) 'First language acquisition' in *Psycholinguistic Series I: Developmental and Pathological* ed. by Morton and Marshall, Elek Science, 1–72

CLARK, H. and CLARK, E. (1977) *Psychology and Language* Harcourt Brace Jovanovich

CLAY, M. (1972) *Reading: The Patterning of Complex Behaviour* Heinemann Educational

DOWNING, J. (1970) Children's concept of language in learning to read *Educational Research* 12, 106–12

DOWNING, J. (1973/4) The child's conception of a word *Reading Research Quarterly* IX (4) 568–82

ELKONIN, D. (1973) 'USSR' in J. Downing (Ed) *Comparative Reading* New York: Macmillan

GIBSON, E. and LEVIN, H. (1975) *The Psychology of Reading* Cambridge, Massachusetts: MIT Press

HADLEY, D. (1970) *An Investigation into Young Children's Concepts about Reading* (unpublished MA dissertation) University of London

HOLDEN, M. and MACGINITIE, W. (1972) Children's conceptions of word boundaries in speech and print *Journal of Educational Psychology* 63, 551–7

HUTTENLOCHER, J. (1964) Children's language: word-phrase relationships *Science* 143, 264–5

KAVANAGH, J. (1972) In discussion section of J. Kavanagh and Mattingly (Eds) *Language by Ear and by Eye* Cambridge, Massachusetts: MIT Press

KARPOVA, S. (1955) 'The preschooler's realization of the lexical structure of speech' in Smith and Miller (Eds) *Genesis of Language* Cambridge, Massachusetts: MIT Press

KINGSTON, A. *et al* (1972) 'Experiments in children's perceptions of words and word boundaries' in Greene (Ed) *Investigations related to Mature Reading* 21st Year National Reading Conference

LIBERMAN, I. (1973) 'Segmentation of the spoken word and reading acquisition' paper presented to the Society for Research in Development, Philadelphia, March 31, quoted in E. Gibson and H. Levin (1975) *The Psychology of Reading* Cambridge, Massachusetts: MIT Press

MASON, J. (1976) Overgeneralisation in learning to read *Journal of Reading Behaviour* 8 (2) 173–82

MAZURKIEWIEZ, A. (1977) Didactic versus discovery phonics instruction effects on speech articulation *Reading World* XVI (3) March, 196–205

MELTZER, N. and HERSE, R. (1969) The boundaries of written words as seen by first graders *Journal of Reading Behaviour* I, 3–13

MICKISH, V. (1974) Children's perceptions of written word boundaries *Journal of Reading Behaviour* VI, 19–22

121

SHATZ, M. (1974) 'The comprehension of individual directions: can two-year-olds shut the door?' Paper presented at the Summer meeting of Linguistics Society of America, July, quoted in H. Clark and E. Clark (1977) *Psychology and Language* Harcourt Brace Jovanovich

VENEZSKY, R. *et al* (1972) 'Studies of prereading skills in Wisconsin' reprinted in E. Gibson and H. Levin (1975) *The Psychology of Reading* Cambridge, Massachusetts: MIT Press

WATERSON, N. (1971) Child phonology: a prosodic view *Journal of Linguistics* 7, 179–211

# Part 4

# Extending reading

# 10   Reading purposes, reading outcomes, and comprehension

## John Merritt, Fiona White and Sue Moore

Very few of the texts we need in everyday life are written just for our personal use. Apart from private letters, most of what we read has been written for a wider audience. It does not, and can not, take full account of our existing knowledge. Nor can it be expected to provide all that we want to know at the time of reading about any particular topic. In addition, most of what we read contains a great deal of information that we do not want – and it is often presented in a form that is not very helpful. We need only to look at the last thing we read for some specific purpose to see how true this is – a travel brochure, perhaps, or even a textbook on teaching reading!

If we wish to develop effective reading, i.e. the ability to read for everyday-life purposes, we must obviously do more than provide the exercises in 'reading comprehension' which are typically found in reading schemes. These exercises usually consist of questions which the author may think are important but which may have very little to do with the interests or purposes of the reader. Apart from this disadvantage, such questions do not teach comprehension – they merely test it.

To develop effective reading we must first examine what is actually involved in extracting information from the texts that are available to us – and then devise ways of helping children to do this. One essential prerequisite is the ability to define what it is we want to know, and the form in which we can make use of that information. The first point is perhaps obvious, but the second may need a little clarification. An example from the experience of one of the authors may help to provide this.

In a recent storm, a garden fence was blown down. The owner knew that the insurance included storm damage, and also damage to fences. What the owner did not know was that it did not include storm damage to fences. This was not immediately obvious from a normal reading of the document. It did become obvious, however, when all the relevant information was extracted and organized in the following manner shown in Figure 1.

Figure 1

*Insurance Cover*

| Item damaged / Kind of damage | Fences | Windows | Roof | etc. |
|---|---|---|---|---|
| Storm | | X | X | |
| Fire | X | X | X | |
| Flood | X | X | X | |
| etc. | X | X | | |

A similar strategy can be used to help children to extract and organize information contained in school texts – provided that they have a well-defined purpose. In the following example a child was asked to read a passage to 'find out about mammals'. Some ideas about how to organize information had already been discussed. The text was as follows:

*Mammals*
Everything can be divided into 'animal, vegetable or mineral', as in the game. The animal we mean is any creature which can move of its own free will, including birds, fishes, reptiles and insects. When we speak of animals in the ordinary way we really mean mammals, which are all the animals which produce their young complete, and nourish them in infancy on their mothers' milk. This book is about those animals, the mammals.

There are, however, some mammals which lay eggs. These are the duck-billed platypus and the spiny ant-eater, or echidna, both of which live in Australia. They are classed as mammals, even though they do lay eggs, because when the young are hatched they are fed on their mothers' milk.
(From Ladybird *Mammals* (1967) Newing and Bowood)

The child's response looked something like Figure 2.

Figure 2

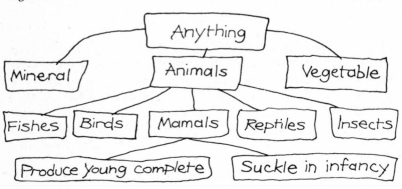

This is a very reasonable response – except that the attributes of mammals are represented as *part* of a hierarchial classification. If more help had been given in defining the information to be extracted it is less likely that this ambiguity in conceptualization would have occurred. The purpose could have been more precisely defined to answer the following questions:

1    How are mammals related to everything else? and
2    How are mammals similar to other animals, and how are they different?

The child's diagram provides an excellent answer to the first question – if the last two boxes are omitted. The second question might have been answered more easily by using a matrix of the kind used in Figure 1 for checking on insurance cover, as in Figure 3.

**Figure 3**

*Mammals and other animals*

| Attributes<br>Animals | Produce young<br>complete | Nourished<br>by mother's milk | Lay eggs |
|---|---|---|---|
| Birds | | | X |
| Fish | | | X |
| Reptiles | | | X |
| Insects | | | X |
| Mammals | X | X | |
|   echidna | | | X |
|   platypus | | | X |

Note how this layout provides a useful format for collecting additional information from any other sources the reader may refer to. Note also how one column has been completed by drawing on previous knowledge. The use of a format of this kind can thus help a child both to relate new information to what he or she already knows and to prepare a sound basis for assimilating further information within a clearly defined conceptual schema.

Summers (1965) provided a very useful review of the range of formats that authors typically provide in different kinds of reading material. His concern, however, was for interpreting visual aids rather than with constructing them. Jenkinson (1966) encouraged the use of a non-prose format in social studies and found this was of value in 'increasing reading power' – but this idea then seemed to languish. A more general approach to the problem of organizing information in non-verbal formats, or models, was presented by Merritt (1975) and Merritt (1977). These ideas were taken up in the Reading Development Course, Open University (1977), and many teachers have now had at least some experience with this approach. The remaining sections of this paper describe experiments in Britain and in Australia respectively in which the values of modelling have been explored. The first was carried out by F. White and the second by S. Moore.

**Pilot Study 1: Report of a pilot experiment carried out in February and March 1978 in two British Schools**
In carrying out this pilot experiment, I wanted to see if a

training in diagrammatic representation would influence reading comprehension and whether or not children would benefit from a training in understanding, interpreting and using such models.

### The experiment

The sample consisted of sixty children – one class of thirty 7½ year olds from one school and a class of thirty 13½ year olds from another school. The children had not previously encountered modelling, nor were the class teachers familiar with this strategy. Their normal comprehension exercises involved reading a passage and answering questions based on the Barrett taxonomy (cited in Clymer 1971). A control group continued with this programme with the class teacher for two hours per week over a period of four weeks. An experimental group, randomly selected, was given training in modelling by the experimenter. Both groups were tested at the beginning and end of the four-week training period.

### The tests

Two tests, Form A and Form B, were specially constructed for the experiment. Each test required the pupil to read a short text and then check a model for omissions and errors against the text. A standardized test, the Gapadol, was also used. This is based on cloze procedure. All the children took the Gapadol test at the beginning and at the end of the experiment. Half of each group took Form A of the specially constructed test at the beginning of the experiment and Test B at the end. This sequence was reversed for the other children. This cancelled out any differences in difficulty between the two forms.

### The training

With the help of the teachers I selected passages from worksheets and textbooks in Religious Education, History and English which the children would be meeting that term. I then set a purpose in reading for each passage.

A systematic training was difficult to organize in the short time available. With the younger children, the starting point seemed to be pictures, picture sequences and some simple diagrams. There was not time to train the pupils with mathematical models although some of the group did make suggestions for using graphs and tables.

With the older children more time was spent on training with maps, scientific and mathematical models. This was possible because they were already familiar with some of these representations. In the time available it was only possible to work with a few models and discuss the potential of some others.

With both groups, the greater part of the sessions was spent in discussion. At the end of the training period all children were tested again in parallel forms of the pre-tests.

*Results*
1    The 'modelling' test: For the 7½ year olds, the scores of the experimental group were *not* significantly higher than those of the control group on the modelling test. For the older children the experimental group *did* have higher scores than the control group on the modelling test. These were significant at the .01 level. (Mann Whitney non-parametric u test)
2    The Gapadol test: For both age groups, there was no significant increase in score in either experimental or control group.

**Figure 4    Effects of training on modelling**

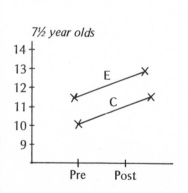
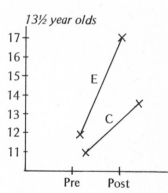

*Discussion*
It is hardly surprising that training in modelling may produce an increase in scores on a modelling test. This could simply indicate that children benefit from training in the interpretation and use of diagrams and need such training if

they are to work with them more effectively. The real question is a matter of educational judgment – does the use of non-verbal formats help children to extract relevant information from a text and organize it effectively? If so, tests of the ability to do just this are, *a priori*, as valid as comprehension tests that resemble comprehension exercises. We may then simply concern ourselves with the question of whether or not the content of the tests represented adequately the formats that are likely to be of real value in everyday life and whether they are suitable for use by children in the age groups studied. The tests included graphs, Venn diagrams, maps, and attributes matrices. It is interesting that the older children who worked with these coped quite well. The younger children were often confused by such diagrams. This could be due to their cognitive limitations. On the other hand, younger children are much less familiar with such formats and a four-week period is too short for effective training.

With regard to the cloze test, these scores do not perhaps provide the best indication of the ability to select relevant information from a text or to impose on it some appropriate conceptual structure. Such tests do not make sufficient demands on the ability to handle substantial quantities of information and more complex conceptual relations. Nevertheless, gains were in fact noted on a cloze test in a second experiment, reported below.

## Pilot Study 2: Kelvin Grove Primary School, Brisbane, Australia.
### February to May 1978
This study, like the study reported above, addressed itself to the question: 'To what extent does training in modelling (the use of diagrammatic outcomes) influence reading comprehension?'

*The experiment*
A total of seventy-two children were involved in this experiment. They were selected from three classes. The classes were Grade 4, Grade 5 and Grade 6 respectively. The ages of the children ranged from nine to twelve years of age. Two groups were established in each class. Each group, 'Control' and 'Experimental', consisted of twelve children.

The control and experimental groups in Grades 4 and 5 were matched in terms of reading scores on the GAP test. In Grade 6, the control group were average readers but the experimental group were below average on this test.

Each group worked on similar reading passages over a period of eight weeks. The control group used traditional, recognized methods for developing reading comprehension, for example predicting, evaluating, using cloze procedure, reading followed by question–answer sessions, skimming, scanning, finding the main idea and summarizing. The modelling group did only modelling exercises.

Each of the six groups met twice per week for half an hour each time. To ensure maximum uniformity in both teaching style and added attention, I did all the teaching for each group.

## The tests

1    GAP – a cloze test, selected for its speed and ease of administration.
2    PAT – a multiple choice test of literal and inferential comprehension, chosen because of its traditional format.

These tests were used at the commencement of the experiment and again at the end.

## The teaching

All of the teaching began from familiar formats. For example, the children drew maps or labelled familiar drawings. We proceeded from these familiar forms to the introduction of less familiar forms, for example Venn diagrams, attributes matrices and graphs.

After about five weeks I became quite discouraged, for on the face of it, I was virtually training the control group to do the tests, for their sessions included substantial periods on cloze texts and comprehension questions on set passages. The experimental group were significantly disadvantaged from the testing point of view for they concentrated solely on modelling.

## Results
Grade 4
There was no significant difference between the two groups

on either test at the start of the experiment. At the finish, the modelling group were significantly higher than the control group on the GAP but not on the PAT.

**Figure 5**

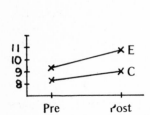

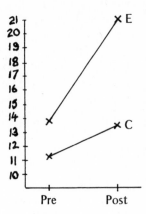

Grade 5
There was no significant difference between the two groups either at the start of the experiment or at the end.

Grade 6
In this class, I wanted to see whether modelling was of particular value to children of low reading attainment. Figure 6 shows the gains of the experimental group – the poor readers who were taught modelling – and the control group of average readers who were given their normal training.

*Discussion*
These observations give some support to the view that modelling does contribute positively to reading comprehension, even on tests which measure a very limited range of comprehension skills. It also supports the view that modelling is of value to poor readers and younger readers. We suspect that larger gains for the modelling groups might have been recorded if the tests used had made significant demands on the ability to extract and organize information.

**Figure 6**

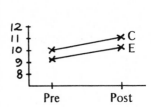

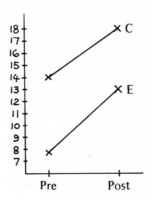

**Conclusion**

Where do we go from here? Educational progress depends upon an adequate evaluation of each new teaching strategy. Research and teaching practice must therefore go hand in hand. First, however, it is important to decide whether an innovation is intrinsically worthwhile. In the case of modelling, we have argued that this is an effective strategy for helping a reader to identify relevant information and for organizing this information. The research reported here tends to support this view and to justify further evaluation studies.

One of the main problems to be tackled in carrying out such studies is that of identifying a wide range of possible models and deciding what models are likely to be most convenient for what kinds of purpose. Next, we need to develop more effective strategies for helping children to use models. These strategies will need to be standardized to some extent so that other researchers can check our findings. A further problem is that it may take a much longer period than we had in the above experiments for children to develop the ability to use this approach effectively. Already, however, a number of teachers are working with us on these various problems. This kind of cooperation between the class teacher and the researcher-teacher may, we hope, produce results that neither could produce in isolation from each other.

# References

CLYMER, T. (1972) 'What is reading?: some current concepts' in A. Melnik and J. Merritt (Eds) *Reading Today and Tomorrow* University of London Press

JENKINSON, M. D. (1966) 'Increasing reading power in social studies' in H. A. Robinson and S. J. Rauch *Corrective Reading in the High School* IRA Perspectives in Reading Series 6, Newark, Delaware: International Reading Association

MERRITT, J. E. (1975) 'Intermediate skills' Reading: seven to eleven *Education* 3–13

MERRITT, J. E. (1977) 'Developing higher levels of reading comprehension' in V. Greaney, (Ed) *Studies in Reading* Dublin: The Educational Company

OPEN UNIVERSITY (1977) 'Developing Independence in Reading' in PE231 *Reading Development* Block 2. The Open University Press

SUMMERS, E. G. (1965) 'Utilizing visual aids in reading materials for effective learning' in H. L. Herber (Ed) *Developing Study Skills in Secondary Schools* Newark, Delaware: International Reading Association.

# 11   Categorization of miscues arising from textual weakness

## Cliff Moon

### Introduction

The work of Kenneth Goodman in the USA and Elizabeth Goodacre in the UK has focused attention on the value of miscue analysis as a diagnostic instrument which can be applied by teachers to assess children's reading strategies. Experience to date suggests that systematic analysis of this kind proposed by Goodman and Goodacre may be a more accurate indicator of reading strengths and weaknesses than conventional tests. Miscue analysis is, in effect, a criterion-referenced test because it assesses what the reader can and cannot process rather than how he compares with external norms. The advantage of miscue analysis is that it can be used with any text which the child happens to be reading and is not necessarily dependent on an arbitrary passage. The content of the child's reading is therefore likely to be more highly motivating because it is probably self-selected according to personal preferences.

This use of miscue analysis – to focus on the reader – is a relatively new technique partly because, as with recent developments in sociolinguistics, it depends upon the use of the tape recorder. As far as we are aware, the technique has not been applied in the opposite direction – that is, to use miscue analysis as an indicator of strengths and weaknesses in the *text* as opposed to the *reader*. The feeling that this might be a fruitful area of investigation grew out of teachers' observations regarding certain word orders, line breaks and page layouts which tended to cause difficulty. Whereas it could be argued that the skilled reader would be able to overcome *any* of these problems, it was felt that if they consistently triggered miscues amongst children at particular stages of reading development then perhaps they were inappropriate at readability levels which corresponded with those stages of development. An obvious example of this arose in respect of 'split words' – words which are broken, usually syllabically, and printed at the end of one line and the beginning of the next in order to evenly align all print on the right hand side of the page. Whereas 'split words' occur in many books for young children and sometimes in the later books of reading schemes, teachers reported instances of miscuing on 'split words' with children who had tested reading ages in excess of ten years.

The concept of *readability* is mentioned above. Just as miscue analysis provides a criterion-referenced test of the reader's performance, similarly it could also provide a criterion-referenced test of certain aspects of readability. In spite of the availability of a large number of readability tests (*cf.* Klare 1963) they do appear to depend upon some fairly arbitrary written language features. For example, mean length of sentence is a criterion widely used in readability formulae whereas Granowsky and Botel (1974) question whether coordination necessarily leads to difficulty especially as children's oral and written language is chiefly composed of strings of coordinate clauses. Granowsky and Botel (*op. cit.* p. 32) write: 'sentence length does not offer a reliable indication of the grammatical make-up and complexity of a sentence'.

Bormuth (1966) points out that although sentence length and complexity are correlated, they both correlate independently with 'difficulty'. Reid (1972) analysed four basic English reading schemes according to syntactic criteria, emphasizing that children learn to read structures and 'grammatical meanings', not lexical units. Both Schlesinger (1969) and Klare (1963) claim that readability studies lack a theoretical basis. They tend to be norm, rather than criterion, based.

It could be inferred that we have been overzealous in our attempts to *measure* readability without having a clear idea of what readability *is*. In other words, we might more usefully attempt a definition of readability based on observation of what does or does not cause difficulty to readers at various stages of their progress in the acquisition of reading skills.

Although the present study would certainly not claim to have reached any firm conclusions along these lines, it nevertheless accords with this direction of thought.

## The context of the investigation

The work described below was carried out during the academic year 1977–8 by a small group of teachers who joined a Bristol University Teacher Research Group to study 'Reading Resources'. The tutor's role was to instigate the research, advise on its progress and assist with statistical analysis. The group initially consisted of ten teachers plus tutor, but from January 1978 only four teachers were involved and these continued until July 1978. The effect of such a drastic drop in numbers was that although pilot studies carried out in the Autumn term 1977 had produced a wealth of relevant data, subsequent experimentation had to be severely limited and a great deal of pilot data remains uninvestigated. The brief of Bristol University Teacher Research Groups is to carry out school-based research in order that teachers may become more knowledgeable about educational research techniques. The results of their investigations is generally considered of less importance than their awareness of research methodology by the end of the year. They are expected to attend group tutorials at the university for one two-hour evening session per week and be prepared to spend an equivalent amount of time outside the sessions carrying out the investigation. It is generally the case that this time is spent in school-based research for two terms and in processing data and writing a report during the third term. In view of these limitations, the thoroughness with which the work has been executed is indicative of the group's commitment to, and enthusiasm for, the project.

## Pilot studies

The 1977 Autumn term was spent gathering data by means of tape-recording children reading aloud in the course of the normal school day within the classes of the Research Group members. At the weekly sessions, these recordings were played and discussed in relation to the texts being read by the children. The ages of the children taught by the investigators ranged from five to eleven and this fortunately gave the group a cross-section of the full primary-school age range. As miscue-triggering features of text arose, they were itemized with actual examples. Towards the end of the term these items had been adjusted several times until the following category list was arrived at. Terms like 'syntactic pattern break' and 'advanced terminal cuing' were coined by the group. All examples actually occurred during the pilot study.

*Categories of miscue caused by text*
1    Line breaks.
     (a) Advanced terminal cuing.
     Relates to the main clause on one line being read as an independent sentence without reference to qualification on the following line, for example:
        Billy tried to get the feather /
        with the stick
     Child read the first line as a complete sentence ending with 'feather'. 'With' started a new sentence.
        To give an 'advance terminal cue' *feather* could appear at the beginning of the second line. The word *the* then provides a cue for continuation.
     (b) Inappropriate line break.
     For example:
        . . . Saul listened. He did
        not know that David had been chosen
        by God.
     'Saul listened, he did.' conformed to Bristol speech convention.
2    Syntactic pattern break.
     Miscue based on syntactic expectation derived from prior text.
     Crystal (1976) refers to this as a syntactic complexity variable of preceding linguistic context. For example:
        Watch
        Watch me
        Watch me hop
        Watch me
        Watch me skip
        Watch *this*
     Child read *me* instead of *this* on the last line
3    Split words.
     Part of word on one line, remainder on following line,

for example:
                Rod-
        erick
Child read this as *Rod and Eric.*

4    Style.
(a) Syntactic.
For example:
    Jennifer held on to the rope too
    to help Johnny pull
This caused repetition, pause and general confusion.
(b)  Semantic.
For example:
    lead (pronounced led) and lead (pronounced leed)
    when cells/batteries mentioned earlier.

5    Tense switch.
For example:
    The children *blow* up the balloons they have bought.
    Mary *blows* hers up until it is very big.
    Jane *blows* up her yellow balloon.
Child substituted *blew* for all three blow(s).

6    Says/said.
(a)  Variations
For example:
    panted, gasped, cackled, hissed etc.
when used in place of says/said.
(b)  Temporal sequence.
'Go to the shop,'  Mother said,  *or* 'Go to the shop,'
said mother.  'Go to the shop.'  Mother said.
The first two forms seem to create less difficulty than the
third because this could be read as 'Go to the shop
Mother...' or 'Go to the shop.' Mother said...

7    Elisions.
(a)  Elision for full term, for example:
    *It is* a pilgrim
    *It is* a Norman
*It's* read for *It is* both times.
(b)  Full form of elision, for example:
    But it *wasn't* a torch
    It was a big pistol
*Wasn't* was read as *was*, a more critical miscue because it
changed the meaning.

8    Idiomatic collocation.

For example:
  *He puffed and blowed* was read instead of
  *He puffed and puffed*

9  Semantically appropriate omission, insertion and substitution.
  Omission:
    we read and *we* write stories
    (*we* omitted)
  Insertion:
    I will sail away
    and look for another island
    I must find an(*other*) island
    (*other*) inserted
  Substitution:
    *Most* of the food was in tins.
    (*Much* was substituted for *most*)
  These miscues could be indicating stylistic weakness and may be related to Category 4(a)

10  Comment clauses.
  For example:
    you know
  (Crystal (1976) also mentions tag question like *didn't he?*)

11  Layout.
  Space between lines. When lines are too close the eye picks up a word from the line below or misses a line when returning to the left hand side of the page.

This list of miscue-triggering categories should not be viewed as complete. It includes those categories the group was able to identify within the available time. In order to carry out controlled experiments a halt had to be called to the pilot study.

### The investigations
From detailed notes on which children had miscued within certain categories the following approximate levels were drawn up. Children's stages of reading development were broadly defined according to tested reading ages and their ability to read fluently various books from the readability stages described in *Individualised Reading* (Moon 1978). 'Reading fluently' refers to the child's ability to read aloud

with a miscue rate of about 5 per cent. The numbers within each of the five levels relate to the categorization of miscue-triggering categories (see above).

| Level | Approx. R.A. | Individualised Reading Stages | Occurrence of miscue-triggering categories |
|-------|--------------|------------------------------|--------------------------------------------|
| 1 | 6.0 | 4 and 5 | 1(a), 1(b), 2, 4(a), 4(b), 5, 6(b), 7(a), 7(b), 8, 9, 10, 11 |
| 2 | 7.0 | 6 and 7 | 1(a), 1(b), 2, 4(a), 4(b), 5, 6(a), 6(b), 7(a), 7(b), 8, 9, 10, 11 |
| 3 | 8.0 | .8 and 9 | 1(a), 1(b), 2, 3, 4(a), 4(b), 5, 6(a), 6(b), 7(a), 7(b), 8, 9, 10, 11 |
| 4 | 9.0 | 10 and 11 | 3, 4(a), 4(b), 5, 6(a), 6(b), 8, 9, 10, 11 |
| 5 | 10.0+ | 12, 13 and beyond | 3, 4(a), 4(b), 5, 8, 9, 10, 11 |

Inclusion of categories indicates that there had been occurrences of these categories at the given level. For example, Category 3, split words, does not appear in Levels 1 or 2 because no books with split words were read by children at these levels.

Also Category 1 (advanced terminal cue) does not occur in Levels 4 or 5 because children at these levels did not misread line endings. They were more fluent readers who, even when reading aloud, were obviously surveying the text beyond the line they were reading and therefore were able to make sense of the text in ways less fluent readers were not able to do.

Out of all five levels and observed categories, the group was able to investigate the following:

| Level 1 | 2 Syntactic pattern break |
|---------|---------------------------|
| Level 2 | 1(a) Advanced terminal cue |
|         | 2 Syntactic pattern break |
|         | 7 Elision |
| Level 3 | NONE |
| Level 4 | NONE |
| Level 5 | 3 Split words |

This indicates the limitations imposed on the investigations. There is still a great deal of work to be carried out on Levels 1, 3, 4 and 5 in particular.

## Method
The method of investigation involved the use of matched texts; that is, story material at the appropriate level was selected and two texts were prepared by 'jumbo-typing' (display typeface) both versions and pasting over the existing text. The texts were kept as close as possible to the original and modifications were made only according to those categories under investigation. Books used for testing were:

Level 1    *It's Fun to Read* Books (Hart-Davis)
Level 2    *Jeremy Mouse* (Dinosaur Publications) and *A Very Important Man* (Benn's Beginning to Read Series)
Level 5    *The Snow Goose* by Paul Gallico (Longman 'Pleasure in Reading' edition)

In each case one version included miscue-triggering categories (the positive version) and one excluded them (the negative version).

Groups of children at the appropriate stage of reading development were tape-recorded reading both texts with a time-lag of two weeks between readings. Half the children read the positive version first and half read the negative version first.

Results were tallied on forms which allowed for *type* of miscue as well as category. These types were coded as follows so that a descriptive as well as statistical analysis could be made:

R    Refusal
$S_1$   Semantically appropriate substitution (e.g. *home* for *house*)
$S_2$   Semantically inappropriate but syntactically appropriate substitution (e.g. *horse* for *house*)
$S_3$   Semantically and syntactically inappropriate substitution (e.g. *has* for *house*)
C    Self-correction
P    Pause
RR   Repetition

O   Omission
I    Insertion

The sub-categorization of substitution was deemed advisable because of the wide variation in importance of substitution miscues. For instance, we seldom compute $S_1$ substitutions for miscue rating at Levels 1 and 2 in everyday practice. It was also felt that pauses, repetitions and self-corrections, significant enough in miscue analysis for study of the reader, were even more important indications of difficulty within the text itself.

## Results and discussion

1   It was generally felt by the group that the most important outcome of the year's work was the mapping out of a research area by formulating the miscue-triggering category list and the broad levels within which these categories occurred. As already mentioned, this delineation of the research problem may form the basis of future work in this area. However, those investigations which led to statistically significant findings are listed below. In each case a two-tailed 't' test was used to determine significance between mean miscue scores obtained on the category under investigation as presented in the positive and negative versions of the texts. The types of miscue which were computed were R, $S_2$, $S_3$, P, RR, O and I.

(a)   Level 1, category 2, syntactic pattern break.
The difference between mean miscue scores was significant at the .05 level. Children made more miscues when an established syntactic pattern was broken. It would appear that they read what they expected to find rather than what was actually printed. It can be argued that, at this level, the ability of the reader to anticipate text is a valuable reading skill and therefore the text ought to confirm rather than contradict the reader's expectations.

(b)   Level 2, category 7, elision.
The difference between mean miscue scores significant at the .02 level. Children tended to read full-form in place of the elision form. This may be due to an over-generalization on the part of the reader, that all printed

material should sound like conventional written form (i.e. without elisions). This over-generalization at a relatively early stage in reading development may be compared to the stage in oral language development when children add an *ed* ending to every past tense verb (e.g. *goed* for *went*).

(c) Level 5, category 3, split words.
The difference between mean miscue scores was significant at the .001 level. The experimental group consisted of sixty upper-junior children and this finding suggests that the split-word convention should be avoided in most reading material intended for children of primary school age.

2    The absence of significant findings in respect of Categories 1(a) and 2 at Level 2 may be attributed to the inclusion of all three categories in the two texts used. It was found that where *one* text was adapted according to *one* category only (for example (a) and (c) above), that text could be 'loaded' with instances of the category. There was then a better chance of miscues occurring within that category. Small numbers of instances tended to produce nil scores for individual children.

3    Whilst it could be argued that reading involves making sense of a variety of print conventions and that sooner or later the reader must encounter all the miscue-triggering categories listed above, the question of what is or is not *appropriate* at a given level seems of paramount importance. If what we are trying to do is to 'make learning to read easy' (Smith 1978) then inappropriate conventions will be avoided at particular levels. Where they become appropriate, or at which point the child should encounter them, would be ascertained by developing longitudinal investigations of individual categories to find their 'cut-off points' – that is, where a particular category failed to trigger sufficient miscues to yield a significantly different miscue score on matched texts. This could be a direction of further research in this field.

4    Although miscue analysis has many advantages as an indicator of both reading ability and readability, it should be

treated with some caution. In reading aloud the child is being asked to perform and this creates a degree of pressure to perform well. There can be no certainty that miscues made during the act of reading aloud are made when the child reads to himself. Self-corrections, pauses and repetitions, for example, may often result from the read-aloud activity and not from the child's inability to read the text silently and fluently. This may be particularly important with reference to *advanced terminal cuing* because the miscue is really one of intonation which possibly arises from reading aloud. In silent reading the miscue, if it occurred at all, would probably be self-corrected very rapidly. It may be better to present text as phrased units of meaning without advanced terminal cues because this encourages the reader to process meaningful units as 'chunks of information'.

5    A further difficulty is that any attempt to examine the text (or the reader) in isolation is to ignore that the reading process involves an interaction between the text *and* the reader. By ensuring that all the children involved in this research were reading these texts with an overall miscue rate of approximately 5 per cent ('instructional' level) this difficulty was partially resolved. However there is no certainty that a miscue which occurred on one of the categories under investigation was caused by the textual category itself. It could equally well have been caused by the child's inability to decode at that point. Even so, if this were the case, the child would presumably have miscued at the same point on the negative version of the same text and there would not then be any difference in miscue score for that category instance.

6    Finally, the aim of the Research Group was to acquaint teachers with research methods by means of a practical investigation. This group achieved far more. The value to *them* lay in finding out more about the children they teach, learning the technique of miscue analysis and, as one member put it, 'realizing that books were not necessarily right'. The research area they have defined may have an important role to play in future investigations regarding what is meant by 'readability' if only as an adjunct to linguistic studies of syntactic complexity. It certainly carries important impli-

cations for those who write material in book or blackboard form for children's use.

## References

BORMUTH, J. R. (1966) Readability: a new approach *Reading Research Quarterly* 1, 79–132

CRYSTAL, D. (1976) *Child Language, Learning and Linguistics* Edward Arnold

GRANOWSKY, A. and BOTEL, M. (1974) Background for a new syntactic complexity formula *The Reading Teacher* October, 31–5

KLARE, G. R. (1963) *The Measurement of Readability* Iowa: Iowa State University Press

MOON, C. (1978) *Individualised Reading* (8th edition) Centre for the Teaching of Reading, University of Reading

REID, J. F. (1972) 'Sentence Structure in reading primers' in A. Melnik and J. Merritt *The Reading Curriculum* Oxford University Press

SCHLESINGER, I. M. (1969) *Sentence Structure and the Reading Process* The Hague: Mouton

SMITH, F. (1978) *Reading* Cambridge University Press

# 12   Pedagogical strategies for fluent reading

## L. John Chapman

Those concerned with the teaching of reading need to consider constantly which is the most appropriate strategy to develop *next* according to the learner's present level of reading ability. That is, there is need to begin the development of the strategy for coping with the next skill in the hierarchy, if such a model is accepted, whilst the learner is almost fully engaged in acquiring and practising skills at lower levels. Whilst noting this we should remember that not all would agree that growth in reading progresses through different stages. Even if there are distinct stages it is necessary to point out that they do not have clear-cut boundaries which those learning to read must negotiate. Growth is perhaps better thought of as proceeding along a continuum, its progress detected by increasing fluency.

It is important to observe that to progress along such a continuum, some readers may have to adopt different strategies, especially if certain pedagogic procedures were used in the first place. For instance, more often than not the learner has been constantly taught – drilled might be a better word – to tackle each letter or individual group of letters to identify a particular word. In general a letter-by-letter, word-by-word process is insisted upon to exploit those phoneme-grapheme relationships that have some regularity. This strategy, whilst of importance at the start, begins to lose its effectiveness as words are more easily recognized and may become, for some children, detrimental as reading skills develop. Indeed, it is preferential for all learners to be taught to tackle the recognition of single words (word-building) within a more global context in the first place. In this way foundations might be laid for later, superior fluent reading.

When reading aloud, the ultimate aim is to achieve fluency which is that readiness of utterance that comes with confidence and which is born of an understanding of the passage being read. Fluency contains within its definition the notion of free flow, and it is important to encourage a strategy whereby learners are enabled to maximize their knowledge of their native language. The vast majority of those learning to read have achieved a basic proficiency in spoken language – a *sine qua non* for reading – as witness their undoubted ability to make their needs known to those around them. The text before them contains many of the same characteristics as are present in their native language. However, in many ways some of these basic language skills have been left out of account in the teaching of reading in its early stages, although they are relied upon implicitly in so many ways. Too often, in the desire to hammer home those sounding skills, the vastly more important strategies that involve the exploitation of language features derived from language itself have been ignored.

The fact that there are high correlations between spoken language ability and the development of reading skills has been quoted in research (but see Weaver 1977); however, as yet, there appear to be few attempts to teach strategies that require learners to draw upon their knowledge of language features that their mastery of oral language has given them. This has to be done in such a way as to make the connections between the language they speak and a reading text *explicit*. Teachers are often adjured to require the child 'to read for meaning', which is after all the ultimate goal of reading –and this is indeed the best overall advice, but how the learner is to be sensitized to those features inherent in the language that assist the transportation of these meaningful messages is left unsaid and more often than not untaught.

As indicated, fluency seems to involve the reader in achieving smooth unimpeded flow through the text; this flow being closely related to the reader's grasp of the meaning of the message being read. If fluency is to be conceived in this way and strategies taught to achieve it, then it becomes important in the first place to look at those linguistic elements present in the text that provide the mechanics of texture – that is, those features that make a text, a text.

To be identifiable as a text, rather than a haphazard

collection of words or sentences, there must be elements and order arrangements, or patternings, that can be shown to provide the text with continuity. Some of these elements, it is suggested, will be part of the learner's implicit language knowledge that has been acquired, like the rules of grammar, in infancy without any direct teaching. They have been absorbed from the language activity of those who have been present in the child's early environment. English children learn – pick up, we say – English from the English-speaking persons around them – Chinese children will acquire Chinese by the same process. With reading the teacher has been inserted into the learning situation to assist in cracking the written code. But all too often the child has been left with the process of code cracking only and *not* the superior language-related strategies. It is perhaps worth noting in this context that some children adapt to reading fluently with little explicit teaching of reading. This occurs presumably in much the same way as a first language is learnt – as Frank Smith puts it, they learn to read by reading. But many do not achieve that level of reading independence which will enable them to read freely in our complex world so as to enjoy all the advantages that literacy can bring.

To become fluent, to achieve a flow, and to apprehend the meaning of a passage as word follows word, requires the ability to *anticipate*. The learner-reader has to look ahead of the actual word being uttered to the completion of a group of words which may be a unit, or sub-unit, of meaning. This in turn leads to the next unit and so on till the final stop at the end of that particular text. This ability to anticipate is notable, and is perhaps the most important characteristic of fluency. It follows then that one of the basic aims of teaching for fluency is to assist the development of this skill of anticipation.

It is comparatively easy to make such a statement of aims, but what are the elements that aid the reader to make predictions as to what is to follow through the text? What are the signals, the clues, or cues that alert the reader to potential anticipatory elements? If these can be identified and spelt out they may well turn out to be the most important teachable elements. Furthermore, the heightening of the learner's awareness to the characteristics of these elements could be the first practical step in a strategy for teaching fluent reading.

## The concept of text cohesion

We are fortunate now, for descriptive studies of English have progressed considerably recently and it is becoming clear that there are many elements in continuous texts that function in such a way to assist anticipation. Any continuous text, whether spoken or written down, is recognizable as a text because it hangs together in certain ways. It is said to cohere. Furthermore, in reading situations the language is visible, so if the elements of cohesion now being described by linguists can be enumerated, the mechanisms which create that cohesion might be revealed as anticipatory cues. In this way, then, it should be possible to appreciate some of the many ways in which the reader is cued to anticipate structural and extra-structural features.

Some of the elements that create cohesion have been referred to in research which analyses reading behaviour, but many others have received scant attention and are not recognized as cohesive mechanisms. One of the features that has begun to receive attention is the process of anaphora which operates both within and between sentences performing strong linkages. The integrative function of anaphora has been investigated, for example by Garrod and Sanford (1976) and Richeck (1976), the latter finding that third-grade children had difficulty in comprehension tasks where anaphoric forms were varied.

Other cohesive elements have been mentioned (Chapman and Hoffman 1977), but little study has been made of the process. In collocation cohesion is achieved through the psychological processes of association – that is, through the association of lexical items that regularly co-occur.

If you look at a recent systematic account of cohesion (Halliday and Hasan 1976) and recall the reading situation, you will soon be impressed by the power of the processes. The main groups of cohesive features are Reference, Substitution, Ellipsis, Conjunction and Lexical Cohesion, and if these are examined in detail it is possible that they will provide a series of particular points in the text which give some of the cues for predicting what is to follow. These could well be the mechanisms of fluency, and could provide practical teaching points. Halliday and Hasan call these features 'cohesive ties'. Some of them can be arranged diagrammatically, as in Figure 1. This illustrates a system of cohesive ties which, it is suggested, cue readers as they read for meaning. (Diagram suggested by J. Pearce (1977), personal communication.)

**Figure 1**

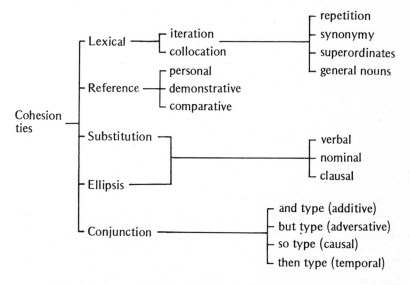

In beginning reading, we envisage progression from left to right across the page, so for elementary prediction purposes we might hypothesize a series of choices from which one is made and then confirmed by later words. The identification of the cohesive element may occur, through one of the five groupings, for example the Reference cues. These cues could be one of three types – personal, demonstrative or comparative. They are defined thus (Halliday and Hasan 1976):

> *Personal* reference is reference by means of function in the speech situation, through the category of *Person*.
> *Demonstrative* reference by means of locations, on a scale of *Proximity*.
> *Comparative* reference is indirect reference by means of *Identity* or *Similarity*. (p.37)

151

The analysis becomes quite complicated to the uninitiated, but the main thrust is clear. (Remember this is a linguistic description, which we are hypothesizing may well provide the basis for psychological processes like anticipation.) Again, Demonstrative reference entails a further cueing effect, i.e. location of some kind. The system according to Halliday and Hasan (1976, p. 57) is as shown in Figure 2.

**Figure 2**

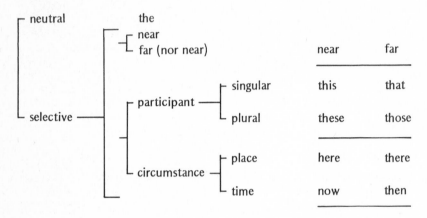

These adverbial demonstratives – here, there, now and then – make reference to location either in space or time; the others – this, that, these, those – are concerned with locating some thing.

Texts can be examined for their occurrence and their cohesive qualities derived. In reading situations their assistance to building up the meaning of a passage is fairly obvious. And so with the Comparatives, as Figure 3 (Halliday and Hasan (1976) p. 76) shows.

Again, the examination of a passage for these cohesive features will help you to appreciate the way in which the system works.

This short account of the elements in a text which are said by linguists to give a text its coherence are, it must be stressed, linguistic description. They have what appears to be obvious connection with the development of reading fluency, but research needs mounting to confirm their

**Figure 3**

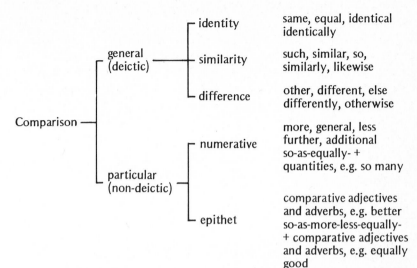

validity for reading in the first place, and to seek out which groups of cohesive ties, or individual elements within groups, are significant. Some progress has been made to this end (see Chapman 1977 and 1978) but a great deal still remains to be done.

However, what is clear, whilst the detail is awaited, is the proposal with which this paper began: that for reading fluency to develop, reading teachers need to prepare their pupils to acquire strategies that will enable them to make use of superior language skills. If reading progress is along a continuum, then awareness of cohesive ties should aid movement along the continuum, for a rudimentary developmental pattern is already clear.

One of the practical ways both to assess whether pupils have mastered some of the processes involved and/or to alert them to these features, is cloze technique. This is the procedure whereby certain words are removed from a passage of continuous text and the reader asked to replace them. [Materials of this nature for children aged eight and nine have been developed and are available from the author at The Open University.] When used sensitively the procedure can be an enjoyable discovery game. Furthermore, when used in group situations it can also provide those involved with useful language discussion work.

Summarising this paper, we might say that the prerequisite for fluent reading is a continuous text. Such a text will inevitably contain connecting features which have been described by linguists as groups of cohesive ties. Pedagogical strategies need to alert readers to the presence of these cohesive elements so as to promote the development of fluency and its attendant comprehension.

## References

CHAPMAN, L. J. (1977) *The perception of language cohesion during fluent reading* Paper read at the Processing of Visible Language Conference, Eindhoven, Holland

CHAPMAN, L. J. (1978) *Alternative outcomes of reading comprehension new verbal strategies* Paper read at the Seventh World Congress on Reading, IRA, Hamburg

CHAPMAN, L. J. and HOFFMAN, M. (1977) 'Intermediate Skills' in PE231 *Reading Development* Block 1, Unit 4 The Open University Press

GARROD, S. and SANFORD, A. (1976) Interpreting anaphoric relations – the integration of semantic information while reading *Journal of Verbal Learning and Verbal Behaviour* 16 (1) 77–90

HALLIDAY, M. A. F. and HASAN, R. (1976) *Cohesion in English* Longman

PEARCE, J. (1977) (personal communication)

RICHEK, M. A. (1976/7) Reading comprehension of anaphoric forms in varying linguistic contexts *Reading Research Quarterly* 2, 145–65

WEAVER, W. W. (1977) 'Linguistic assumptions and reading instruction' in A. J. Kingston (Ed) *Towards a Psychology of Reading and Language* Athens: University of Georgia Mass. 64–70

# 13 Further thoughts on relevance

## Mary Hoffman

It is impossible for something to be relevant full-stop. It has to be relevant to something or somebody. The examples which I collected for my monograph (Hoffman 1976) were cases of relevance to somebody more often than to something. It is a way of looking at teaching similar to that which replaces the formulation 'I teach French' or 'I teach Maths' with 'I teach children'. Relevance to something involves one kind of professional competence but relevance to somebody demands in addition a very close and particular knowledge of all the people who make up your class.

In *Reading, Writing and Relevance*, the principles on which examples of relevant reading and writing materials were included were as follows:

1 The activities should be relevant to the children themselves so that they can see *why* these often difficult processes should be necessary and worthwhile and not just have to accept the teacher's word for it.
2 The children themselves should be involved in the planning of the activities, regardless of how that work originated.
3 There should be some inherent reward in the work which is realizable within the anticipation-span of the children undertaking it.
4 The vocabulary involved should be familiar to the child and interesting enough to be worth remembering and using again.

Margaret Donaldson, in her recent book *Children's Minds* (1978) paints a gloomy picture of what happens to children in education. She says:

There is no denying that, in spite of the enlightened concern of our primary schools with happiness, schooling somehow or other turns into a distinctly unhappy experience for many of our children. From it, large numbers of them emerge ill-equipped for life in our society and inescapably aware of it. So they either regard themselves as stupid for failing, or else, in an understandable effort to defend against this admission, they regard the activities at which they have failed as stupid. (p. 14)

Donaldson is talking about education in general but I will leave it to your experience to judge how apposite her remarks are for teachers of reading. Her main thesis is that children progressively as they pass through school do not understand the purpose or often the nature of the tasks they are set. So often they are presented with abstract problems at which they fail but it has been shown that if the same problems are presented in terms which make more what Donaldson calls 'human sense', children can cope with them perfectly well. So then, a relevant reading or writing activity might be further defined as one that makes 'human sense' to the children involved, which it is almost bound to do if it meets the criteria set out above.

Since collecting the examples for the monograph – which was, incidentally, very hard to do, since teachers are diffident and could not believe that I really wanted to hear about their own daily practice – two main points have emerged. One is that certain types of activity described there are both easy and worthwhile to replicate. It was my avowed purpose *not* to offer blueprints to teachers. Since one example began with a death and another with a flood, I hope that this will be obvious even to readers who skip introductions. However, I have since then come across several excellent booklets prepared by secondary schoolchildren to introduce newcomers to the school and allay their fears and worries. This is similar to the example 'Writing for a change' in the monograph (Hoffman *op.cit.* No. 27 pp. 89-92).

The other main point to emerge is one which has very much influenced my choice of materials for this paper. If you look at the criteria listed above you will notice that there is nothing about them which inherently applies only to what has come to be known as 'functional reading'. And yet the monograph was largely composed of functional examples. I have not found since then many examples of whatever the complement – notice I do not say opposite – of functional reading is. Call it imaginative or creative or what you like; I am not trying to coin a new term, merely indicating a recognizable phenomenon. The kind of reading and writing which extends a person's view of herself and the world, something which takes you to a destination that you may not have known existed when you set out, on a journey as important as any for which you are likely to consult a railway timetable.

The crux is criterion three – the inherent reward within the child's anticipation-span. A child makes and writes a card for his mother's birthday and gives it to her the next day; relevance, human sense, a point to literacy, all are plain to see. But a child reads a poem about a bird, say. What then? If it leads on to a huge project-folder on wildlife-conservation then it's relevant, isn't it? If the child, when he leaves school, goes to work in Regents Park Zoo, is it still relevant but with a very long anticipation-span? Or he reads another poem, about something quite different. Or he becomes a poet. Or, when he is in his thirties, he finds a richness in Hopkins' poem 'The Windhover' that he might never have known if he had not read that first one about the skylark or the nightingale or the budgie. You see how absurd this kind of question can be. The point is that one cannot, as the teacher, always legislate for criterion three. One must do one's best, but remember that the children are going to surprise you about what kindles the spark for them. Suggest, guide, help as much as you will, they still need to be trusted with the matches if the rocket is ever to go up.

So, in keeping with the Conference theme of 'Growth in Reading' I have chosen examples of what I think are relevant reading and writing activities which contribute to the emotional and imaginative growth of children in school. There is not always a clear-cut distinction between this and the growth of functional competence; I am not talking about a dichotomy.

One of the most important things about growing up is grasping concepts of time. Time has a nasty habit of not standing still and waiting to be grasped. Not just in the past, present and future, but the mysterious way in which this slippery phenomenon strikes differently at different times, time goes fast or slowly, seems a long way off or like only yesterday. Here are some thoughts on this subject by six and seven year olds at a London primary school:

1 When I was eight months old I always used to go to sleep and I had lots of toys and I couldn't walk so my mum had to push me in the pram. And I had one kitten and only three teeth and now my kitten is a big cat and I have twenty-four teeth.
2 The best thing to do when you are a baby is to suck a bottle.

These bits of writing were part of a project 'When we were babies' in which the whole class was involved. Any primary-school class would enjoy this and find it easy to relate to their experience and vocabulary. Many of the children have younger siblings, photographs could be brought in and a baby/child matching competition held, with the teacher not exempted. An exhibition could be held and many reading and writing activities could result. This is all part of seeing one's place in a repeated pattern of birth and growth and preparing for the eventual stage when the child becomes a parent.

As well as the parent in the child there is also the child in the parent and even, incredibly, in the grandparent to be discovered. There is an excellent example written up by Sally Purkis in the *History Workshop Journal* (Purkis 1977) which began with a photograph and led to an under-standing of history in children aged seven and eight. This Cambridgeshire teacher showed her class a picture taken outside the school in about 1908 showing a row of girls dressed in black stockings, lace-up boots and hats. The children could recognize the spot but were puzzled by the strangely-dressed pupils. 'Funny' was their reaction. Working backwards on the number-line principle which they had used in maths, the children were able to work out that, at that time, their own grandmothers would have been the age of the children in the photographs. This was the same age that the class was now. Had their grannies dressed like that at their age? So a questionnaire was constructed, asking simple questions about clothing, food, school, entertainment and so on. The children administered it to their grandparents over the half-term.

'Grandma' was taken in the broadest sense to refer to any member of that generation who was willing to cooperate. The information from the questionnaire was pooled and the teacher began to read the results to the whole class at story time and to put them up on the wall under subject headings. There is no reason why this shouldn't have been done by the children themselves, as perhaps the teacher would realize when she came to evaluate this work. There, in the simple language of the grandmothers, was a wealth of detailed historical information unavailable from any textbook that these children could have managed to read – with the added thrill of being given by people they knew. For example:

1 Girls wore a vest, bodice, drawers, three petticoats and a pinafore.
2 My mother did the washing in a galvanized bath on the kitchen table with a washboard made of wood.

The muffin man, tiger nuts, whips and tops were all recollected by the grandmas. The children made a scrapbook and collected a museum of clothing, flat-irons, toffee-hammers and so on, and finally held an exhibition to which the grandparents were invited. What a splendid introduction to reading and understanding history and an early antidote to the idea that that subject is only about monarchs and politicians, battles and Acts of Parliament.

My next two examples are from eleven year olds in the Midlands. The first is of a girl who decided to read a book which was difficult for her. It was Gavin Maxwell's *Ring of Bright Water* and she had been recommended to read it by the school caretaker, a marvellous resource person who also contributed much information to another project, on the Second World War – but thereby hangs another tale. This child found the text demanding. In one single paragraph (p. 121) describing a seascape, there were three words which she didn't know – 'madder' (as applied to colour), 'intermediary' and 'anaemic' (referring to 'the pale, anaemic roses of the South'). But her interest in the whole book carried her over these hard words and the grasp on her imagination kept her going. She is now reading *Tarka the Otter* by Henry Williamson, a very hard book indeed. Now a teacher, trying to meet criteria one, two and four might not hand either of these two books to a child of this age and ability. But criterion three had come into powerful operation. There *was* sufficient inherent reward for that child and perhaps only she could have known it. Perhaps the caretaker had a better sense of the child's imaginative life than the teacher did. Please note that the Maxwell book, which fired this child's imagination, is *not* a work of fiction.

The second eleven year old example is one where the imaginative and functional aspects have developed side by side. A group of children from this same school in the Midlands went to visit Newstead Abbey, the ancestral home of Lord Byron. Out of their own need for information couched in a form they could understand they decided to prepare a brochure appropriate for subsequent visits made by younger children. The children drew up their own list of necessary information, some of it very functional, such as the site of lavatories, cafes, picnic areas etc. But they also included material about Byron. Why was he famous? Who was he?

The children interviewed others lower down the school as part of this vital planning stage, and drew on the resources of Newstead and the school library. They also worked to a purpose/resource grid, which would not look unfamiliar to students of the Open University's Reading Courses. Each child concentrated on whatever interested her or him and the results were pooled. In evaluating the outcome of their work, the children interviewed the younger ones who had used the brochure to see if it had been effective. They also reviewed their own selection of materials – why had some articles been rejected and why had certain styles been adopted.

They had no lesson on nineteenth-century history or architecture or Romantic poetry but, out of this project, in addition to the brochure, grew a great variety of reading and writing, sparked off by it. Some of these children are voluntarily reading biographies of Byron and some of his poems. Others have found themselves led on to learn more about architecture as a result of what they discovered at

Newstead. This kind of work has a beginning and a middle but not necessarily an end.

My last example is both sad and thought-provoking. It is of a Jamaican girl in a south London suburb. She is fourteen, attends a comprehensive, will leave school in two years' time, and wants to be a typist. She has been attending remedial reading groups for over two years and does not think her reading has improved. Her teacher says she reads 'clumsily, brokenly and with difficulty' and her writing 'though intelligible, is awkward, laborious, full of technical errors' (Richmond, 1977). But the girl, whom I shall call Barbara, excels as 'an organizer, leader, inspirer, manipulator and sometimes intimidator of others', again in her teacher's words.

Barbara and her friends created a play as an item for the school concert, at the request of a teacher. It was videotaped and caused a great deal of interest among the pupils and teachers, because of the language and the situation. It is called *Brixton Blues* and is about the life of the Black West Indian community in a South-East London suburb. It is funny and sad and wry and perceptive. But most striking of all it is linguistically rich and diverse to an extent never before seen in the school work of these fourteen year olds. It is a dialect play, mainly in Jamaican patois but also including much Standard English, Cockney and what the teacher calls Black South London.

The centre of control of these varieties of language is Barbara, who plays the Mum, who switches register and dialect as she talks to an invisible stallholder, a policeman on the 'phone, rouses a congregation in the church and, at the emotional and dramatic climax of the play, extemporizes an impassioned thirty-five line monologue on the cost of living, loyalty, betrayal, parenthood and pain. As her teacher says, you are looking at an artist in language.

The play aroused so much interest that Barbara and her friend decided to transcribe the tape. They were the only people capable of this skilled and arduous job. Barbara controlled the tape recorder, played a stretch at a time and dictated it to Sharon, who wrote it down. They consulted about all spelling of Jamaican dialect words, such as 'unnuh' and 'fastey', and words where the pronunciation was sufficiently different from Received Pronunciation to warrant a different spelling, e.g. nuttin (nothing) and sarve (serve). A third friend typed the result. This first exercise took eight hours. The girls read through the transcript and were not satisfied with it. So they did it again. This second version took five hours. And yet one so often hears about children of this age and ability that they 'can't concentrate'. These girls were capable of this complex activity of writing, reading and rewriting because the material was relevant to them. The language was their own, the world was their world. Barbara had a chance to come into her own powers, to combine for the first time her considerable social and personal abilities with an aspect of literacy encouraged by the school.

Barbara has since been expelled. I don't know why; not all kinds of charisma are congruent with the school ethos. It would be easy to see her as a martyr or victim. But I cannot help seeing her as an example of a wasted opportunity for someone whose talents did not find a relevant hold on anything in her school work except for that glorious once. But, in keeping with the Conference theme, I ask you to think of the many others who never glimpse that once and to resolve to encourage growth in, through and because of reading, writing and relevance.

### References
DONALDSON, M. (1978) *Children's Minds* Fontana/Collins
HOFFMAN, M. (1976) *Reading, Writing and Relevance* Hodder and Stoughton
MAXWELL, G. (1960) *Ring of Bright Water* Longman
PURKIS, S. (1977) Oral history in the primary school *History Workshop Journal* 2, 113–17
RICHMOND, J. (1977) *Language Alive in School (Brixton Blues)* mimeographed
WILLIAMSON, H. (1927) *Tarka the Otter* Putnam

# Part 5

# Reading in the later years

# 14  Reading for learning – simplifying the process

## Keith Gardner

### Introduction

The improvement of reading for learning has been regarded largely in terms of programming the reader to adopt certain strategies. Study reading procedures, such as SQ3R have been emphasized; library techniques have been taught to enable pupils to select appropriate materials; note taking has been stressed as a means of consolidating reading.

However, the *Effective Use of Reading* project (Lunzer and Gardner 1979) recently completed at Nottingham University has produced some evidence that such approaches may not, in themselves, be sufficient to foster adequate reading for learning across the curriculum.

### Some obstacles to reading for learning

For the purposes of this paper, three issues raised by the *Effective Use of Reading* project will be considered. First, a survey of existing classroom practice indicated that reading for learning is rarely used in lessons other than English. Pupils are not required to read continuously, or reflectively. Indeed, 90 per cent of their observed reading was of less than thirty seconds' duration; the most common reading purpose was to answer a question – which was normally accomplished by transferring a small section of a text into the pupil's own handwriting. Whatever the full implications of this finding it is clear that reading for learning is not practical in the classroom. It may be assumed, therefore, that even if pupils are taught 'strategies' for learning such teaching is unlikely to have beneficial results if essential practice is lacking. In fact, some confirmation of this was obtained. Pupils trained in using a resource area rarely used their 'reading strategies' in project work.

Second, it was apparent that pupil attitude and motivation was of paramount importance. This is not an unexpected finding but, in relation to reading for learning, it requires careful consideration. It may be assumed that when intrinsic motivation is high a reader will strive to overcome difficulties inherent in the text. On the other hand, when intrinsic motivation is low the reverse is likely to be true. If, then, it is also conceded that only a small minority of pupils will be highly motivated to read all materials, from History through to Physics, it is apparent that there will be problems in some areas of the curriculum for most pupils. Such problems will not arise from lack of reading techniques alone; rather, they will stem from an unwillingness to attend and to reflect. Moreover, teaching reading strategies in itself will not be a solution.

Third, an examination of the readability levels of materials used in secondary schools across the curriculum showed a mismatch between the probable reading capability of the pupils and the texts in common use. In a word, many pupils were frustrated by the reading they were offered, and this would serve to aggravate the problems suggested above.

## Some interim suggestions, and their limitations

The enquiries carried out during the *Effective Use of Reading* project indicated that reading with discussion, utilizing prediction, cloze and sequencing techniques, was a useful way of improving reading comprehension. Such techniques clearly provided the practice in handling text that was lacking, and the response of pupils was encouraging. However, the problem of textual difficulty remained.

It was to examine this, and other issues, that funding for a new project was sought and obtained from the Schools Council. This new project, *Reading for Learning* (Lunzer and Gardner), will study the reading-with-discussion procedures more closely, and will also attempt to describe what makes a text 'difficult'. Preliminary work has focused on the latter point and it is to a consideration of our initial discussions that the rest of this paper is devoted.

### The text as an obstacle to learning

We started from the point that readability measures indicated that many school texts were too complex for 11–13 year pupils. What happens when such texts are simplified?

Early enquiries have alerted us to certain dangers. First, a simple text, in terms of word and sequence length is not necessarily more comprehensible – or, for that matter, more interesting – than a complex text. In short, reducing the readability level of texts may not be a solution.

There are a number of possible reasons for this. For instance, one effect of producing an information text that deliberately avoids long words and complex constructions may be to increase its density. Then, the reader is overwhelmed by facts. It may well be that a degree of redundancy is necessary. Or, the simplified text may, in fact, contain little that requires attention. For example, the following extract seems to induce mechanical rather than reflective reading:

> The Normans charged again. But still they could not defeat the English. Then William thought of another plan. He told his men to shoot their arrows high into the air. One hit Harold in the eye.

Second, ability to read a text perfectly and comprehension (i.e. ability to answer questions on the text) do not seem to be related in a simple way. This is not an original thought as Thorndike said something similar seventy years ago. However, one is reminded that reading accuracy and reading comprehension do not correlate perfectly. Hence, whilst reducing readability level might also increase reading accuracy, this, in itself, does not result in improved comprehension. It seems reasonable to suggest, therefore, that textual problems go rather deeper than surface difficulty. But in what way?

There is the concept of grammatical cohesion which sounds as though it might be a useful way in. The non-cohesive passages might prove to be difficult to comprehend and the cohesive passages more simple. Unfortunately, passages which pupils found difficult were grammatically cohesive, but the actual testing of the idea threw up another possibility. It was noticed that sentences within a paragraph could be described as either:

1    carrying on the meaning of the previous sentence, or

2    not continuing the meaning of the previous sentence.

Within the project team we assigned the term 'semantic cohesion' to this property of sentences, and we found we were able to describe a paragraph in terms of its 'semantic cohesiveness' with a reasonable degree of unanimity. So far so good. Then it was found that simple prose in information textbooks frequently exhibited low internal 'semantic cohesiveness' – but narrative prose was invariably highly cohesive.

This matter requires fuller explanation. Here, time allows for but one example taken from an Environmental Studies text (River and Canal Transport, Blandford):

Sentence 1    People were carried on special barges called fly boats.

Sentence 2    These made regular journeys along certain canals. (Probably cohesive although 'these' can be referred back to 'People'!)

Sentence 3    Fresh horses were ready every few miles, and 'flies' could travel much faster than stage-coaches which had to struggle along steep muddy and rough road ways. (Non-cohesive)

Sentence 4    The bows of some fly boats were fitted with a large sharp knife to cut the tow line of any barge that blocked its way. (Non-cohesive)


When pupils were asked to re-write such paragraphs to make them easier to understand some interesting results are obtained. A thirteen year old pupil offered this:

Sentence 1    Special barges called 'fly-boats' carried people along certain canals.

Sentence 2    They travelled more quickly than stage coaches because fresh horses were ready every few miles and canals were easier to move along than the muddy roads of that time.

Sentence 3    To speed the journey even more, some boats were fitted with a sharp knife that cut the tow-line of a barge that blocked its way.

Other pupils rated the re-written extract 'easier to understand' than the original.

We would conclude that it is necessary to examine texts more closely. One common fault seems to be the habit some writers have acquired of merely setting down strings of facts which are only barely related.

There are, of course, many other textual features to consider. Among them, layout, subheadings, and length of section. All seem to have a bearing on 'readability'. But, in beginning to study texts, we have been alerted also to another issue. A pupil's response to a text is governed, in part, by what he already knows. When the distance between the knowledge of the reader and the content of the text is great, then the quality of the text is critical. When this distance is narrow, then the reader is apparently carried over textual problems.

This raises some further problems. Reading for learning may be considered in terms of initiating learning: that is, the reader will not be familiar with the content of the text. Or, reading may be used to summarize what the reader has already learned: that is, the reader is likely to be quite familiar with the content of the text. The two conditions are quite different. It may well be that reading is more efficient in the latter case than the former, unless the reader is both able and highly motivated. If this is so, the role of reading for learning in the classroom needs to be planned carefully.

Again, one example can be given. The writer introduced the topic of glaciers to a class of first-year secondary pupils. One half of the class were given a text to read. The other half spent some time looking at a set of film slides before reading the text. (The slides illustrated certain glacial features.) Even this simple device resulted in a difference in test scores following the reading of the text. What is being explored here is the relationship of reading to a total learning situation.


## Conclusions

In the study of reading for learning the text itself cannot be ignored. It seems that some texts are written in a way that inhibits, rather than promotes understanding and retention. At this time, it might be suggested that:

1 The use of discussion techniques across the curriculum would promote pupil attention and reflection.
2 Whilst many texts in current use are too complex for average readers to handle unaided, the simplification of such texts in terms of current readability measures may not ease the situation for the reader.
3 The issues of density and cohesion in a text have been raised. These are important matters, but much more study is required before conclusions can be put forward.
4 Ease of reading could be furthered by greater attention to the planning and layout of texts. The work undertaken by the Open University should be noted in this context.
5 The role of reading in a total learning situation needs to be considered. It has been suggested tentatively that reading may be better adapted to summarizing what has already been learned, than for initiating learning.

## References
LUNZER, E. A. and GARDNER, K. (1979) *The Effective Use of Reading* Heinemann Educational
LUNZER, E. A. and GARDNER, K. (ongoing) *Reading for Learning in the Secondary School* A Schools Council Project at Nottingham University School of Education

# 15 Comprehending reading: the dynamics of learning conversations

## Sheila Harri-Augstein and Laurie F. Thomas

The Bullock Report (1975) has recommended the implementation of programmes for improving language use and reading comprehension. Here one such programme is outlined. It is designed to encourage greater self-organization in learning by reading. Originally aimed at students in sixth forms and in tertiary education, the techniques have been adapted and developed for use in primary and secondary schools, and in industry and commerce.

Early laboratory research on how students read (Augstein 1971) had shown, almost inadvertently, that increased awareness enabled learners to break free from long-established habits and begin to experiment with a wider range of strategies and tactics. This resulted in greater flexibility in their use of reading as a learning skill. Tutors of some of the students taking part spontaneously enquired what had been done to so improve their approach to learning. Review of the researcher's experience and discussion with subjects, revealed that the debriefing conversation had a marked impact.

In the next phase of research the originally crude techniques for recording reading behaviour and for describing the structure of meaning in a text were improved, and additional tools were developed. The *ad hoc* debriefing conversations were also studied to refine the process by which 'talk-back' through the behaviour and experience of reading produced significant changes in learning ability.

Thus a programme of laboratory and action research projects spanning a ten-year period was launched. This systematically investigated how conversational methods can enable learners to explore, review and develop reading competence. Action research courses were carried out in schools, colleges of education, one technical college, one university and in training departments in industry. (Grants for the research programme were obtained from DES, the Nuffield Foundation, SSRC and various industrial organizations.)

## Learning conversations: method, model and tools

Earlier work by the authors (1974) demonstrated that students operate well below their reading-for-learning potential. This supported Perry's findings (1959) that Harvard freshmen exhibited either 'obedient purposelessness' or 'positive misconceptions' about purposes and strategies of reading. Despite massive practice in reading, students' descriptions of how and why they read are vague and fragmented. They lack the language and skills to analyse the processes involved and to diagnose their reading difficulties. Most adolescent and adult readers are unable to move through the levels of organization (word, sentence, paragraph, whole text) to appreciate the location of difficulty. Confronted by their inadequacies, they react with bewilderment, anxiety, anger or even alienation from reading as a method of learning. When a negative attitude combines with inadequate skills to produce prolonged experience of ineffectiveness, difficulties become self-perpetuating, resented but unrecognized.

The wealth of literature on models of reading (Clymer 1968) and on intervention programmes (Roettger 1974) yield little evidence on which to base a programme of action research designed to develop competence in using text as a resource for learning. Most psychological research on reading and language acquisition has focused on short-term, serial and recognition learning which fails to tap the complexity of comprehension. Such orthodox statistically-based investigations use comparatively simple stimuli which are completely known to the experimenter. However, by adopting less conventional approaches, evidence is gradually accumulating about the sophisticated cognitive processes involved in reading. Morton and Saljo (1976) and Augstein (1971) have demonstrated the complexity and variation in reading outcomes. Goodman (1970), Thomas and Augstein (1972) and Lunzer (1977) interpret comprehension as an active process whereby meaning is generated and checked against the words on the page using personally-relevant criteria. The process applies equally to word recognition and to the appreciation of all levels of syntactic and semantic structure. Each of these works report the need to involve the subject personally in the ongoing experiment, which means that the experimenter has to relinquish complete control.

*The conversational method*
Objectivity normally demands repeatability of events, prior specification of conditions and the pre-selection of measures. But studies aimed at increasing self-organization demand that the learners have freedom to explore opportunities in their own terms. As the learners begin to exercise greater choice, so the researcher loses the capacity to insist on a pre-planned design. If the researcher does so insist, the highly-structured short-term events yield data which trivialize the experiences of the learner. Concern with experimental control can also lead the researcher to lose personal contact with the subjects. This reduces the reality and relevance of the research findings. But the freely-chosen experiences of learners as they move towards greater self-organization, do not lend themselves to the collection of systematically-comparable performance data. Thus a simple view of objectivity and the pursuit of self-organization would appear incompatible. This brief statement of the paradox within educational research led the authors away from an exclusively before-and-after, statistically-based experimental format, towards a conversational research design.

The first move is to involve the learners in the purpose of the research. They generate personally-relevant feedback about their own performance at each phase of the teaching/learning programme. But the information obtained by the learners also serves as research evidence. There is much to be said for this approach, but it suffers from the 'pollsters' dilemma'. The research data is fed back into the learning process which is therefore polluted by the assumptions of the researcher and the learner. The universality of this 'experimenter effect' is now fairly widely acknowledged (Rosenthal 1963). The researchers moved towards greater involvement in the teaching/learning events. Conscious of their influence they observed this and used their understanding to enhance the learning conversation. This is the method of action research. Because the researchers moved into the role of active adviser to the learners, they became involved in their real problems and loss of objectivity is traded for access to rich mines of experience.

The action-research methodology took on a new dimension as the learners were encouraged to become more self-organized. They became their own personal scientists. Self-assessment procedures take over many of the functions of traditional research. In deciding their own purposes, recording their own reading behaviour, assessing their learning outcomes and deciding their overall strategies for researching personal processes, the learners took over much of what the experimentalist calls research, and the researchers took on a more advisory role. Moving into this role, they began to formulate ideas about the supervision of the learner's self-organized researching of personal processes. The researchers began to research the conversational process. Traditional before-and-after results became part of an ongoing conversation, which also yields results of a different order. Within course tests, pre- and post-course and follow-up measures were used to evaluate course effectiveness and also provided ongoing feedback about learning processes. These results are reported elsewhere (Thomas and Augstein 1976b).

This combined approach of measurement for evaluation and feedback changes the whole conception of experimental method. One major assumption on which the conversational methodology is built is that awareness of process requires a language in which the process can be discussed. Pask (1976) has called this the meta-language. Most of the learners who have taken part in the research programme had no awareness of how they read to learn and had no language in which to talk about it. As personal scientists they were inarticulate and therefore could not create their own learning opportunities. As a general rule the authors believe that the meta-language must grow out of the shared experience of researcher/teacher and learner. The researcher uses a model of the process to negotiate a language with the learner as he or she researches personal reading processes.

*A model of the process language of reading-for-learning*
The basic components of the reading-for-learning process are considered to be the *person* and the *resource*: *purpose*, *strategy*, *outcome* and *review* (Thomas and Augstein 1973). This is illustrated in Figure 1. Reading can be viewed as the construction of relevant, personally valued and viable meanings (Augstein 1971). The reader, as personal scientist, checks out his theory of the ideas in a text against the words on the page. Figure 1 illustrates this: A1, A2, A3 are successive meaning generating activities. The content of the 'A' can be graphemes, words, phrases, sentences, paragraphs, or larger sections of the text. If the attribution of meaning is personally adequate (i.e. what is being compared matches), then the reader reads on. If it is inadequate (i.e. mismatches) then the reader attempts to generate more appropriate meaning. Such mismatch is revealed in the structure of his strategy. Changes in process result in a different level of monitoring. If A1, A2 and A3 are sentences, then mismatch may lead to monitoring some of the phrases. Search and comparison at this lower level may then lead to match at the higher level. Match leads to closure, so that the meaning generated becomes incorporated into the long-term store to form part of the reader's personal knowing. The alternative 'structures of meaning' which a reader can generate from a finite set of words is infinite. In the short term, meaning depends on the immediate purpose and that part of the text being processed. In the longer term, it relates to the higher-order purposes and to the whole text. Thus, purpose within a hierarchy of purposes forms the basis against which comparisons are made and match is achieved.

The learner has to think about the reading process as co-existing at several levels. The process can be understood in terms of how units of meaning are generated and get linked together, smaller units into larger units, and so on. During reading one is continually moving up and down through this network of organization. In perceiving the reading process

## Figure 1 The process of reading for learning

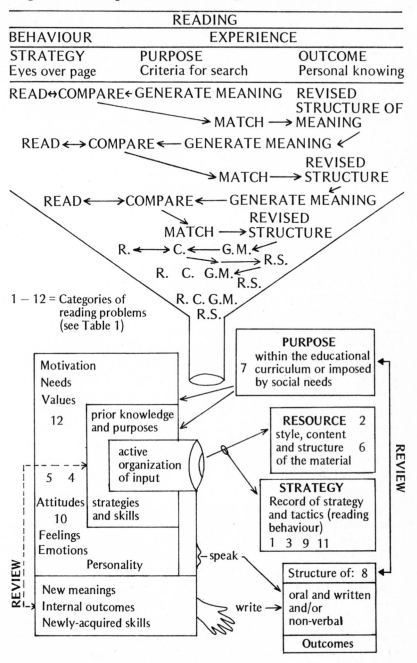

and thinking about it, one must be prepared to move between levels within any one component, or to move within one level from one component to another. The ability to do this enhances self-organization in reading-for-learning. Starting from this simplified model the negotiation of a meta-language enables learners, often for the first time, to become aware of, and to review, the quality of their reading for learning. As the meta-language develops, the simplified model of process is refined and elaborated (Augstein 1971). It becomes a powerful descriptive system for examining and changing long-existing habits, creating greater flexibility. Using the model as a conceptual framework, tools can be used to offer feedback about personal reading processes. This generates an awareness-raising conversation based on the learners' own experiences.

*The conversational tools*
Learners are encouraged to research their own reading. A series of investigatory tools which evoke relevant learning events have been developed for use by such personal scientists. Each tool is used to record and organize a specific experience to offer personally-relevant feedback about the process of reading. Understanding created out of direct experience enables the learner to experiment and change. This is very different from attempts to apply 'research findings' reported in the literature. Such reports usually provoke only verbal understanding and do not achieve the heightened awareness which enables the reader to break out of habitual models of operating (Thomas and Augstein 1976b).

1   *A taxonomy of reading problems*
The first step in developing reading competence is to help individuals identify their reading problems. Within this programme two procedures have been employed. These are reported elsewhere (Augstein 1975a). A category system of student reading problems is presented in Table 1.

Group-initiated categorization can be used to raise awareness of individual reading difficulties. As the group 'talk through' the categories using the model (Figure 1) as a reference, they become aware of how *purpose, strategy, outcome*

**Table 1   A classified list of student reading problems**

| Major category | Number of responses | Average number of responses per person | Sub-categories | | |
|---|---|---|---|---|---|
| 1 Process | 83 | 1.38 | Learns better if reading accompanied by discussion with peers or staff. | Confused by author's style. | Unable to review the reading experience. |
| | | | More reading leads to less understanding. | Unaware of author signposts. | Slow at reading. |
| | | | Too much time spent on note making. | Requires rest after periods of from 15–45 minutes. | Has difficulty in reading aloud. |
| | | | Ignores details. | Needs to re-read a number of times. | Nothing going in, lack of comprehension. |
| | | | Gets too engrossed and cannot put book down. | Reads too quickly. | Tries to be selective but unsure of criteria. |
| | | | | Emotional pressures lead to unintended bias. | |
| 2 Structure, organization and layout of resource | 69 | 1.15 | Forced to use too difficult material. | Doesn't like large chapters without sections. | Inadequate summaries in the text. |
| | | | Difficulty in pulling out features (major and minor). | Author assumes a certain basic knowledge. | Despair at pages full of words. |
| | | | Complicated writing, waffly. | Inadequate knowledge of references. | Poor relationships between diagrams and the text. |
| | | | | | Irritated by small print. |

**Table 1** (*continued*)

| | | | | | |
|---|---|---|---|---|---|
| 3 Selection and relevance | 42 | 0.70 | Conflicting priorities for reading. | Pressure of other assignments. | Has never been taught how to use a library, therefore unable to select the right books. |
| | | | Gets sidetracked into reading irrelevant texts. | Difficult to connect suggested reading to the rest of the course. | Never reviews accessing skills, tends to handle all books in same way, therefore unable to effectively select relevant parts. |
| | | | Often unable to use semantic clues in text. | | |
| 4 Hang-ups | 37 | 0.62 | Couldn't be bothered to have eye test. | Don't like glasses. | Don't care about poor lighting, prefer dark atmosphere. |
| | | | Hang-ups about seating positions, got to smoke, got to scratch my head. | | |
| 5 Distraction | 36 | 0.60 | Finding time to read. | Bar, women, music, family, shopping. | People talk to me. |
| | | | Can't read in silence. | | Noise whilst reading. |
| 6 Terminology | 28 | 0.47 | Irritated by excessive jargon. | New terminology not defined in text. | Differing terminology in same subject. |
| | | | Reading words wrongly; incorrect meanings. | | |
| 7 Reading purposes | 27 | 0.45 | Unable to articulate a specific purpose for reading. | Unable to distinguish between formal and informal reading. | Equate reading for pleasure with novels and reading for learning with textbooks. |
| | | | Textbook reading has to do with summarizing. | Seldom review outcomes against purpose. | |
| 8 Outcome | 21 | 0.35 | Slow in remembering. | Cannot bring material to mind when wanted. | Forget detailed information such as dates, names, places etc. |
| | | | Remembering different things at different times from the same text. | | |

**Table 1** (*continued*)

| | | | | | |
|---|---|---|---|---|---|
| 9 Passivity | 20 | 0.33 | Often inadequately defined purposes for reading. Never thinks about *how* to retrieve information from a book. | Allows the author to take over, abdicates responsibility. | Provisional plans seldom followed through and seldom reviewed afterwards. |
| 10 Boredom | 19 | 0.31 | Loses interest at the sight of a textbook. Hard to get interested, or to get started, need to be in the mood. | Gets bored, tired, sleepy, when reading anything. Disinterest in reading for mundane information! | Finds it difficult to concentrate. |
| 11 Inflexibility | 17 | 0.28 | Only vaguely aware of reading method. Tends to read any book or article from beginning to end. | Cannot adapt method to text or purpose. | Usually go through set routine of using a library. |
| 12 Physiological and physical | 16 | 0.27 | Tired eyes. Physically tired. | Poor lighting. | Uncomfortable seating. |
| 13 Miscellaneous | 12 | 0.20 | | | |

and *review* influence their comprehension of the printed resource.

Basic reading skills are taught in primary schools but more complex skills are acquired mainly by happenstance. Unreviewed, the reading process falls out of conscious control and the reader ceases to be aware of the cues and skills that he or she is relying on to attribute meaning to a text. The reading robot takes over (Thomas and Augstein 1976b). Habits which are limited in range and effectiveness dominate the person's reading behaviour. The effective use of text as a resource for learning depends on a capacity to get in touch with the complex processes involved in reading, so that these can be reviewed and developed. This group participation technique proved useful at the early stages of learning conversations for the identification of personal reading problems and for initiating change.

2   *The Kelly repertory grid: reading purposes*
The repertory grid can be used to help students explore and review the dimension in which they think about purposes for reading. During intensive individual discussion at the beginning of a course, each student identified nine purposes. These were used to elicit personal constructs. The resulting repertory grids were used conversationally to elaborate the students' range of reading purposes. Figure 2 shows Gwen's grid reorganized for feedback (Thomas 1976). Gwen's nine purposes grouped into four clusters (C1/C3/C6, 2/C5, 4). As she reflected on this distilled display of her own views of reading purposes a reappraisal of her approach to reading became possible.

Grid conversations consist of three phases. In the first phase, the learner is asked to name a range of 'elements' which could define a 'universe of discourse', in this case 'purposes' for reading. To facilitate this the tutor can take the learner through a diary of reading events, covering a day, week or month. Each event can be explored to identify a personally meaningful purpose for reading. The learner is then moved on to the second phase, when 'constructs' are elicited and all elements or purposes are rated to the poles (v and x) of these constructs (Thomas and Augstein 1977a). Learners become immediately more aware of the topic and the framework in which they perceive it. However, the third

180

# Figure 2 Gwen's focused grid: purposes for reading

ELEMENTS

| CONSTRUCTS Pole 1 | Pole 2 | 5. To feel how Dylan Thomas experienced Xmas as a young child | 7. To learn about the social habits of rabbits | 4. To learn what Richard Burton makes of King Lear | 2. To learn the photosynthesis equation | 6. To check a mathematical proof | 3. To find out how to do the experiment | 9. To learn the names of German rivers and towns | 8. To check a reference for an essay | 1. To find out what materials a plant requires for photosynthesis |
|---|---|---|---|---|---|---|---|---|---|---|
| 1 To answer factual questions | To elucidate my own view | X | X | X | ✓ | X | X | ✓ | ✓ | ✓ |
| 3 To instruct myself how to do something | To reflect on something | X | ✓ | X | ✓ | ✓ | ✓ | ✓ | ✓ | ✓ |
| 6 Everyday reality | Entering someone else's world | X | X | X | ✓ | ✓ | ✓ | ✓ | ✓ | ✓ |
| 2 Practical | Imagery | X | X | X | ✓ | ✓ | ✓ | ✓ | ✓ | ✓ |
| 5 Work | Enjoyment | X | X | X | X | ✓ | ✓ | ✓ | ✓ | ✓ |
| 4 Appreciate the logic | To fantasize | X | X | ✓ | X | ✓ | ✓ | ✓ | ✓ | ✓ |

phase, involving talk-back through the focused grid as a whole, initiates a highly meaningful awareness of the learners' views of the topic. Elements and constructs are resorted and clustered according to maximum match of responses (v and x). The whole pattern of such similarities in the grid can be explored (Thomas 1976).

A series of such grid conversations with one learner (Gwen) resulted in an extension of the range and quality of her ideas about reading purposes. Some of these include:

to examine style to see how feelings are evoked;
to evaluate the author's argument;
to draw inferences from factual material;
to empathize with another's feelings for despair, and
to share vicariously in a life and death adventure.

**Figure 3   The Brunel Reading Recorder**

3 *The Reading Recorder: reading strategy*
The Reading Recorder (Figure 3) provides a record of how a

text is read. The record shows changes in pace, hesitations, skipping, back-tracking and note-making. One read record is shown in Figure 4 . An analysis of reading records has led the authors to identify five ideal types of 'read'. Actual records often contain a mix of these, but nevertheless they serve to provide a common terminology for conversational exchange. These have been described in detail in a previous publication (Thomas and Augstein 1972). Behavioural records of reading can be effectively recruited to enable students to explore, review and develop their self-organized capacity to learn from print. Students are seldom aware of the cognitive and affective processes which underlie their reading behaviour. To the extent that they remain unaware, reading becomes a marionette-like mechanical activity. By guiding learners into contact with their own processes, they can become more aware of the existing state of their skills and attitudes towards reading and bring these under review. A read record used haphazardly in a Learning Conversation does not allow a participant to achieve significant states of awareness. The uninitiated learner is unable to make accurate inferences. The teaching participant in the conversation must either be prepared to offer these, or to help the learner acquire the perceptual skill to make them for himself. The quality of the Learning Conversation depends on this sensitivity to the information in the record.

In interpreting the read records the learner attempts to reconstruct the original reading experience. Briefly, this is achieved as follows:

The learner is talked through the read record by the researcher/teacher.
'. . . you started at line (X) and read evenly through to line (Y) where you began to slow down and read at half your original speed until line (Z). Here you stopped for ten seconds. Was this of any significance? . . .
Now on line (P) you stopped and skipped back to line (E) and made a note. Why was this? . . .' and so on.

Organized talk-back through the read record enables the reader to identify key habits and to challenge these, so that new strategies can be developed. But experimentation with one's personal reading skills requires support. Learners

Figure 4  Mapping a read record onto a Flow Diagram of text

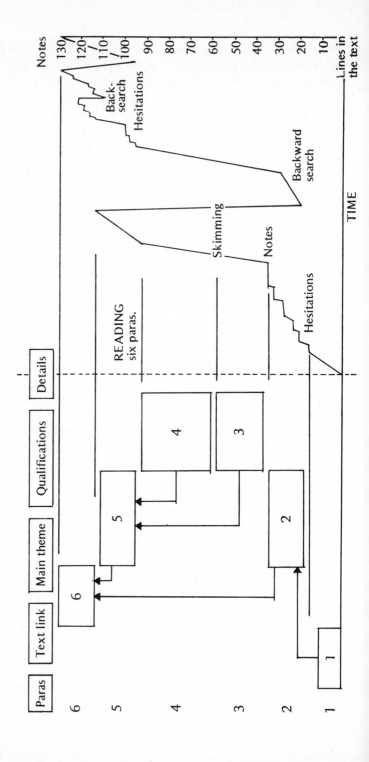

experience anxiety as they become aware of the limits of their skill. In attempting to improve they may often start by getting worse! Old habits must disintegrate before new skills can be developed. Part of the conversational skill is to empathize with the reader. Is he reliving the reading experience, or is he simply going through the motions of reproducing the behaviour? Talking a person back into the reading-for-learning experience is an important component of the awareness-raising technique.

4 *The Flow Diagram Technique: strategy and outcome*
Whilst words run serially across the page the reader is expected to store facts and relationships and use the cues in the text to create a complex pattern of meaning in his head. The significance of reading behaviour cannot be fully understood until this structure of meaning can be described. The Flow Diagram Technique was developed to exhibit in a structured form, the non-linearity of the meanings which the reader attributes to a text (Thomas and Augstein 1973). The Technique can be used to analyse a sentence, a whole book or any unit of meaning in-between. Students have found one of its most creative contributions to be the identification of how structure at one level, say a paragraph, is created by the patterning of structures from the lower level, say sentences, and from the context of its position in the higher-level structure, say a section.

The process of comprehending a text is essentially subjective. The Flow Diagram Technique can be used to enable learners to display the meanings which they attribute to texts. Having created an awareness of the process of reading by talk-back through the read record, the Flow Diagram can be introduced into the Learning Conversation. By constructing a personally relevant flow diagram and mapping this onto the read record (Figure 4), the learner becomes explicitly aware of the ways in which meaning is attributed as he hesitates, slows down, and skips forward and backward through a text. Together the tutor and reader reflect upon the read record and flow diagram by relating these to each other, to the original text, and to the purpose for reading.

5 *Structures of meaning: reading outcome*
The primary outcomes of reading are changes in the

thoughts and feelings of the reader. Often, the reader is only vaguely aware of the range and richness of the 'structures of meaning' he generates. A series of heuristics for displaying such structures involves eliciting items of meaning, defining the relationship between items and organizing this into a patterned structure. This different approach to express meaning in contrast with essays and other linear expositions pulls the reader out of a fixed acceptance of ideas in language and challenges him to reflect anew. Aided by the tutor, the reader becomes more aware of the complexity of structure in even the simplest meanings. The procedure is described in detail elsewhere (Thomas and Augstein 1976a). This tool represents an important move away from standardized tests, criterion-referenced tests and informal teacher tests. Such tests are more concerned with selection and prediction of ability and are for teacher rather than learner diagnosis. Structures of meaning measure learner-based comprehension and as such can form an essential component of informal reading inventories (IRI).

Given a structure of meaning, the reader can begin to question how this relates to the purpose of reading, and to a read record of the text being read. Relating the emergent pattern to external criteria can provide the reader with further insights. He can begin to relate his personal understanding to public experiences, the teacher, other learners, and experts in a field. The importance of this procedure is that whilst remaining centrally located in his own understanding, a learner can explore and relate this to the thoughts and understanding of others. Two or more individuals can agree to share a given purpose for reading a text and proceed to exchange their understanding. This exchange process depends on specific procedures, whereby each participant gains new insights and personal meaning is restructured.

*Other tools*
Many techniques currently in use in reading courses can be recruited as conversational tools for awareness-raising and review of reading-for-learning processes. The cloze procedure is one such example. Provided the tutor negotiates with the reader, the range and nature of the cues he is using and offers a meta-commentary on this, using for example

such referent terms as 'forward/backward acting', 'syntactic/semantic', and 'inter or intra sentence', the procedure becomes elevated as a tool for sharpening the reader's awareness of the meaning attributing process. Unfortunately, all too often this commentary is withheld from the reader and the potency of the procedure becomes diminished. A purpose taxonomy such as Barrett's (Clymer 1968) or Bloom's (Bloom 1956) can similarly be recruited, provided this is seen as one referent against which the reader can evaluate self-chosen purposes. Tutors of reading-for-learning should aim to invent specific conversational tools for individual needs. The basic requirements include: some observational record of that aspect being investigated; a display which facilitates 'talk-back'; a facility for the negotiation of a meta-description of behaviour and experience; and a procedure for gradually weaning away from dependency on the tool, with an enhanced perception of the process.

### The conversational results

Short- and long-term evaluation measures are reported elsewhere (Thomas and Augstein 1976b). Changes in response to a questionnaire show that after the programme, 'students question more what they read; plan their reading more rigorously; search for organization in a text; make fewer notes and find reading more enjoyable'. Records of reading behaviour show that participants have become more flexible and use a wider repertoire of tactics. Improvements in reading performance and academic performance are highly correlated. The opinion of staff was that participants are more active in tutorials and that the organization of their written work had improved.

Conversational research leads to *conversational results*. Whilst the 'evaluation results' appear valid and objective, these measures throw a camouflage of uniformity over individual sets of experience. The conversational method accepts the researcher/tutor and the learner as equal participants. The learner observes his own experiences and recruits the skills and technology of the researcher/tutor. Together they act as 'personal scientists' using 'theories' about how they read and learn as the basis for action, reviewing the consequences of action to revise their theories. Rigour arises from a continually negotiated agreement to proceed with agreed tools and a joint model of the enquiry. The conversational results yield a power to predict or to intervene and influence, similar to those of traditional physical science. But in social science identical events do not produce identical consequences. The 'subject matter', man, is self-regulating and adaptive. He can be thought to be self-programmed. The 'invariant facts' of conversational method are the models, processes, languages and tools from which mutual programmes are created to allow the participants to achieve their purposes. The developing science of conversation articulates the 'rules' of interaction by which mutually agreed self-regulation is maintained (Thomas 1977).

The focus of such 'learning conversations' is reflection upon process; the learner reflects on his learning; the tutor monitors this and reflects on the management of the conversation. The tutor's function can be described as 'mirroring' the process to the learner. Mirroring leads to heightened awareness and this enables the learner to explore the skill, so that movement towards greater competency and creativity is achieved (Augstein 1977).

An appreciation of 'man in process' requires a new system of language. Rogers (1969) comes close to this with his unconditional positive regard, empathy and congruence, but whilst he shows deep understanding of the conditions required for personal growth he pays little attention to the mechanisms by which personal meaning is constructed. Kelly's theory (1955) focuses on personal meaning, but his method (the repertory grid) deals exclusively in thoughts and feelings. Pask's theory (1976) of conversation attempts to bridge the gap between thought and action but the formality of his approach appears (but only appears) to distance the learner from the central points of action. The author's approach enables the learner to take control progressively of his own learning, by helping him to invent a language and methods to achieve this.

*Meta-language*
The skeletal model in Figure 1 offers a starting framework for each conversation. This is used to elaborate a more sophisticated personal model and to negotiate a personal

system of operational meta-language. Effective language is personal, based in direct experience, but it must be

Table 2 Levels in a meta-language for achieving conversational control

| Researcher language | Negotiate | Learner language |
|---|---|---|
| | *Conversational process* | |
| ... process, feedback, learning-to-learn, tutorial, mirroring, referent, support, self-generated feedback, trust, buffering, empathy, personal knowing, tacit knowledge, shared meaning ... | | how I do it, check, reflect, see myself, compare with, help, I believe, feel–I know, sympathize, know how, agree, mutual |
| | *Model of reading-for-learning* | |
| ... needs, hierarchy, heter-archy, *purpose*, *strategy*, tactics, *outcomes*, taxonomy, structures of meaning, internal review, generative process, meaning attibution, prior knowledge, elements, constructs, problems ... | | want, wish, levels, Purpose, Strategy, style, Outcome, method, stance, tricks, knack, habit, understanding, pattern, making sense, appreciate, construct, invent, reading diffi-culties, skill, craft |
| | *Specific terms* | |
| *purpose* ... rote, translation, in-terpretation, supplementation ... | | parrot fashion, paraphrase, own words, go beyond, select, |
| ... recognition, recall recon-struction, problem solving, repertory grid analysis, synthe-sis, criteria, referents, levels, internal cues, external cues, specific facts, factual items, problems, main points, sum-marize ... | | ah ha, O.K., remember, suss out, take to bits, put together, reasons, example, basis, attention, to note, pointer, details, ideas, themes, argument, lay out, precis |
| *strategy* ... read record, hesitation, flip back, flip forward, rate of reading, change in rate, line number, position in text, structure of meaning ... tactics, smooth, search, small item, large item, check read ... ... monitoring, decision point, input, data processing ... | | graph, stop, went back, skipped, speed up, word in text, straight line, squiggle, stepped, aware, decide, take in, think about |

189

**Table 2** (*continued*)

| | |
|---|---|
| *outcome* . . . criteria, multiple choice, objective test, recall, recognition, free response, cloze procedure, comprehension, summary, essay-type . . . | 1 line tests, remember, write, gaps, understand, sort out, map of text, |
| . . . flow diagram, link, main theme elaboration, qualification, example, dialogue argument . . . | correction, style, details, author's points, groups, mapping, congruent, between us, agree, out loud, doing, scribble, visible, |
| . . . meaning structures, items, relations clusters, mapping, pattern interpersonal, two person sharing . . . | |
| . . . written, verbal, behavioural, internal, external. . . | |

negotiated with others if experience is to be shared. To convey the flavour of this negotiation, examples of terminology are given in Table 2.

When existent language is not sufficient the tools are used to help raise awareness of the process of reading-for-learning. They provide unusual perspectives which help to break self-perpetuating habits. This direct experience is shared and negotiated into living specialist languages which elaborate and refine the learner's consciousness of process. Whilst there is obviously no objective check on the validity of the re-creation of the experiential process of reading, there are numerous corroborative indicators. Spontaneous remarks which relate to the content of the text and to the monitoring and decision-making processes, together with the reader's apparent recognition of his earlier experience, all add up. Part of the skill in the Learning Conversation is to be able to talk a reader back into his earlier process with evaluative commentary attached. He is thus able to re-view the process of learning. The terminology is not enough, it must be syntactically and semantically linked with the tools to provide a facility equivalent to that by which the craftsman relates to his materials and tools. Conversational events involving group discussions on reading problems, repertory grids, the taxonomy of reading purposes, the reading recorder, flow diagrams and structures of meaning, have been offered earlier in this paper. The conversational technology incorporating these can be articulated as an action–verbal–diagnostic–empathic–decision-making process which is shared between two (or more) people. Being two (or more) autonomous nodes of control neither can independently predict the precise content and exact flow of the conversation. But to the extent that they share an overall model of their activity they can achieve their mutually agreed purposes. This requires a meta-language in which to articulate the process. A more detailed report of conversational events is published elsewhere (Thomas and Augstein 1977b).

### The dynamics of the Learning Conversation

Courses and other research in this programme have revealed two directions in which this science of conversation can be articulated. Different levels of discourse can be identified in a Learning Conversation (for example, Life, Tutorial and Learning-to-learn). These can be identified and examples examined for the cues which indicate when to move from one level to another. Within the conversation at one specific level, for example learning-to-learn, it has been found useful to identify three interwoven dialogues. Together these reflect the learner's cognitive processes back to him, support him through painful periods of change and encourage him to develop stable referents which anchor his judgment of the quality of his self-assessment.

1 *The 'commentary on process' dialogue* raises the learner's awareness of his own reading-for-learning activities. It requires that learners explore their needs, resources and opportunities and then negotiate these into viable learning purposes. As the learners begin to recognize their purposes, they are able to explore their own behaviour and experience, identify strategies and explore the nature of their tactical decision-making. They are then encouraged to examine how they evaluate learning outcomes. Finally, as they become more aware of this whole process, they are encouraged to bring it under a continuing review.
2 *The 'personal support' dialogue* deals with the emotional context of learning. Carl Rogers's ideas indicate one approach to the freeing and regulating of emotion. But there are other directive techniques which can be used to help people over difficult periods (Augstein 1975b). The

191

language of personal support is only partly verbal. Gesture, expression and posture contribute to the communication in which there is a mutual testing out of beliefs and intentions. Gradually, a supportive relationship is built up. Teachers/tutors differ in their ability to generate this dialogue of personal support and much teaching flounders when it is not developed. Experience indicates that it can be learned.

3 The *'referents for evaluating competence' dialogue* is about the quality of learning. It is designed to help the learner to articulate the dimensions of quality. This process is partly reliant upon self-assessment using subjective criteria and partly upon the identification of referents in the outside world. Such referents can take the form either of significant other people with whom the learner compares himself, or more abstract indicators deriving from professional or peer groups. This dialogue about quality and referents can easily degenerate into the advocation of a dogmatic system of rules. For the dialogue to remain active a language is required in which to articulate the developing dimensions of quality and the ways in which these relate to the referents in the learner's world.

The structuring of conversational courses into immediate shorter and longer events has led us to a hierarchical view of the *conversational encounter*. Three levels have been differentiated (Thomas and Augstein 1976b, 1977a):

1 The *'learning-to-learn conversation' is primarily concerned with re-negotiating the skills by which personal understanding is achieved.* The detailed interaction by which habits can be broken, reviewed and improved skills rebuilt, becomes the focus of attention.

2 The *'tutorial conversation' on the other hand is more concerned with the longer-term strategic aspects of learning*; the planning of goals and the execution of purposes. It depends on the establishment of explicit learning contracts where the content of the learning is negotiated. Needs are articulated into specific purposes, the resources identified and the strategies developed. The deployment of basic learning skills (when to sit down with others and think, to pick up a book, to look things over, to peruse in the

library, to tune into broadcasts, or to make notes etc.) form part of this conversation. It can also question when a student should spend time raising his level of competence in any one skill. It is when such decisions are made that the 'tutorial conversation' refers back to the 'learning-to-learn conversation'.

3 In the final analysis education is only justifiable if it enhances real *life conversations*, and this contributes to the quality of life and the competence of individual and group enterprises and to society as a whole. Thus 'learning-to-learn conversations' and 'tutorial conversations' are only supportable if they contribute to greater capabilities in learning from and with experience, as an individual interacts within and extends his chosen world.

*The self-organized reader*
During the learning conversation the tutor acts as *articulator* of the *dialogues* and *manager* of these as the learner explores the resource. Gradually the learner internalizes the conversation and develops a capacity to articulate this with himself or herself. In reading, the self-organized learner is able to identify and define personal needs; translate these into purposes which form part of a wide-ranging repertoire of ever-expanding purposes; recruit effective strategies; interact with the text by generating alternative purposes and strategies depending on its structure and organization; treat texts that challenge and frustrate differently to those that fit easily into existing understanding; and assess the quality of learning outcomes within the context of the whole process. The self-organized learner acquires the ability to be flexibly aware of the process of learning. He or she can relax into the non-conscious use of reading skills without losing the ability to bring these back into conscious review. Finally, he or she can identify the dimensions of problems – intellectual, attitudinal, skill – so that appropriate assistance can be sought. In so doing, a learning network made up of books, tutors, peers, experts and a whole range of other resources are created.

**Implications for education**
Conversational methodology promises to become a productive alternative to more content-specific

programmes for promoting the development of reading as a learning skill (Polanyi 1967; Pask 1975; Thomas 1977). The tools used to raise awareness of process, already effective, will be refined, developed and supplemented as more operational experience is channelled back into the psychological tool-makers. Complex models of language usage such as information theory, phrase structure, deep structure or even cybernetic/logic systems have not in our experience proved useful to personal scientists setting out to research their own processes. Pragmatic positions such as GPID (Merritt 1974) and SQ3 (Robinson 1961) are too didactic and rigid to serve as vehicles for developing personally meaningful explanations. Simple process models such as that offered earlier, being capable of infinite expansion and variety, best serve the Learning Conversation; students are free to harness their own mythologies of the process of reading into expanding personal models and meta-languages. These provide them with sufficient insight to achieve individually valued changes in learning capacity. Models and their meta-languages are thus valued within conversational theory as conceptual tools for effecting change and maintaining flexibility.

In offering 'language experience' and 'experience exchange' in the classroom, three basic questions need to be faced; what variety of language, type of experience, and form of exchange? In the authors' view, meeting this challenge depends on elevating the quality of transactions so that learners of every age group are enabled to attain a *metaview* of what learning is about.

### References

AUGSTEIN, E. S. HARRI- (1971) *Reading Strategies and Learning Outcomes* Ph.D thesis. Brunel University

AUGSTEIN, E. S. HARRI- (1975a) *An Investigation into Reading-for-Learning Problems: the Development of Two Awareness Raising Tools* Centre for the Study of Human Learning, Brunel University

AUGSTEIN, E. S. HARRI- (1975b) *Towards a Theory of Learning Conversation and a Paradigm for Conversational Research* Paper read at Annual Conference BPS. Centre for the Sutdy of Human Learning, Brunel University

AUGSTEIN, E. S. HARRI (1977) *'Reflecting on structures of meaning: a process of learning-to-learn'* in F. Fransella (Ed) Proceedings of Second Int. Kelly Congress, Oxford: Academic Press

BLOOM, B. S. (1956) *A Taxonomy of Educational Objectives Vol. 1: The Cognitive Domain* Longman

BUZAN, T. (1975) *Use Your Head* BBC Publications

CLYMER, T. (1968) *'What is reading?: some current concepts'* in A. Melnik and J. Merritt (Eds) *Reading: Today and Tomorrow* University of LondonPress/The Open University Press

DES (1975) *A Language for Life* (The Bullock Report) HMSO

GOODMAN, K. S. (1970) *Innovation and Change in Reading Instruction* University of Chicago Press

GOODMAN, K. S. (1970) Behind the eye: what happens in reading *Reading Process and Programme* Illinois National Council for Teachers of English

KEEN, T. and REID, F. (1977) Guided learning: a discussion *PLET* Vol. 14, 1

KELLY, G. A. (1955) *The Psychology of Personal Constructs* Vol. I and Vol. II New York: Norton

LUNZER, E. A. (1977) *The Effective Use of Reading* Schools Council

MERRITT, J. E. (1974) *What Shall we Teach?* Ward Lock Educational

MORTON, F. and SALJO, R.(1976) On qualitative differences in learning: outcome and process *British Journal of Educational Psychology* 46, 4–11

OSGOOD, C. E. (1952) The nature and measurement of meaning *Psychology Bulletin* 49, 197–237

PASK, G. (1975) *Conversation, Cognition and Learning* Amsterdam: Elsevier

PASK, G. (1976) Conversational techniques in the study and practice of education *British Journal of Educational Psychology* 46, 12–25

PENDLETON, D. (1976) 'Intervening in the teacher/learner dialogue' in J. Gilliland *Reading: Research and Classroom Practice* Ward Lock Educational

PERRY, W. E. (1959) Students' use and misuse of reading skills: a report to faculty *Harvard Educational Revue* 29, iii 193–200

PIAGET, J. (1950) *The Psychology of Intelligence* (trans. by M. Piercy and D. E. Berlyne) Routledge and Kegan Paul

POLANYI, M. (1967) *The Tacit Dimension* Routledge and Kegan Paul

POPE, M. (1977) *'Monitoring and reflecting in teacher training: a personal construct theory approach'* in F. Fransella (Ed) Proceeding of Second Int. Kelly Congress, Oxford: Academic Press

RADLEY, A. (1976) 'Living on the horizon' in D. Bannister (Ed) *Perspectives in Personal Construct Theory* (Vol. II) Academic Press

REVANS, R. (1976) Action learning *BACIE Journal*

ROBINSON, F. P. (1961) *Effective Study* New York: Harper and Row

ROETTGER, D. (1974) 'Intervention programmes' in *New Horizons in Reading* Proceedings of the Fifth IRA Congress, Vienna Delaware: International Reading Association

ROGERS, C. (1969) *Freedom-to-Learn* Merrill

ROSENTHAL, R. (1963) On the social psychology of the psychological experiment *American Scientist* 51, 268–83

THOMAS, L. F. (1969) *McQuitty: A Computer Program for Hierarchical Cluster Analysis* Centre for the Study of Human Learning, Brunel University

THOMAS, L. F. (1976) *Focusing: Exhibiting Meaning in the Grid* Centre for the

Study of Human Learning, Brunel University

THOMAS, L. F. (1977) 'A personal construct approach to learning' in F. Fransella (Ed) *Education, Training and Therapy* Proceedings of Second International Kelly Congress, Oxford: Academic Press

THOMAS, L. F. and AUGSTEIN, E. S. HARRI- (1972) An experimental approach to the study of reading as a learning skill *Resources in Education* 8 (Nov.) 28–45

THOMAS, L. F. and AUGSTEIN, E. S. HARRI- (1973) *Developing Your Own Reading* The Open University Press

THOMAS, L. F. and AUGSTEIN, E. S. HARRI- (1974) 'Reading to learn' in *New Horizons in Reading* Proceedings of Fifth World Congress in Reading, Vienna Delaware: International Reading Association

THOMAS, L. F. and AUGSTEIN, E. S. HARRI- (1976a) *Structures of Meaning: an Educational Kit* Centre for the Study of Human Learning, Brunel University

THOMAS, L. F. and AUGSTEIN, E. S. HARRI- (1976b) *The Self-Organised Learner and the Printed Word* Monograph (SSRC) Centre for the Study of Human Learning, Brunel University

THOMAS, L. F. and AUGSTEIN, E. S. HARRI- (1977a) 'Learning-to-learn: the personal construction and exchange of meaning' in M. Howe Wiley (Ed) *Research in Adult Learning*

THOMAS, L. F. and AUGSTEIN, E. S. HARRI- (1977b) *The Art and Science of Getting a Degree: a Student's Workbook* Centre for the Study of Human Learning, Brunel University.

# 16 Functional reading and the school

## William Latham and Owen Parry

### Introduction

In the Green Paper *Education in Schools – a Consultative Document* (Cmnd 6869 1977) it was argued that 'schools must prepare their pupils for the transition to adult life and work'. If such a preparation is accepted as one of the duties of the school, it seems reasonable to expect secondary schools to prepare their pupils, as far as may be possible, for the functional reading (i.e. reading associated with a task or role) which will be required of them when they first leave school. For instance, the pupil leaving school at 16+ should be prepared for functional reading related to his/her role as a job seeker or worker (and, one might add, as consumer and citizen).

Unfortunately, it is not reasonable to expect the secondary school to prepare pupils for functional reading related to any of the roles mentioned above, as the reading tasks involved have yet to be identified and classified; and, obviously, no tests exist to assess the pupil's progress towards success in functional reading or diagnose his/her difficulties.

In September 1977 Sheffield City Polytechnic, in association with Sheffield Metropolitan District Council, initiated a research programme aimed at providing Sheffield schools with both information and assessment and diagnostic tests related to functional reading in the areas of job seeking and employment.

### The research programme

The research programme has the following three objectives:

1 the identification and classification of reading tasks associated with job seeking and employment in Sheffield, which a 16+ year old school leaver faces immediately he leaves school;
2 the construction and validation of a criterion-referenced group test based on the reading tasks identified in achieving objective (1) above;
3 the construction of diagnostic tests to be used with individuals who fail to reach the criterion scores on the group test.

A fourth objective, subject to discussion with the schools, will be the production of materials to be used in teaching related to functional reading. The progress of the research towards objectives (1) and (2) above is described below.

### The research

In order to investigate the reading requirements of job seeking and employment, we must first ask what areas of employment take on school leavers at 16+; what sort of jobs the leavers seek and enter; and what are the reading requirements involved. To answer the first of these questions, the help of the Sheffield Careers Service was sought. They kindly provided statistics relating to the 'occupational destinations' of school leavers since the raising of the school leaving age. We have found it useful to use the categorization of types of employment and types of job to which these statistics are related. Types of employment are categorized by the Standard Industrial Classification (SIC) (Central Statistical Office 1968) (see Table 1); and types of job into the categories shown in Table 2.

Table 1 gives a breakdown of numbers entering the various areas of employment. The metal working and engineering industries combined are gaining a larger proportion of leavers over time, whilst certain manufacturing industries take fewer leavers every year. The Distributive trades continue to take on the largest number in any one category. There is some change within groups, however: 'Engineering' and 'Engineering Small Tools' have taken on fewer and fewer leavers in the past few years, whilst 'Other Metal Manufacturer' has increased greatly.

**Table 1**     Analysis of school leavers' first jobs; 1976/7

| Industry | Total | Percentage |
|---|---|---|
| Agriculture | 32 | 0.58 |
| Mining | 41 | 0.74 |
| Food, Drink and Tobacco | 193 | 3.52 |
| Chemical and Allied Industry | 9 | 0.16 |
| Metal Manufacture | 487 | 8.84 |
| Engineering | 139 | 2.52 |
| Electrical Goods | 54 | 0.98 |
| Vehicles | 8 | 0.15 |
| Engineering Small Tools | 206 | 3.74 |
| Hand Tools | 230 | 4.17 |
| Cutlery | 434 | 7.88 |
| Other Metal Goods | 385 | 6.99 |
| Textiles | 14 | 0.25 |
| Clothing | 109 | 1.98 |
| Bricks, Pottery and Glass | 27 | 0.49 |
| Timber and Furniture | 73 | 1.32 |
| Paper, Printing and Publishing | 56 | 1.01 |
| Other Manufacturing Industries | 28 | 0.51 |
| Construction | 419 | 7.60 |
| Gas, Electricity and Water | 47 | 0.85 |
| Transport and Communications | 78 | 1.42 |
| Distribution | 1209 | 21.94 |
| Insurance Banking and Finance | 194 | 3.52 |
| Professional and Scientific Services | 273 | 4.95 |
| Miscellaneous Services | 193 | 3.52 |
| Hairdressing | 96 | 1.74 |
| Motor Repairs | 229 | 4.16 |
| Public Administration | 247 | 4.48 |
| *Total* | 5510 | 100.01 |

**Table 2**     Definitions of job types

| | |
|---|---|
| Apprenticeship | in which articles of apprenticeship are signed and agreed, with national regulations, block and/or day release training |
| Professional: | recognized training in one of the professions, e.g. articled clerk in accountancy |
| Clerical: | general office and clerical duties which may or may not include any training |
| Operative Training: | specific, on-the-job training for a minimum period of two months |
| Others: | no formal training longer than two months, or none at all; non-clerical |

## Sampling

It was proposed to take a proportional stratified sample of each industrial category. Before doing this, however, it was decided to try and decrease the number of categories to be considered, as many areas employed few school leavers at 16+. All categories employing less than 1 per cent of the total number of school leavers (1976/7) were excluded for the following reasons:

1 This will exclude categories which have previously only accounted for 4.71 per cent of all school leavers in 1976/7 (260 persons, see Table 1).
2 The number of categories is reduced to nineteen, which will save research time and effort reasonably employed elsewhere.
3 No excluded category represents more than 1.5 per cent of any job type and therefore specific job-related reading materials from these categories would be of limited value.

It was felt that random sampling within each category might well result in the 'swamping' of the sample with small firms. This was considered undesirable as it was thought that the reading requirements of jobs in larger firms may be greater than in smaller firms, where there is likely to be greater oral communication. Further, small firms, *per se*, are less likely to take on school leavers in any significant numbers. Therefore, firms employing less than a certain number of employees (all employees, not just school leavers) were to be eliminated from consideration in this sample. The data kindly made available by the Employment Service Agency did not include firms with less than thirty employees; this was therefore taken as an appropriate cut-off point, after due consideration.

Firms were then stratified according to size, into 'Small', 'Medium' and 'Large' categories; 'Small' firms usually had 30 to 100 employees, 'Medium' had 101 to 500 employees and 'Large' had 501+ employees. Occasionally, however, eight or nine firms appeared in the data for a single employment category as having 1000+ employees. Rather than group all of these very large firms with smaller ones, it was decided that, for groups where there were several 1000+ firms, they should be the 'Large' size category, whilst 'Medium' would be 101 to 1000.

A further problem was that of heterogeneity of industries within a category; for instance, the very mixed set of employments grouped together under the heading 'Miscellaneous Services'. With a limited number of firms to be sampled from each category, it might well be that not all industries in a highly heterogeneous category would be sampled, or that less important industries, in terms of the number of school leavers employed, would be included in the sample at the expense of the more important. With this in mind, some of the more heterogeneous categories were examined in more detail and certain areas of employment excluded, usually on the grounds of the small number of school leavers employed.

The category 'Public Administration' needed special consideration. It is, again, a fairly heterogeneous category. It was felt that access to branches of the Civil Service (except in relation to job seeking, i.e. Job Centres) would be difficult and that the time and effort involved in adequately covering this organization was not justified by the small number of school leavers employed by it. The Armed Forces remove their recruits for training elsewhere and so may be discounted. Also, in Local Government Service the Police and Fire Services recruit very few school leavers at 16+ years of age. Therefore, in its study of 'Public Administration' the project confined itself to Sheffield Metropolitan District Council, its collaborating institution; the nature and scope of that study to be determined in conjunction with the Council.

With the above considerations in mind, a proportional, random sample, stratified by sic category and by size, was taken. The role of Industry Training Boards (ITBs) and Group Training Associations (GTAs) is a key factor in the sampling method. ITBs all exist to provide standards within their industry, but many also provide basic training, as do the GTAs. Such training may be 'off the job' at a special training centre, 'on the job' at the workplace, or a combination of these two. With little exception, block or day release to a College of Further Education makes up some part of this training. There are often limits placed on the types of employee allowed to go on such courses, however; typically, all apprentices attend, as do many operative trainees. It is useful to take those categories covered by a Training Board or Association and consider them separately.

**Figure 1   Sampling model for employment**

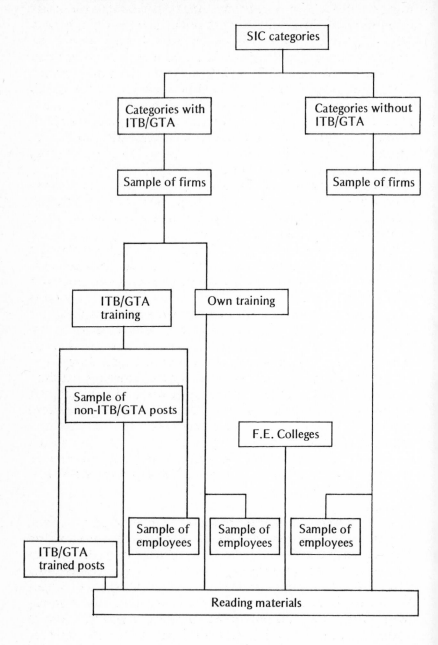

The Sampling Model for Employment (Figure 1) shows how this aids the obtaining of reading materials and the sampling of employees. From the sample of firms in categories with ITB/GTAS, firms will be divided up into those that use the ITB/GTA training schemes (or related schemes) and those that do their own training. Of the former group, information can be gained direct from the Board or Association whilst job types for which they provide no schemes will require separate investigation. Further Education courses are also a source of information concerning reading requirements. In short, there are five routes to the gaining of reading materials from employment for test design: via ITB/GTAS; via firms using these schemes; via other firms in these categories; via firms in other categories; and via Further Education college courses. Job Centres and Trade Unions add further dimensions to test design.

Nineteen categories were finally selected; fifteen are covered by a Training Board or Association, four are not. The proportion of the sample allotted to each category was determined by the proportion (of the total) of school leavers entering employment in that category. The data in Table 1 have been used to arrive at the number of firms to be samples from each category. Whilst it is recognized that the data in Table 1 include all school leavers, including those leaving at 17 and 18+, it was felt that the sampling method was sufficiently accurate for the purposes of the study. A sample of the 116 firms, plus departments of Sheffield Metropolitan District Council, was taken.

In summary, we have attempted to use a sampling model which will give widest possible coverage of job-related reading tasks encountered by school leavers in Sheffield.

*Contacts*

Before each SIC group was contacted, representatives of the relevant ITB were seen and asked to give their opinion on the representativeness of their area of the sample. In three cases this meant that resampling to replace a firm had to take place. Replacement was for such reasons as recent takeovers, bankruptcies etc. not mentioned in the original data from the Employment Service Agency. Where applicable, details of the ITB/GTA scheme were noted so that relevant personnel could be interviewed at a later stage.

Information was also obtained about the sort of data which might be encountered in that industry, such as the type of training systems used etc.

The Sheffield Careers Service was again most helpful in allowing names of contacts for each firm to be extracted from their files. One hundred and three names were obtained in this way, or provided by the ITB/GTAS. To date, of the firms contacted, twenty-five have declined or been unable to help, but sixty-five interviews have been successfully completed. Firms were contacted one SIC category at a time, in order of importance; but beginning by joining all the metal working and engineering industries together (41 per cent of all school leavers). Initially, four areas of cooperation were requested:

1 an initial discussion between the firm's representative and the Research Assistant to the project;
2 the inspection of reading materials actually used on the job by school leavers;
3 discussion with some of the firm's recent school-leaver employees about the situations on the job in which reading is required;
4 observation of some of the leavers at work in situations which require reading.

It was found, however, that the latter two areas were inappropriate at that time of year (March to July), as most school leavers are taken on in the August–September period and, hence, the material being used was not the initial material in which we were most interested. It was decided, therefore, that a second stage of interviewing of a sub-sample of school leavers, later in the year, would fulfil the requirements of the discussion and observation stages. This second round of interviewing has the added advantage of coming at a time when areas of overlap in reading requirements will have been discovered, thus cutting down on the work involved.

In parallel with the collection of job-related reading materials and information concerning their use, detailed work has been carried out on the factors involved in item construction. Presented with the wealth of material from the sample, it is necessary to sort out the materials which are representative of the jobs undertaken by school leavers and to construct items which reflect reading tasks performed by them. The factors involved are discussed below.

*Item construction*
It is proposed to classify materials according to a system developed by Sticht and his associates in their work with the United States Army (Sticht *et al* 1972). Using this classification system, we can then relate reading materials to job type and employment area and construct items which adequately represent the range of reading tasks involved. The classification is given in Table 3.

**Table 3    Content-type categories**

1    Tables of content and indexes

2    Standards and specifications

3    Identification and physical description

4    Procedural directions

5    Procedural checkpoints

6    Functional description


The definition of each of these content-type categories follows:

1 *Tables of content and indexes*
Content designating the location of information within a publication.
An example would be use of a telephone directory.
2 *Standards and specifications*
Content setting forth specific rules or tolerances to which task procedures or the completed product must conform.
An example would be conditions in an insurance policy.
3 *Identification and physical description*
Content attempting to represent symbolically an object via an identifying code (stock, nomenclature) and/or by itemizing its distinguishing physical attributes.
An example would be an inventory or price list.

4 *Procedural directions*

Content which presents a step-by-step description of how to carry out a specific job activity. Essential elements are equipment/materials/ingredients to be used, and how they are to be used, with presentation organized in a sequential step-wise fashion.

A good example is a vehicle maintenance manual.

5 *Procedural checkpoints*

Content which presents a key word or highly summarized version of what should be done in carrying out a task rather than how it should be done. This content differs from the content classified under Procedural Directions in that it assumes the user knows how to carry out the steps once reminded that the step exists and/or reminded of the decision factors which determine whether the step is required.

Here, a job card related to an industrial process is a good example.

6 *Functional description*

Content which presents an operating (cause and effect, dependency relationships) description of some existing physical system or sub-system, or an existing administrative system or sub-system.

A description of an industrial process, say in a training manual, would be an example of this.

Certain factors are of importance when considering which types of test item – multiple-choice, sentence completion, cloze procedure etc. – are appropriate for the assessment of ability in this area. Firstly, the pupil cannot be expected to bring prior technical knowledge to the test (technical not only in content but also in the sense of special jargon or vocabulary). The main focus of the items, therefore, must be on the different content-type categories given above and the pupil's ability to cope with them despite unfamiliar terms. Secondly, items must try to represent real reading requirements of jobs, of the sort actually undertaken by school leavers. As an example, cloze procedure would be an inappropriate form of item, as no employee is ever required to fill in blank spaces in a written passage, while an item that requires ticking off items on a price list does represent an appropriate item, this being a fairly common task at work.

Various forms of multiple-choice items (where the questions refer to some action the reader might have to take, for example asking for the next step in a sequence of instructions) and 'action-type' items (such as a filing exercise of the ticking off on a list already mentioned); these seem to be the most appropriate types of item, though not all the material is yet in from the sample to completely confirm this.

## Item banking

Also in parallel with work already mentioned is the work on item banking. If the items constructed exceed in number the items actually used in the final test or tests (as seems likely), it would seem useful to keep all the items for future use, for example the construction of parallel forms. Some item-banking projects are far advanced (for example the NFER Project on Item Banking), but it is not proposed to enter into such complexities in this study.

Items will be filed by assigning each a number, which will relate to a set of data about the item stored by the computer. This data will consist of a 'history' of the item (where the material was derived, which employment area, which type of job), classificatory data (content-type, item-type, key etc.), and 'usage' data (number of testees, per cent correct answer, date of last use, number of users etc.). Such data will assist test construction, as specific types of item can be swiftly selected, and simple statistical calculations performed as necessary.

## Work to be carried out in the immediate future

An outline of the next stages of the research is given below.

## Job Centres and Trade Unions

After the completion of the interviews in the employment areas, job seeking will be considered, via interviews with Job Centre personnel. Relevant Trade Unions will be contacted about documentation they may provide for school leavers starting work.

## Content validation

It is proposed to use panels of employers to obtain content validation of items as representatives of tasks in their areas; and of linguists to examine the structure of the tasks for any

207

undue complexities in the questions and underlying structures not previously considered in the construction of the items.

*Piloting and further validation*
Items will be piloted amongst the target population in the autumn term, leading to initial measures of reliability. A sweep test of the target population will be carried out in the following term. A predictive validity study is planned, to consider the relationships between test performance and adequate job performance.

## References

CENTRAL STATISTICAL OFFICE (1968) *The Standard Industrial Classification* HMSO

Cmnd 6869 (1977) *Education in Schools – a Consultative Document* HMSO

STICHT, T. G., CARLOY, J. S., KERN, R. P. and FOX, L. C. (1972) Project REALISTIC: determination of adult functional literacy skill levels *Reading Research Quarterly* 7, 424–65

# 17 Reading and the consumer

## Alma Williams

### The size of the problem – theirs and ours

'Illiteracy is no longer the unhappy privilege of the developing countries,' UNESCO's Director-General pointed out on the occasion of the Eleventh International Literacy Day. The statistic of one adult in three who cannot read or write is an average figure. It embraces not only developing countries – where the map of illiteracy coincides with the map of poverty – but also many industrialized nations which have recently begun to suffer relapses in their own midst.

In Britain, we do not have the problem of dealing with an illiteracy rate of over 80 per cent which affects countries like Ethiopia, Afghanistan and Guinea-Buissol. But even in our so-called advanced Westernized society we now have to admit to an estimated two million people out of our population of fifty-seven millions who have severe difficulties in reading and writing. The United States appears to face similar difficulties in reaching acceptable standards of functional literacy and the general competence it implies. A survey carried out by the US Office of Education and quoted in *The Guardian*, 31 October, 1975, finds that:

> ... There were fifteen million people who could not address a letter well enough for the postal service to be able to read it; sixteen millions could not write a personal cheque; forty-five millions were unable when presented with a typical airline timetable to decide which flight to take to arrive at their destination by noon and return one and a half hours later and ... nearly twenty millions could not work out the change they would get from a twenty-dollar bill after they had

been given the receipt for their purchases by a drug store.

It may, however, be true that other sophisticated societies who still retain compulsory military service fare better, since young male adults can then be induced to learn to read and write at the point of a metaphorical bayonet. There is, therefore, a growing recognition that reading can provide the key to competence: as a young Moroccan worker pointed out in an unpublished UNICEF study, 'When one knows how to read, one feels the master of one's own destiny.'

### Getting people moving – the motivations for learning to read

Learning to read brings about a fundamental difference in life-style. Yet it is an effort to face change, especially in the midst of poverty and a struggle for survival. And for some change in behaviour and attitude can seem to be an admission of previous error: it still takes a lot of guts in Britain today to say you can't read. So the wish to read has to be personally desired and not externally imposed if its effects are to last. In most parts of the world (except where literacy is politically undesirable) there is an increasing recognition that reading can provide the key to practical competence, to activity and a sense of fulfilment at home, at work and at leisure. Participation in religion is also an important motivation for many: 'So that I can read the Koran' is a commonly given reason in Eastern countries for learning to read.

In UNESCO's proposals for a new social and economic order, literacy plays its part by encouraging – *inter alia* – greater and more meaningful productivity, with many of its schemes bringing immediate, tangible returns in the form of better crops and more money. The most successful ventures on the whole are those where a community is involved, where rural villagers and urban neighbours organize their own services without an excess of external intervention. Self-help of this kind is the reason for the success of the 'Barangay' experiments in the Philippines where villagers themselves, after a basic training, are responsible for the elimination of malnutrition, which is closely tied in with the need for reading, understanding and critical awareness.

In Britain the practical difficulties that face our illiterates and semi-literates do not usually cause them to die of malnutrition, though a six-week old baby died recently because its mother could not read the instructions on the baby milk powder tin; but they are not going to be able to vote, read a newspaper or undertake any truly skilled work. They find it difficult to read road signs, bus timetables, street names and maps. They cannot understand a hire purchase agreement, a legal document, sign a cheque or fill in a form. They cannot claim benefits to which they may well be entitled. The major motivation of our 100,000 new literates is that of getting and keeping a job; but there are also strong family, social and consumer reasons for wanting to learn to read.

A look at the reasons given during literacy campaigns in South-West Hertfordshire produces the following comments: 'Reading means being able to go shopping on your own and write a list and compare things – and not make mistakes like buying cat food for tinned fish'; 'It means that I can check up on estimates and quotes and things like that and know I'm not being cheated'; 'It means I can save more money by knowing what I'm buying and getting'; 'It means I can do and make things because I can read instructions'; 'It means I can be private and independent in the forms I have to fill in'; 'It means I can call my life my own.'

These are not so very different from the reason given by a young Moroccan worker who wanted to learn to read, 'So that I cannot be fooled and made to pay more than what I have to by law', or that of a Bombay textile worker, 'So that I shan't be cheated', or a Senegalese migrant mother in Paris, 'So that I can know what medicine to give my child and how much the dose is.'

**The growing need for functional competence**
None of the citizen-consumers quoted above are likely to have heard of UNESCO's Declaration of Persepolis in 1975 which declared that, 'Literacy is linked to meeting Man's fundamental requirements.' Nevertheless, to all of them, reading is an essentially practical thing rather than an abstract accomplishment with an undefined purpose. It is part of the competence of everyday living which is

becoming inescapably and even agressively complex in most parts of the world. Such newly-necessary functional competence may well mean learning new basic skills – detecting and rejecting adulterated foodstuffs in India, or spotting bogus brands of soap and toiletries packed and advertised in Malaysia. Competence now often depends on reading ability, for an enormous amount of information – of the order of 60 per cent – is transmitted in written form. Those who cannot read are therefore deprived citizens and consumers, ignorant and exposed to malpractices in health, hygiene, safety and nutrition, so that ultimately the happiness and well-being of a family can depend on the printed and, accordingly, the semi-permanent word.

## An ongoing challenge

One of the problems in literacy campaigns is people's reluctance to sustain their reading and writing skills once these have been achieved. There is often a rapid falling off in standards, and the rejoicing at Indian village candle-lighting ceremonies – which mark the attainment of full literacy – is short-lived. 'But when literacy is functional or work-orientated,' says UNESCO, 'it has been found that the drop-out rate is very low.' It is pretty difficult to opt out of being a consumer with all the daily reminders and repetitions, written and visual, that confront us. Consumer communications, from menus to means-tested benefits, emphasize the need for maintaining and improving reading skills – a challenge often, and maybe also a cause for concern in their frequent and unnecessary, possibly even deliberate, incomprehensibility. Our own British adult literacy resource materials provide multi-media examples – such as tickets, telephones, trains and toilets – which in their direct relevance to daily life help to prevent wide-scale slipping back.

It is also more likely that literacy will progress if it is community-based rather than externally imposed, as I pointed out earlier. Kurt Waldheim emphasized this on International Literacy Day 1977: 'The acquisition, and equally important, the retention of literacy is intrinsically bound up with the individual's participation for himself and his community.' For in acquiring new skills in reading and writing people also assume new ways of thinking: more important than the tricks of any trade is a critical awareness that will enable new literates to make and transform their own existence and eventually that of other people. Reading produces and stimulates activism, the capability of participation, and the possibility for change.

## Consumer motivations in the classroom
British education has recently come under heavy fire for failing to turn out school leavers equipped to deal with the routines of living, working and voting. First, reading standards were attacked, and then in March 1978 there was an onslaught on numerical achievements.

Consumer education can help to improve both reading and mathematical skills by introducing a multi-disciplinary relevance and urgency not just into traditional Home Economics lessons but also into Language, Science, Business and Social Studies, Commerce, the Humanities, even into Religious Education. Reading as a means to an immediate and personally appropriate end can be seen to have a point even by the most turned-off fourth-year renegade: motor-bike manuals, maps, menus, mail-order catalogues have instant as well as 'investment' appeal. But the choice of such unconventional materials depends on a teacher's knowledge of students far beyond their classroom attainments, on the avoidance of condemnation, and on an ability – sometimes intuitive – to assess a need immediately it develops. If Peter acquires a dog by fair means or foul at the weekend, it is now on Monday morning that he wants to know about dog licences and diets and distemper, not next Thursday. Emergencies like this have to be coped with, but others can more conveniently be created or situations manipulated to fit in with an accumulation of relevant consumer and community materials such as forms, instructions, guarantees, leaflets, labels and so on.

## The Open University's contribution
There is a strong consumer component in the Open University's new Diploma in Reading Development. There are two set books: *Reading, Writing and Relevance* (Hoffman 1976) and *Reading and the Consumer* (Williams 1976). Two course units, 11 and 12, by the same authors develop some of the ideas expressed in the books in further detail. Unit 11, for

example, helps teachers to ensure that their children can read and deal competently with the 1500 or so advertisements they see around them each day. Manufacturers and their agencies certainly don't intend their ads to be an inducement to learn to read, but it can happen that a child who fails to be inspired by *Janet and John* will happily learn to read from petrol signs, cornflakes packets and *Guinness* posters. Reminders are all around – in a world often more compelling than that of school – and different communications media provide an educationally effective multi-media system, even if culture is sacrificed to competence.

## Cause for concern

Unit 12 in the Open University's course leads on to consideration of wider consumer issues, casting a critical eye upon public and semi-public communications. Documents, often unsolicited and undesired, come through our letter boxes from the Inland Revenue, the Government, the Water Board, the Vatman. Many of them are not in continuous prose, but appear as forms to be filled in, questionnaires to be completed, tables to be interpreted. Other printed materials on which we depend daily also appear in a format different from that of normal reading materials: road maps, street plans, underground plans, train timetables with small print, long lines and columns of figures, coded exceptions, abbreviations and symbols – all have to be decoded, understood and applied. Even fluent adult readers have difficulty in understanding some of the communications they may need to read: insurance policies, income tax returns, house purchase documents, landlord – tenant agreements, hire purchase contracts.

In the course of preparing Unit 12, the Open University analysed (Flesch 1948) the mean reading age of a number of the kinds of texts that most of us are confronted with from time to time. The Bank of England's (then) Notice to Travellers with a reading age of 24.4 was ony marginally more difficult than a typical example of a personal travel insurance policy at 23.4. The Save-as-you-Earn form and prospectus did not fare too well at 22.3. Fortunately, there were good examples at the other end of the scale with the Office of Fair Trading's leaflet on 'How to put things right' scoring 13.8, the National Gas Consumers' Council's 'Gas, the law and you' 13.6, and the Metrication Board's 'Going Metric' 11.9.

Improvements are being brought about because organizations are beginning to work together and consult, to understand and sympathize with the vulnerability of those with low reading skills. Since 1974 the Impact Trust has worked with Liverpool City Council's Area Management Unit to produce a simplified version of five commonly needed benefit forms, all in a single booklet of large print with a reading age of not much more than 7. Impact developed the following criteria for writing 'readable' prose:

Shorten sentences.
Omit long or uncommon words and phrases.
Avoid complicated grammatical structures.
Use active verbs, not passive.
Restore to full length sentences which can be artificially shortened such as: 'State relationship to applicant or if lodger'.
Omit unclear or forbidding directives.
Use design techniques to induce reading fluency.
Consider design and wording of forms at the same time.

Not far away from Merseyside, following the Impact tradition, reading and other problems are being solved in Salford on a person-to-person basis at the Form Market – formerly a shop, in a busy street in an old inner-city area with high unemployment. Consumer pressures, like these in the North-West, are bringing about conditions under which the Government is beginning to respond. The Department of Health and Social Security and the Supplementary Benefits Commission, for example, have worked together to produce a new series of consumer-tested leaflets on benefits. These are very much simpler than anything previously produced by these departments.

We are accordingly one step nearer the fulfilment of the United Nations' Commission's Charter on Human Rights, which now includes among its consumer entitlements the right to information. But the fact remains that the right to information is not in itself enough: it must also include the right to communications in a form and in terms that the majority of citizens can understand.

# References

FLESCH, R. F. (1948) A new readability yardstick *Journal of Applied Psychology* 32, 221–33

HOFFMAN, M. (1976) *Reading, Writing and Relevance* Hodder and Stoughton

WILLIAMS, A. (1976) *Reading and the Consumer* Hodder and Stoughton

# Part 6

# Assessment and evaluation

# 18 Improving reading through counselling – Royal Road or cul-de-sac?

## Peter Pumfrey

### Introduction

In presenting this paper, I must first declare my interest. Currently I organize and contribute to a course of training in guidance and counselling for experienced teachers at the University of Manchester. I have also been involved in the remedial teaching of reading for many years. Hence the suggestion that counselling might help certain children overcome their reading difficulties has, for me, a considerable appeal. This is largely because such a hypothesis focuses attention on the all-too-easily ignored affective aspects of reading and on the importance of interpersonal relationships in fostering learning.

The teaching profession suspects, and certain sections of it believe, that there are many pupils under-achieving in reading (Moseley 1975; Moseley and Moseley 1977; Little 1978). The search for methods and materials that will minimize reading skills within the context of a balanced curriculum is a continuing challenge to the profession. The history of the teaching of reading is well symbolized by imaginative innovation, dedication – and an ocean of bathwater containing abandoned babies (Morris 1973). Is counselling of pupils with reading difficulties an important 'baby' or merely muddy water; a Royal Road or a cul-de-sac?

In this paper I indicate briefly some conceptual and empirical problems inherent in the title, outline research findings and suggest some promising lines of development.

## Conceptual and empirical problems
The major conceptual and empirical problems that occur when discussing the possibility of improving reading through counselling arise from the following four considerations:

1 There are many conflicting views concerning the nature of reading development. From this it follows that equally marked differences exist about the nature of failure in reading and in how reading difficulties can be assessed and alleviated (Lessinger 1970; Singer and Ruddell 1976; Spache 1976).
2 There are many schools of counselling, each with a distinctive theoretical basis and techniques (Patterson 1966; Stefflre and Grant 1972; Krumboltz and Thoresen 1976).
3 A range of rationale underpins the claim that the reading difficulties of certain children can be alleviated by counselling. One particularly important phenomenological approach involving the self-perceptions of poor readers leads to the following related set of conceptual problems.
4 The self-image, ideal-self and self-esteem are terms that can be defined conceptually and operationally in various ways. Their relationship with reading attainment is a matter of controversy. In part, this is because our ability to measure particular aspects of these concepts is not well advanced despite considerable efforts in this field (Wylie 1974; Wells and Marwell 1976). Interesting studies have nonetheless been reported (e.g. Wattenburg and Clifford 1968; Andrew 1971; Williams 1973).

Lest the reader feel somewhat chastened at the problems in studying this area, he can take comfort in the notion that an acknowledgment of ignorance is the prime condition for developing knowledge. By this token we are well placed, if we so wish, to discover something about the effects of counselling on children's reading difficulties (Berretta 1970; Quicke 1975).

## Research findings
The effects of counselling on children's reading attainments

have been reported in a wide range of studies. Following a brief mention of selected reviews, the major part of this section will be devoted to some recent exploratory work done in Britain.

Frequently articles on the effects of counselling on children with reading difficulties do not give much detail of the interactions that actually took place between the counsellor and the client. Counselling becomes so inclusive a term as to lose its meaning. It can easily become all things to all people. We must move to a detailed operational specification of what behaviours are involved in effective counselling of pupils with reading difficulties (Winkler *et al* 1965). Techniques deliberately aimed at modifying the pupil's self-image as reader form a huge spectrum. The techniques may derive from a wide range of theoretical orientations. All can claim to be counselling. Any teacher arranging activities and materials to improve the pupil's reading self-concept is seen as carrying out a counselling function by some writers (Sanacore 1975). Perhaps the word counselling should be proscribed by Act of Parliament in the interests of clarity.

In looking at articles and research reports in this field it is essential that the reader discriminate between evidence based on enthusiastic but unsupported claims, studies that do not use control groups and studies that have control groups. This strategy was adopted by the authors of a review article in which a number of researches on the relationship between counselling and reading attainment are considered (Pumfrey and Elliott 1969). The assessment and enhancement of the pupil's reading self-concept has been recently discussed in *The Reading Teacher* (Sanacore 1975). An annotated bibliography of work in this field is also available, although its contents are rather dated (Lang 1976). More substantial material on self-concept and reading can be found in an International Reading Association (IRA) publication by Quandt (1972). A thoughtful consideration of some of the interaction between pupils' self-perceptions and reading abilities, also published by the IRA, has been prepared by Jason and Dubnow (1973). Finally, Coles's thesis contains an extensive critical review of the literature (1976). Unfortunately, theses in university libraries are not readily accessible to many readers. The review of the literature in a later journal article based on her thesis is inevitab!v very condensed, but the bibliography is a valuable source (Coles 1977).

Turning to recent British research, Lawrence started from the premise that a child with reading difficulties is likely to see himself both as an inferior reader and an inferior person. He aimed to investigate the effects of conventional remedial teaching and a form of individual personal counselling derived from Rogerian client-centred theory with such pupils (Rogers 1965). In his first experiment forty-eight children with reading difficulties from four typical village schools were divided into four matched groups – three treatment and one control group. Group 1 received only remedial reading; Group 2 was given remedial reading and counselling; the third group was counselled by a psychologist; Group 4 formed a control. After six months, changes in reading attainments in all four groups were compared. Additionally, change in the personality profile of Group 3 was tested using the Children's Personality Questionnaire (Porter and Cattell 1959). In terms of reading attainments the counselled group had made the most progress. It is also claimed that, 'The difference between this group and other groups proved to be statistically significant in each case except when compared with the group which received remedial reading combined with counselling' (Lawrence 1971, p. 123). Group 3 pupils' scores on the 'O' factor of the Children's Personality Questionnaire (hereafter CPQ), were markedly reduced. The 'O' factor measures 'troubled, guilt-prone behaviour associated with a poor self-image'. Hence it was inferred that counselling had led to improved self-images and improved reading attainments in this group.

In Lawrence's next experiment (a pilot study for subsequent work) the use of lay personnel as individual counsellors of children with reading difficulties was investigated. Twenty-eight children from two schools were divided, within schools, into an experimental group receiving once-weekly individual counselling and a control group. After eighteen weeks the results in both reading improvement and change in the CPQ profile are interpreted as supporting the efficacy of the experimental treatment,

221

although the increase in reading attainment under the counselling condition was significant in only *one* of the two pilot study schools. According to Lawrence: 'It would appear to be possible for non-professional personnel to carry out successful individual counselling of retarded readers, with only the minimum of training.' (1973, p. 60)

The third experiment was an expansion of the second. Four schools, whose headteachers had shown interest in the pilot project, were selected. From each school two matched groups, each of six retarded readers, were identified. One group was to act as a control. Each headteacher recruited a local volunteer (all were women) to take part in the experiment. The volunteers were briefed as to their function and each was met three times by the researcher during the two-term programme of once-weekly individual counselling. At the end of the experiment three of the counselled groups showed statistically significant increases in reading attainment.

In reviews of this series of experiments, various individuals expressed reservations concerning the validity of Lawrence's conclusions (Westwood 1974; Pumfrey 1974). These reservations were based on weaknesses in the design and analyses and on what appeared unjustified generalizations from his data. On the basis of a careful reading of the available articles and book, and carrying out a number of analyses of the data contained therein, it seemed to me that Lawrence had overstated his case. A further point was that no follow-up study had been carried out. The transitory nature of the short-term effects of almost any intervention aimed at improving reading skills is well documented. Lawrence stated that, with regard to the absence of a follow-up study, one had been completed by July, 1974, that the results were encouraging and would be published shortly. As yet I have not had the opportunity of seeing these data.

Lawrence carried out a further small-scale study involving twenty-four retarded readers in one school. Its rationale and results are as follows. It is possible that some of the purported benefits of counselling children with reading difficulties are offset when the client is subsequently faced with traditional reading materials. If counselling was followed by the use of a reading situation different in character from that associated with previous failure, might not the benefits of counselling be enhanced? Lawrence set out to investigate this possibility. Four groups were matched for chronological age, reading age and IQ. Group 1 received individual counselling from a non-professional. Group 2 received individual counselling followed by a novel reading scheme known as the Blagg Games Project (hereafter BGP), a graded series of reading games. The third group received only the BGP programme. Group 4 was allowed to play non-reading games of their own choice without adult supervision. The study lasted for four months during which each of the groups received only eight experimental treatments. 'The results tentatively suggest that, on this occasion, the gains from counselling were magnified by the carefully controlled reading situation following it' (Lawrence and Blagg 1974, p. 62).

During 1975, Coles decided to compare the relative efficacy of conventional remedial teaching and counselling of junior school children with reading difficulties, extending Lawrence's first experiment. The same four categories of treatment as used by Lawrence were specified, namely counselling only, counselling and remedial reading, remedial reading only and a control group. Children with reading difficulties were identified from an LEA survey of all first-year junior pupils. Twenty-one members of the LEA Remedial Education Service took part. Briefing on a Rogerian counselling approach was given. Each teacher opted for whichever of the three methods they felt they could use most effectively. The subjects were drawn from a wide variety of schools. All were second-year junior school pupils with reading difficulties. A sample of fifty-three was used. Both reading tests and the CPQ were used before the experiment, at the end, and also three months later in a follow-up. Attitudes to reading and attendance were also monitored. The treatments took place weekly, lasted for forty minutes and finished after one term.

The results revealed no differential treatment effect. However, all four groups had improved their reading attainments over the period of treatment and follow-up. No changes in these pupils' scores on the 'O' factor of the CPQ were found. No changes in classroom behaviour as rated by class teachers were identified. There was, however, significantly greater attendance in the groups receiving counselling or an element of counselling (Coles 1976; 1977).

Coles discussed possible reasons for these largely negative findings. She concludes that further research into the effectiveness of counselling children with reading problems is needed. Her study was well planned, more sophisticated in design, and allowing greater generalization than any of Lawrence's four researches. Lawrence has replied, somewhat acerbically, to Coles's work (Lawrence 1977). Insofar as a researcher's *raison d'être* is to stimulate constructive criticism, both Lawrence and Coles have been successful.

There is disagreement as to the youngest age of clients with whom a verbal counselling technique offers promise. Self-awareness is seen by certain workers as a prerequisite of effective counselling. It has been stated that children are unlikely to be aware of failure in reading until it has been experienced. Therefore counselling will not be necessary before the junior school stage of education. This is approximately the age at which many children begin to think at the concrete operational level, with all this implies in terms of the relinquishment of egocentric for operational (reversible) thinking. Being able, in part, to appreciate things from other people's points of view would appear to constitute a necessary but not sufficient condition for effective counselling. Lawrence's work with junior school children supports this contention (Lawrence 1971; 1972; 1973). Lawrence has described the type of counselling provided in his experiments by himself and by the untrained lay personnel used in some of his research. Recognizing limitations, but aware of the value of mobilizing community resources, in experiments 2 and 3 Lawrence utilized the services of five women considered by the headteachers of the schools as 'suitable', plus one known to the psychologist and acceptable to the teacher. The lay personnel were briefed by the psychologist and headteachers. These briefings reflected the influence of Carl Rogers's client-centred theory of counselling, although the techniques utilized were not strictly Rogerian. The purpose was to help children with reading difficulties regain the natural curiosity and motivation to read that it was believed most children possess. Of the method, Lawrence says, 'The sort of counselling envisaged here is in many ways a replication of a normal, happy, instinctive, spontaneous, mother–child relationship' (Lawrence 1973, p. 29). According to Lawrence, no expert psychological or psychiatric knowledge is required. He states that the personal counselling he describes could 'probably have been carried out by any sympathetic, intelligent layman, with a brief instruction in the techniques' . . . (Lawrence 1971, p.124).

In Coles's work the briefing, along similar lines to Lawrence's, of trained, qualified and experienced members of a Remedial Education Service was undertaken by an expert in counselling theory and practice. However, bearing in mind the limitations of time, neither group of counsellors could be deemed 'fully trained' or even adequately informed.

To varying unknown degrees, they could empathize, be congruent and show unconditional positive regard to their individual clients. In summary, the counselling involved an expression of tender loving care for the individual. The non-specific nature of this intervention is currently under serious criticism. One cause of concern is that it does not allow the counsellor behaviours to be satisfactorily specified, analysed, taught and evaluated. The assumption that the psychological equivalent of the disinfectant *TCP* was TLC, or tender loving care, is suspect. It avoids the behavioural analysis that progress requires. Indeed, counsellors such as Vriend and Dyer argue that for certain clients such an approach can be counter-productive, reinforcing the child's self-defeating reading behaviours and attitudes (Vriend and Dyer 1973).

This point is supported by Lane (1976). He reports an experimental study of the influence of personality on response to counselling (of an unspecified variety) in a group of secondary school pupils with reading difficulties. A distinct pattern appeared. Those pupils scoring in the direction of high 'tough-mindedness' and low 'neuroticism' were the poorest responders. Using the same personality test as Lawrence, but suited to adolescents, Lane found that the failing group rated low on 'anxiety' and 'guilt proneness'. In contrast, in Lawrence's first study all except two of the twelve children in the counselling group showed a high level of guilt at the start of the programme. In Coles's sample, high 'O' scale scores on the CPQ were *not* characteristic of

225

poor readers and this might have been a factor in the non-differential response to counselling she reports. As Lane notes: 'In order that pupils are not given remedial reading and then fail, and are then given remedial reading and then fail again . . . a more selective use of techniques is necessary' (1976, p. 121).

Recent work into the relationship between self-evaluation and reading progress indicates the influence of the social context on a child's response to reading progress. The researcher used sixty-three subjects from schools with a high and low proportion of pupils with reading difficulties. Their first conclusion was that the relationship between self-evaluation and reading progress is more complex than Lawrence allows. A child with reading difficulties does not necessarily have a lower self-evaluation than his more competent peers. Secondly, the influence of the social context is marked. If they are surrounded by a relatively large number of children equally retarded in reading, children with reading difficulties may not see themselves as of less worth than competent readers (Nichols *et al* 1977). Whilst the authors rightly suggest that their findings be treated with caution, they do point to further work that must be done if we are to identify effective interventions for pupils with specific characteristics.

## Some promising lines of development: locus of control, counselling for personal mastery and the alleviation of reading difficulties

Locus of control refers to the manner in which an individual perceives the control that his actions have on the rewards he receives, whether *Smarties*, approval or the satisfactions of competence. The notion is derived from social learning theory. The child who attributes such rewards or reinforcements as he experiences to 'fate, luck, chance or the intervention of powerful others' is deemed to have an external locus of control belief. In contrast, the person who considers that his own actions are an important causal agent in achieving goals and obtaining rewards, is considered as having an internal locus of control belief (Rotter 1966).

The development of a child's belief concerning locus of control appears to move gradually from externality towards internality, although the locus of control belief can vary with the particular aspects of behaviour and associated reinforcements under consideration. For example, activities in which the child sees himself as competent are usually viewed with an internal locus of control belief.

Of particular concern in the present context is the relationship between locus of control belief and academic attainments. Techniques have been developed to assess the locus of control belief (Nowicki and Strickland 1973). It has been shown that internal locus of control belief is associated with high achievement (McGhee and Crandall 1968; Messer 1972; Nowicki and Walker 1973). Well-known counsellors have also worked in this field (Dyer and Vriend 1975). In relation to reading, it appears that internality is associated with more advanced reading skills (Shaw and Uhl 1970). The individual who believes his own efforts can contribute little compared with the power of external influences in the achievement of a goal is likely both to learn less and also learn to devalue himself. The individual's locus of control belief can become a potent determinant of performance and attainment (Winschel and Lawrence 1975). An excellent source of information on recent work based on locus of control belief is available (Lifshitz and Ramot 1978). These ideas have also been adopted and developed by the school of counselling inspired by Vriend and Dyer. They emphasize the importance of an internal locus of control belief in the development of the fully functioning individual. Their training programme for counsellors outlines the means whereby the counsellor can help the client to move progressively through five clearly defined stages towards what they term 'Personal Mastery'. It is interesting to note that they consider competence in reading to be attainable by 95 per cent of the school population. This will, however, only be achieved if the individuals involved are at, or moving towards, personal mastery. This requires the development of a belief in themselves and their own abilities. The condition could be roughly paraphrased as having moved towards an internal locus of control belief. The strength of Vriend and Dyer's work is their specificity in operationally defining the processes in, and behaviours of, both counsellor and client that lead to personal mastery (Vriend and Dyer 1973). Whilst their work has been mainly with adolescents and older age groups, it could be extended into the primary sector.

It has also been demonstrated that there is an important interaction between locus of control and shifts in the climate of success within which the pupil is working. Climate of success can be positive or negative. The phrase refers to situations in which the participants are informed that they are, or are not, likely to succeed in a task. Thus contrasing climates of success and of failure can be set up. Groups characterized by an internal locus of control belief produced a significant gain in performance when the climate of success was changed from success to failure. They persisted in their endeavours. In contrast, those characterized by an external locus of control belief showed a reduced performance and reduced persistence. When the shift in climate of success was in the opposite direction, namely from failure to success, the externals showed a larger improvement in performance than any group in any of the other experimental conditions (Miller 1961). That this work was done with mentally retarded children on serial learning tasks does not, in my opinion, detract from its importance when considering children with reading difficulties. The idea that children who accept some responsibility for their own success or failure show greater persistence and initiative in achieving educational and other goals than children who attribute such achievements to factors external to themselves is worthy of further study.

The means of developing an internal locus of control belief have been empirically investigated using a wide range of techniques. The aim of such studies is usually to explore the means and outcomes of moving children from an external to an internal locus of control belief.

Children with reading difficulties and poor self-images of themselves as readers, may well attribute their problems to events outside themselves. 'It's the teacher, she's no good at teaching me to read.' 'It's the books; they're too tatty and boring.' Whilst these statements may not be true, one can see that subjectively an external locus of control belief may be operating. This can justify the pupil's poor reading, excusing him from responsibility and supporting his current self-image. The pupil's motivation to read will be impaired in such circumstances and his chances of becoming a competent reader reduced.

If one considers children with reading difficulties who also have poor self-images, it is suggested that many will have an external locus of control belief. Using the counselling strategies advocated by Dyer and Vriend to help these children develop an internal locus of control belief may well contribute to improving their reading attainments and enhancing their self-image.

The orientation and strategies needed for such counselling cannot be acquired overnight. Their mastery requires the investment of considerable effort and time by the potential counsellor. Additionally, the content of the counselling programme would need to be oriented towards language abilities in general and reading skills in particular. Thus a knowledge of the materials and methods available in the learning of reading would be essential. Given these prerequisites, there is much to be said for both individual and group school-based and teacher-conducted experimentation (McCollum and Anderson 1974).

It is well known that exposure of individuals with poor self-concept to experiences of success in an activity as perceived by an observer does not necessarily improve the self-concept or performance of the pupil. Frequently, such successful experiences are ignored, denied or distorted. This reaction is typically associated with an external locus of control belief. The child who sees himself as a poor reader yet who reads something successfully may attribute his success to 'luck', or deny his performance, for example, 'I can't *really* read that well.' It appears that the experience of success in reading or reading-related tasks for the particular group I have specified must be accompanied by a form of counselling aimed at fostering an internal locus of control belief. Put more prosaically, the child must be helped to learn to have faith in himself and in his own abilities. The experience of success with reading tasks from an observer's frame of reference may be insufficient by itself.

There are many difficulties, many conceptual, empirical, political and organizational problems to impede such a programme. As these have always existed in the past and have been overcome by interested individuals, I can see no reason why the suggested programme could not be mounted. The willingness of the Manchester Schools

Psychological Service and the staff of its Remedial Education Service to carry out the research mentioned earlier into the relative efficacy of counselling and remedial teaching in alleviating reading difficulties, is but one example (Coles 1976; 1977). Lawrence's work is another (Lawrence 1973; Lawrence and Blagg 1974). It is good to know that teachers and educational psychologists in this country are planning further research into this exciting area. We should give them every support in their endeavours.

Studies using counselling techniques specifically aimed at fostering personal mastery and an internal locus of control belief in the classroom situation have been outlined. The use of such an approach with some clearly described groups of children with reading difficulties would be of both practical and theoretical interest.

## Conclusion

Returning to the title of this paper, 'Improving reading through counselling – Royal Road or cul-de-sac?', a number of important reservations have been expressed and justified. The pioneers, the enthusiasts, can all too readily overstate their cases. Evidence so far available does not justify some exaggerated claims that have been made. The clarification of complex situations is a major function of research and experiment in education. However, much as we might wish it to be, clarification is not synonymous with simplification. In my opinion our natural tendency to oversimplify the relationship between counselling and the alleviation of reading difficulties is dangerous. It is dangerous because it can lead to unjustified expectations by teachers. The subsequent disillusionment can lead, metaphorically, to one more promising baby going down the drain of fashion (Pumfrey 1974).

On the positive side the issues raised by the use of counselling, whether alone or in combination with other activities bring to the fore the importance of interpersonal relationships in facilitating learning. In emphasizing the importance of the self-image and locus of control belief, teachers of reading are sensitized to the importance of the internal frame of reference, to the way things are perceived by the child with reading difficulties and an impaired self-image.

Counselling as a strategy for dealing with reading difficulties is not a panacea. In the teaching and learning of reading no one approach can ever be the Royal Road to functional literacy for all. On the other hand, it will only become a cul-de-sac if we turn it into one by virtue of an unwillingness to undertake the necessary systematic investigations and experiments based on sound research design (Farr *et al* 1976).

Those who have worked, are currently working or intend doing so in this area deserve our constructive criticism, our respect and, above all, our support in their endeavours. There are still far too many unrecognized 'Dibs' in our schools for this work not to continue (Axline 1964).

## References

ANDREW, R. J. (1971) The self-concept of good and poor teachers *The Slow Learning Child* 18, 3, 160–66

AXLINE, V. M. (1964) *Dibs: In Search of Self* Gollancz

BERRETTA, S. (1970) Self-concept development in the reading programme *The Reading Teacher* 24, 3, 232–9

COLES, C. M. (1976) *A Replication and Extension of Lawrence's Work on the Effects of Counselling on Retarded Readers* Unpublished M.Sc. thesis, Division of Educational Guidance, Department of Education, University of Manchester

COLES, C. M. (1977) Counselling and reading retardation *Therapeutic Education* 5, 1, 10–18

DYER, W. and VRIEND, J. (1975) *Counselling Techniques that Work* Washington: American Personnel and Guidance Association

FARR, R., WEINTRAUB, S. and TONE, B. (Eds) (1976) *Improving Reading Research* Newark, Delaware: International Reading Association

JASON, M. H. and DUBNOW, B. (1973) 'The relationship between self-perceptions of reading abilities and reading achievement' in MacGinitie, W. H. (Ed) *Assessment Problems in Reading* Newark, Delaware: International Reading Association

KRUMBOLTZ, J. and THORESEN, C. E. (Eds) (1976) *Counselling Methods* New York: Holt Rinehart and Winston

LANE, D. (1976) Limitations of counselling with retarded readers *Remedial Education* 11,3, 120–21

LANG, J. B. (1976) Self-concept and reading achievement: an annotated bibliography *The Reading Teacher* 29, 8, 787–93

LAWRENCE, D. (1971) The effects of counselling on retarded readers *Educational Research* 13, 2, 119–24

LAWRENCE, D. (1972) Counselling of retarded readers by non-professionals *Educational Research* 15, 1, 48–54

LAWRENCE, D. (1973) *Improved Reading through Counselling* Ward Lock Educational

LAWRENCE, D. (1977) A comment on Clare Coles' article *Therapeutic Education* 5, 2, 44–5

LAWRENCE, D. and BLAGG, N. (1974) Improved reading through self-initiated learning and counselling *Remedial Education* 9, 2, 61–3

LAWRENCE, E. A. and WINSCHEL, J. F. (1973) Self-concept and the retarded: research and issues *Exceptional Children* 310–19

LESSINGER, L. M. (1970) *Every Kid a Winner: Accountability in Education* New York: Simon and Schuster

LIFSHITZ, M. and RAMOT, L. (1978) Towards a framework for developing children's locus-of-control orientation *Child Development* 49, 85–95

LITTLE, A. N. (1978) *Educational Policies for Multi-Racial Areas* Goldsmiths' College Inaugural Lecture

McCOLLUM, R.S. and ANDERSON, R. P. (1974) Group counselling with reading disabled children *Journal of Counselling Psychology* 21, 2, 150–55

McGHEE, P. E. and CRANDALL, V. C. (1968) Beliefs in internal–external control of reinforcement and academic performance *Child Development* 39, 91–102

MESSER, S. B. (1972) The relation of internal–external control to academic performance *Child Development* 43, 1456–62

MILLER, M. B. (1961) Locus of control, learning climate and climate shifts in serial learning with mental retardates *Dissertation Abstracts International* 22, 2887

MORRIS, R. (1973) (amended edition) *Success and Failure in Learning to Read* Penguin

MOSELEY, C. and MOSELEY, D. (1977) *Language and Reading among Underachievers* NFER

MOSELEY, D. (1975) *Special Provision for Reading* NFER

NICHOLS, S. L., NICHOLS, K. A. and BURDEN, R. L. (1977) The relationships between self-evaluation and reading progress: some paradoxical findings *Remedial Education* 12, 4, 191–3

NOWICKI, S. and STRICKLAND, B. R. (1973) A locus of control scale for children *Journal of Consulting and Clinical Psychology* 40, 148–54

NOWICKI, S. and WALKER, C. (1973) Achievement in relation to locus of control: identification of a new source of variance *Journal of Genetic Psychology* 123, 63–7

PATTERSON, C. H. (1966) *Theories of Counselling and Psychotherapy* New York: Harper and Row

PORTER, R. B. and CATTELL, R. B. (1959) *Technical Handbook for the Children's Personality Questionnaire* Illinois: Institute for Personality Assessment and Testing

PUMFREY, P. D. (1974) Review of Lawrence's 'Improved reading through counselling' *Reading* 8, 2, 40–42

PUMFREY, P. D. and ELLIOTT, C. D. (1969) Play therapy, social adjustment and reading attainment *Educational Research* 12, 3, 183–93

QUANDT, I. (1972) *Self-concept and Reading* Newark, Delaware: International Reading Association

QUICKE, J. C. (1975) Self-concept and the diagnosis of reading difficulties *Remedial Education* 10, 2, 77–81

ROGERS, C. R. (1965) *Client-centred Therapy: its current practice, implications and theory* Boston: Houghton Mifflin

ROTTER, J. B. (1966) Generalized expectancies for internal versus external control of reinforcement *Psychological Monographs* 80, 1

SANACORE, J. (1975) Reading self-concept: assessment and enhancement *The Reading Teacher* 29, 2, 164–8

SHAW, R. L. and UHL, P. (1970) Control of reinforcement and academic achievement *Journal of Educational Research* 64, 226–8

SINGER, H. and RUDDELL, R. D. (Eds) (1976) (2nd edition) *Theoretical Models and Processes of Reading* Newark, Delaware: International Reading Association

SPACHE, G. D. (1976) *Investigating the Issues of Reading Disability* Boston: Allyn and Bacon

STEFFLRE, B. and GRANT, W. H. (1972) (2nd edition) *Theories of Counselling* New York: McGraw Hill

VRIEND, J. and DYER, W. (1973) *Counselling for Personal Mastery* (an eight cassette programme) Washington: American Personnel and Guidance Association

WATTENBERG, W. W. and CLIFFORD, C. (1968) Relation of self-concepts to beginning achievement in reading *Child Development* 35, 461–7

WELLS, L. E. and MARWELL, G. (1976) *Self-Esteem: its Conceptualisation and Measurement* New York: Sago

WESTWOOD, P. (1974) Review of Lawrence, D. 'Improved reading through counselling' *Remedial Education* 9, 2, 93

WILLIAMS, J. H. (1973) The relationship between self-concept and reading achievement in 1st Grade children *Journal of Educational Research* 66, 378–80

WINKLER, R. C., TEIGLAND, J. J., MUNGER, P. F. and KRANZLER, G. D. (1965) The effects of selected counselling and remedial techniques on underachieving elementary school students *Journal of Counselling Psychology* 12, 4, 384–7

WINSCHEL, J. F. and LAWRENCE, E. A. (1975) Locus of control: implications for special education *Exceptional Children* 41, 483–9

WYLIE, R. C. (1974) *Self-concept: a Review of Methodological Considerations and Measuring* Vol. 1. Nebraska: University of Nebraska Press

# 19  Monitoring of language performance in the schools of England and Wales

## Tom Gorman

What I would like to do in the time available is to outline briefly the work of the Language Monitoring Project which is being undertaken by a research team at the National Foundation for Educational Research on behalf of the Assessment of Performance Unit of the Department of Educational Science; and to comment on the rationale underlying the construction of the measures that are being developed to assess reading ability.

The Assessment of Performance Unit (APU) was set up by the DES in 1974 to promote developments relating to assessing and monitoring the achievement of children at school and to seek to identify the incidence of underachievement. The assessment programme in language is being carried out in collaboration with a Steering Group of subject specialists and officers of the APU and with liaison groups of teachers in different parts of the country. The work of the Steering Group is, in turn, coordinated with that of other groups by the Coordinating Committee of the APU and is scrutinized by a National Consultative Committee appointed by the Secretary of State.

The overall assessment programme being planned in language is, therefore, part of a more extensive programme that differs from previous efforts to assess levels of performance on a national basis in a number of ways. Firstly, what is being sought is a cross-curricula picture of performance initially in areas such as language, mathematics and science. Language is therefore regarded not simply as the product of the English lesson but also as servicing and being developed in other areas of the curriculum. Secondly, the methods and instruments used to assess performance are far more varied than those used in previous undertakings. In each subject area a wide variety of instruments will be used to measure different aspects of performance: in language, for example, we are currently focusing on reading and writing, but will subsequently investigate the feasibility of assessing listening and speaking skills. Whenever possible the instruments will, however, be linked or calibrated so that in any one area it will be possible to report on performance on different tests in terms of the same units of measurement.

This approach is possible because the concern is not to assess the performance of one child as against another or one school against another – indeed our terms of reference explicitly exclude any method of reporting that could permit individual children or schools to be identified – but to build up a picture of national performance using instruments that adequately reflect the complexity of the subject area and to develop a system of assessment that will subsequently make it possible to monitor changes over time in such performance.

I said earlier that the work being done differs from that previously undertaken in a number of ways and I would like to elaborate this point somewhat. Since 1948, a number of national or large-scale surveys have been carried out in England and Wales which have provided generalized information about reading standards. Two instruments have been employed in a number of surveys: the National Survey Form Six (NS6) and the Watts-Vernon test, both of which require pupils to select the appropriate terms to complete a set of incomplete and contextualized sentences. The selection of the appropriate word requires the child to make use of knowledge of both syntactic and semantic meaning and pragmatic knowledge of the world. What such an exercise does not involve is knowledge of what Chomsky would term discourse grammar – that is, the ability to interpret the meaning of a text (the logical form and propositional content) as this is developed in a series of sentences linked by a network of devices such as reference, substitution and conjunction; and linked also in terms of rhetorical devices by which, for example, a writer indicates which parts of a sentence he wishes to topicalize or to give emphasis to.

These are some of the general considerations that we had in mind when developing item-types to be used in the experimental tests of reading ability. An initial emphasis has been laid on such items as can be used to assess a pupil's ability to comprehend passages of continuous prose as a whole and in relation to information provided in passages on related themes. [A somewhat different approach – focusing on component skills such as those involved in graphic decoding – would need to be adopted in the preparation of diagnostic tests and tests for pupils in the initial stages of learning to read; and we are keeping open the option of developing additional tests such as tests of word meaning which have high construct validity but low face validity and content validity in curricular terms, if this proves to be necessary.]

The basic test instruments developed to date for use at primary level take the form of short booklets containing passages relating to a common theme. The themes relate to topics that pupils might encounter in more than one area of the curriculum and were selected after discussions with teachers in liaison groups and pupils. The reading passages in the booklets are selected or adapted from textbooks, works of reference, and works of literature of a kind likely to be employed or referred to by teachers of eleven year old children. The re-usable booklets are attractively illustrated. We think it important the children should find the materials attractive to look at and interesting to read – and our initial experiments indicate that this appears generally to be the case.

Each booklet has a table of contents and an index. In completing the booklets pupils are asked to carry out reading tasks analogous to those they are required to undertake in the classroom. Basically, these tasks involve the use of what I have termed skills of interpretation or interpretive skills; and the use of reference skills by which, for example, pupils are asked to determine the relevance of a passage to the question by identifying its general theme or gist, or to locate information relevant to a particular topic in one or more passages and to interpret or evaluate it in the light of information derived from the passage as a whole or from other passages they have read. They are also asked in some cases to apply the information gained by drawing a diagram or completing a crossword. They may be asked to reinterpret information provided in one passage by information given in charts or diagrams.

At the secondary level, the initial materials prepared are also in booklet form. The passages are, however, drawn from a wider range of written work than are the primary booklets. One experimental measure, for example, takes the form of a holiday brochure containing information about the historical background, geographical setting, and major activities and industries of a town, together with train timetables, information about hotels, and other information the pupils will be expected to employ in using the brochure.

I will not elaborate further here on the range of questions that will be asked. It will be apparent that we are concerned in this exercise to present the children with tasks of the kind that they and their teachers will be generally familiar with as readers. Further information about this consideration is available in the document on *Language Performance* recently published by APU.

An alternative approach would have been to have constructed items with reference to a taxonomy of comprehension skills – though I know of no taxonomy that has empirical validity in measurement terms. It would also have been feasible to have prepared sets of items to investigate systematically the pupil's understanding of different aspects of the meaning of the texts, for example the positional or referential meaning, and what some linguists would currently term pragmatic, textual, con- textual and discoursal meaning. Both of these approaches hae been rejected in favour of the approach adopted; but we will subsequently undertake data analysis which will, insofar as is feasible, take account of the types of meanings pupils are asked to respond to, and which may ultimately serve to provide a more coherent theoretical basis for the pre- paration of items of different levels of difficulty.

Perhaps I should emphasize here that we do not assume that the reading activities itemized about will be found to involve the application of distinct sub-skills. It is our view that, at this level, reading comprehension is best regarded as a unitary trait that is amenable to objective measurement in the sense that it can be measured independently of the item-types employed. In the initial item analysis that is being undertaken we will, however, be examining the behaviour of items within and across the categories of item types that have been specified and it may subsequently be possible by this means to determine whether these categories can be said to have discriminant validity in measurement terms. In this and other respects, therefore, the development work that is being undertaken may in the long term contribute to one aspect of our knowledge about the reading process. Our main concerns are practical ones, however, and the research we are doing is directed specifically toward the production of valid and reliable measures of assessment.

## Further developments
It may subsequently be necessary to supplement the reading materials already prepared with materials that measure component processes of reading or discrete skills such as are involved in letter and word recognition. A decision will be taken after the results of the pilot tests are available as to whether further measures relating to component processes of reading will be developed to take account of the fact that some children in the sample may not have attained the state of initial literacy that we have predicted in preparing the booklets.

We have additionally begun to investigate the possibility of developing measures in which groups of three children are given a set of reference books by an observer and asked to extract information efficiently from these. We will be interested in the strategies they adopt to do this as well as the results of their efforts. In this case the reading exercise will be preceded by explanation and discussion and followed by discussion and writing – one member of the group will record the answers formulated by the others. We are conscious of the fact that our description of performance in reading cannot ultimately be divorced from the description of pupils' behaviour in other aspects of language per-formance.

We are also currently developing an attitude-scale and questionnaire that will give us information about a pupil's undirected reading and writing activities outside the class-room and his or her attitudes to reading and writing generally.

Whether it will ultimately be possible to incorporate all these experimental measures into a monitoring programme remains to be seen, but at this stage it seems appropriate to experiment with the widest possible range of measures rather than to adopt a methodologically cautious approach.

The main point I wish to stress, in conclusion, is that the range of measures devised will not, we believe, serve to restrict teachers' concerns and practice in the teaching of reading. It is indeed possible that they will provide a stimulus to good classroom practice. In the past the use of a single measure of reading ability of the type initially described may well have had adverse consequences, but the range of measures to be employed in the projected surveys of performance should be such as to minimize detrimental backwash effects. It is, moreover, conceivable that even greater flexibility can be achieved in the future by the allocation of assessment measures to pupils on the basis of information provided by teachers about their language attainment; and, ultimately, it may also be possible in some cases to take pupil preferences for particular topics or subject areas into account when allocating reading tasks.

Let me end by saying that your comments, verbal or written, on those aspects of the monitoring programme I have outlined or on the more comprehensive outline given in the APU pamphlet on *Language Monitoring* would be welcomed. These have to be made direct to me or sent to Mr D.T.E. Marjoram, HMI, the Head of the APU, at the Department of Education and Science.

*Footn.*

Dr Tom Gorman is Principal Research Officer for the Language Monitoring Research Project. The other members of the team are Alison Tate, Denis Vincent and Peter Davies.

# 20 Reading – penance or pleasure?

## James Ewing

### Reading isn't just words

The heading of this section is part of a quote from an eight year old boy who was asked, along with his class, to explain what reading is and to express some opinions about it. The full quote is, 'Reading isn't just words, you can read traffic lights, or Morse Code.' Such a view expressed by an eight year old is particularly mature, and indeed uncommon, even among teachers. As part of an investigation I am involved with, I have been inviting pupils and teachers to comment on what they think reading is and how they feel about it.

With the teacher there is still a widespread view that teaching reading is the sole responsibility of the infant class and remedial teachers at the primary level and of the English class and remedial teachers at the secondary level. One primary headteacher justified this view by saying, 'Teachers of non-infant classes do not teach reading, they give children opportunities for practice.' At secondary level, a Technical teacher justified his lack of involvement in reading by saying, 'I leave reading instruction to the professionals', and a Geography teacher was clearly in doubt about what he should be doing. He reported, 'For a long time we've been adjusting our subject to take into account poor reading abilities, which is perhaps wrong.'

The views expressed by pupils are no less revealing and several trends emerged from the interviews and discussions. Reading aloud is largely unpopular, particularly amongst the poorer readers. There were many expressions of embarrassment, discomfort and fear of ridicule and guilt from school pupils at both the primary and secondary stages. One eleven year old girl in her last year at the primary school openly admitted, 'If you can't read, you feel ashamed.'

A further trend was very marked. Pupils view with considerable emphasis the functional nature of reading – that is, the necessity of being able to read for purely practical purposes, or as a nine year old boy expressed it, 'I have to learn to read because it's part of your adult life.' An even younger respondent, an eight year old girl, views the necessity for reading this way, 'I need to be able to read because everybody else can read', and a widely popular expression is summed up by the view 'You have to read so that you can get a job when you leave school.'

The functional aspects of reading are not limited to pupils, however. One teacher of Technical subjects views reading as, 'a method of getting information' and, 'to further the subject, to cope with instructions'. The intrinsic pleasure of reading is not completely ignored, however. A ten year old girl claims, 'When I read, I am in a trance', and a twelve year old considers that, 'Reading is very comforting when you are down.'

A somewhat contrary view is also expressed both by pupils and teachers. An eleven year old boy says, 'When I read, I feel like battering my book', and a Mathematics teacher is prepared to elect out of reading, 'If I was given the opportunity of reading a book, or doing a mathematical problem, I'd take the mathematical problem any time – it's far more stimulating.'

These views expressed by a small sample of school pupils and their teachers are probably not untypical of more widely held opinions. There is general reflection of limited pleasure to be gained from reading, this being replaced by a strong feeling of the necessity for reading. It would be difficult to say where this view originates, in the home or in the school, but it is certainly present. The views of teachers and parents are very strong indicators of consequent pupil attitudes and we cannot criticize pupils too much for having poor attitudes to reading. It may not be entirely their fault. Perhaps this is adequately indicated by a quote from an eight year old boy, whose assessment of the connection between school and reading may contain some truth: 'You learn to read so that you can go to school.'

### What are attitudes?
A very simple answer to such a question might be that

attitudes are just the way we feel. With respect to reading, can we say, therefore, that we 'feel' one way or another, or that we have feelings which we can describe? It may be quite difficult for some to describe verbally their own personal feelings about reading. This becomes particularly true when you ask the apparently simple question, 'Do you like reading?' Children as young as eight or nine years, although they can normally respond 'Yes' or 'No' fairly readily, frequently ask supplementary questions like, 'Do you mean reading at school?', or 'What kind of reading do you mean?', or 'Do you mean reading aloud?' It is probably true, therefore, that for most people, children and adults alike, a straightforward liking or disliking of reading does not adequately reflect that person's attitude to reading. An attitude, although something personal, goes far beyond a simple liking or disliking. Some would suggest that attitudes include a person's interests, values, judgments, emotional reactions etc.

This approach to attitudes to reading indicates a fairly complex picture of inner or internal dimensions of the individual. These internal dispositions are capable of combining in different ways when the individual is involved in a variety of reading situations. That is, a person's potential attitudes exist in some form inside the individual, ready to be expressed when the occasion arises, and the whole range of situations which are available will produce an equally diverse range of reactions. The mechanisms by which a person's attitudes manifest themselves lie somewhere between the external situation and the response to that situation.

Despite the variety of ways in which a person's attitude to reading may appear, there is probably some overall pattern operating. So a child who dislikes reading aloud will probably avoid such situations, whatever the context. Similarly the child who enjoys light reading will likely feel this way all the time and consequently indulge in the activity over a wide range of situations.

A further way in which the pattern may operate is indicated in the following example. A fifteen year old girl, following a non-certificate course, was involved in reading and copying down a passage which included sections like 'Vitamin $B_{12}$ is stored in the liver, or converted to coenzymes, which, with folic acid, are involved in the replication of cells during division'. In a following class the reading required was of a poem. On being questioned afterwards, the girl expressed positive feelings towards the first experience, indicating how she thought the experience was good, valuable and important, as being what school should be about, whereas with the second experience calculated by the teacher to give pleasure, she claimed a general dislike. This indicates the possibility of a higher-order structure which makes the pupil react favourably to all functional reading situations related to what she thought school should be about. She was apparently favourably disposed to that, irrespective of content. Any reading which is not so directed figures much less positively with this pupil.

The extent to which a single person feels positively or negatively about a large number of reading experiences may therefore be an indication of the overall attitude to reading. Although an individual may have some positive feelings and some negative feelings about reading, it is very likely that the balance shows a distinct tendency towards either the positive or negative side. This means that we can, theoretically, assess a person's attitude to reading as being, in general terms, positive or negative.

For example, if various statements about reading are made, children can be asked to indicate agreement or disagreement with them. There is evidence to suggest a general tendency for replies to indicate straightforward agreement or disagreement with statements such as 'Reading is boring unless you want to find out something', rather than to opt for a middle-of-the-road or 'not sure' response. There is also a definite tendency for children to respond fairly consistently either in the direction of exhibiting a favourable general attitude to reading or in the direction of exhibiting a poor general attitude. There are always, of course, those who genuinely hold neutral attitudes to

Table 1    Pattern of responses to a measure of attitudes to reading

| Number of children responding consistently favourably | Number of children responding consistently unfavourably | Number of children responding consistently neutrally | Number of children responding inconsistently |
|---|---|---|---|
| 39 | 12 | 5 | 14 |

reading and those whose views are mixed or inconsistent, as Table 1 indicates.

The figures in Table 1 are based on approximately equal numbers of primary-school children and secondary-school children and indicate quite firmly that the majority (51 out of 70) of respondents show a definite positive or negative attitude to reading. The number who respond consistently neutrally is low, and this confirms that attitudes towards reading are, by and large, polarized. Of the 14 pupils whose responses show inconsistency, i.e. neither a definite bias towards the positive or negative end, those at the primary level showed wider fluctuation than the secondary-school pupils.

Another issue which is often raised is whether attitudes to reading are in any way linked with pupil attainment. It is widely accepted that you can assess pupil attainment in reading, either to give a single dimension or reading ability or to indicate a profile of performance of different reading skills. If it is possible to assess attitudes similarly then examination of such findings should be able to indicate the degree of correspondence between the two measures. I have administered these measures to groups of children at both primary-school and secondary-school levels, and the findings are summarized in Table 2.

Table 2     Comparison of reading attainment with pupil attitudes

| | Number of children with favourable attitude | Number of children with unfavourable attitude | Number of children with neutral attitude | Number of children with inconsistent responses |
|---|---|---|---|---|
| Above-average attainment | 3 | 2 | 0 | 0 |
| Average attainment | 27 | 5 | 4 | 6 |
| Below-average attainment | 9 | 5 | 1 | 8 |

The measure of reading attainment used was the *Edinburgh Reading Tests*, which for the younger aged primary-school children was found to be difficult. This partly accounts for the low number of pupils showing an above-average attainment.

In broad terms the majority of children showing a positive attitude towards reading have an average or above-average attainment. Taking all the remaining children, i.e. those with a definite poor attitude, a neutral attitude, and those whose responses are inconsistent, it could be said that they do not have a positive attitude to reading. A substantial proportion of them (14 out of 27) perform at a below-average level in reading.

Reading attainment is a reasonably objective measure of pupil performance in class and appears to be related to the pupils' attitudes. This is not the same, however, as an indication of how the child sees himself as a pupil in the class. Do children who assess themselves as among the most able pupils also indicate a positive attitude towards reading? Similarly, do children who rate themselves as unsuccessful in classwork produce negative attitude ratings?

It is not easy for a child to make a public assessment of his own ability or performance, either in terms of openly admitting to his own position, in both directions, or in terms of accurately assessing his level. The difficulties with young children tend to lie in their inability to make accurate judgments, whereas with older children there may be a greater reticence in making such a statement, perhaps because of their greater awareness of the truth, or as a desire for conformity.

Such a comparison, despite the difficulties, may give added information about pupil attitude to reading. A group of primary-school children were asked to assess how they saw themselves as pupils at school and the findings are given in Table 3.

Table 3   Comparison of pupil self-rating with attitude to reading

|  | Number of children with favourable attitude | Number of children with unfavourable attitude | Number of children with neutral attitude | Number of children with inconsistent attitude responses |
|---|---|---|---|---|
| Above-average self-ratings | 28 | 2 | 2 | 2 |
| Neutral self-ratings | 11 | 6 | 2 | 8 |
| Below-average self-ratings | 3 | 4 | 3 | 5 |

From the figures in Table 3, it can be seen that there is a spread of pupil self-ratings indicating a fair reflection of reality. Although some pupils must inevitably give an inflated self-rating, or take retreat in the average category, more than 20 per cent have indicated a below-average self-assessment.

It is therefore worth noting that the majority of pupils with an above-average self-rating also have a positive attitude to reading. Further, of those with a below-average rating, the major part fall into the three non-positive attitude categories.

### How can you measure attitudes?
In the previous section, I have referred to measures of attitude to reading which can be administered to children. After having tried out a variety of approaches I have finally decided to use two methods which appear to be fairly reliable and reasonably valid measures of attitude to reading.

One method requires the pupil to indicate his or her agreement or disagreement with various statements pertaining to reading. Such statements can relate to school-based reading, or reading out of school. As I am presently looking at attitudes essentially within the school, I have restricted the statement to that context. Some sample statements are:

I am glad I learned to read.
There is too much reading to do in school.
Reading books is the best way to learn things.

The scoring of such scales is fairly simple and straightforward and allows a total attitude 'score' to be calculated for an individual child. After having experimented with several forms of this scale, some used in primary schools and some in secondary schools, I have now reached the stage where a single form has been produced for children aged eight to sixteen years.

The second method I have used involves identifying a number of reading situations or reading experiences which are familiar to school pupils, such as:

Reading aloud in class.
Reading to find out facts or information.
Reading books, chosen by myself, for pleasure at school.

The pupils are required to make a number of judgments on each of these situations, designed to gauge the individual's view of liking, usefulness and importance. The value of this approach is that a number of dimensions of attitude can be assessed independently, whereas with the first method mentioned above, a much more unidimensional measure is being taken. It is also particularly relevant that all the judgments are made in regard to actual reading situations which can normally be easily identified by the respondent. Evidence I have to date indicates that the three dimensions of liking, usefulness and importance are sufficiently different to be worth measuring separately and yet close enough to be grouped as an indicator of attitude to reading. The form I have finally produced can be used with pupils at both primary and secondary levels.

## Conclusions
The assessment of attitude to reading remains a difficult area but there are some clear indications that such measures can be achieved. Of the two types which I have mentioned, i.e. the unidimensional agreement/disagreement scale and the multi-dimensional reading situation evaluation scales, which is the more appropriate for the classroom teacher? The unidimensional measure has some value in comparing one individual child against another, or even one group with another, but the multi-dimensional approach enables a much clearer picture of individual attitudes to be examined. When teachers are currently more and more concerned with curricular implications of research findings, it might be useful to mention one further dimension of the reading situation measure. As well as requiring each pupil to evaluate on the basis of liking, usefulness and importance, a fourth assessment was required in terms of how often the pupil thought he was involved in each reading situation. Information about a pupil's judgments on liking, usefulness and importance coupled with the pupil's perception of the regularity or frequency of certain reading situations should

then enable the class teacher to do two things. Firstly it can help the teacher to clarify what he is providing, in curriculum terms, for pupil learning experiences. Secondly it should enable the teacher to modify the provision for any one pupil in respect of the reading situations from which he might usefully benefit. It might help the teacher identify some of the areas in which the pupil requires greater motivation. For example, using such a technique, a teacher may find that reading poetry is universally regarded as unimportant. If we accept pedagogically that such a reading activity is important then the teacher may be able to modify his approach to reading poetry in a variety of ways in order to improve pupil attitudes.

Essential to these observations about the reading curriculum is the assumption that attitudes are indeed measurable and clearly identifiable. Further, the relationship between attitude to reading and reading performance or pupils' views of their own ability has been demonstrated to some extent in the work described. The extent to which this is useful to class teachers will depend, to some degree, on their willingness to accept attitude measures as providing meaningful information about individual pupils. There is very little evidence of such measures currently in use in schools, and their introduction must of necessity be with caution. Their contribution to the classroom can only be considered as useful if there follows an improvement in teaching.

# Part 7

# International perspectives

# 21 Reading research in the Soviet Union

## John Downing

> Why is it that a child who knows the characters and their sounds still cannot read the word or syllable they compose? This strictly speaking is the riddle of the reading process ... One could demonstrate that the entire history of methods of teaching reading is one of hypotheses about this riddle.
>
> Elkonin (1973a)

This passage from Elkonin's chapter in *Comparative Reading* is characteristic of the personality of this distinguished Russian psychologist. Although he has broad theoretical and research interests, a great part of his life's work demonstrates his fascination with the riddle of the reading process. When one is working with him in the Academy of Educational Sciences in Moscow or in his experimental classrooms in the Moscow city schools one has the impression of being picked up and swept forward by the surging wave of his curiosity about this riddle.

When we planned the *Comparative Reading* project (Downing 1973) clearly the USSR had to be one of the countries included in our comparison of children's experiences in learning to read in different cultures and languages. Elkonin was the obvious choice for the Russian member of our team, as he was the leading researcher on reading in the USSR and some of his work already had been published in English (Elkonin 1963; 1971). Fortunately, Elkonin accepted our invitation to participate. His contribution turned out to be especially rewarding. It opened a window on the reading scene in the Soviet Union. What we saw through it was very thought provoking. An avenue of research was being followed that appeared to be strikingly different from the focus of investigation in other countries. Elkonin and other Russian psychologists seemed to be placing much greater emphasis on the child's reasoning processes in learning to read. Furthermore, some quite unusual methods of teaching were being used in experimental classes – methods designed to help children understand the tasks of literacy acquisition.

Elkonin's report prompted the question – how did he arrive at this point in his research? This question led, in turn, to the realization that in the English-speaking world very little was known of the Russian reading research literature. This reflection led me to go to work with Elkonin in Moscow under the Canada-USSR exchange agreement. I discovered that his report in *Comparative Reading* was really a quite modest account of the research programme in Moscow.

During my visit to Moscow I suggested to Elkonin that we should try to give reading specialists in other countries a picture of how Soviet reading research had developed to its present position. He agreed. A few days later he produced a list of publications that he considered to be landmarks in the history of reading research in the USSR. The next step was an application to the Canada Council for a grant to finance the translation of these and other Russian books and articles on reading research. This was obtained in 1977 and the Soviet Reading Research Project was established at the University of Victoria. We are well on with the work and the book that will make available the information that we have collected has been accepted for publication as *Reading Research in the Soviet Union* (Downing, in press).

I have explained how this study of Soviet reading research came into being. Now let us take a peep at some of the fascinating thoughts of our Russian colleagues that are coming to light. They can be only glimpses because our project is still in progress and this is merely a preliminary report of current work.

## Some preliminary findings

There appears to be a division of opinion between teaching methods specialists and educational psychologists in the USSR. This, of course, is no novelty outside that country. Also, as in other countries, this problem is exacerbated by the momentum of school traditions and the pedagogical folklore that surrounds them. Thus, in the USSR we have the all-too-familiar spectacle of psychological researchers in verbal battle with 'practical' educators over how to teach reading. A recent example is the attack on Elkonin's research reports by Goretsky, Kiriushkin and Shanko (1972) who defend the traditional methods of teaching that are typically used in the schools of the Russian Republic. Their strongly worded criticism of the Academy's experiments is reacted to with equal sharpness by Elkonin (1973b). This struggle between the purveyors of teaching methods and psychological researchers occurs everywhere because change is a threat to anyone whose claim to authority is based on special knowledge of the conventional methods.

Although the struggle between researchers and methods experts is quite familiar in other countries, the similarity fades in some ways when one studies the content of the Russian theoretical and research publications on how children learn to read.

A key figure in the development of reading education in the USSR was Ushinsky (1949). It was over a century ago that he introduced his method of teaching reading in Russia. (Note that the date, 1949, relates to the publication of Ushinsky's *Collected Works.*) Ushinsky's approach was a kind of phonic method but it was very advanced in several ways. It was not just a matter of teaching children the sounds of letters. He wrote that his aim was to utilize 'those common psychological processes that are effective in all languages and to children of all nationalities'. In particular, Ushinsky wanted to make children familiar with the phonemic system of the language. He wanted reading instruction to be *a language study*. For this reason, initial methods of reading instruction had to take account of transfer of learning – would the initial teaching methods help or hinder children's later linguistic development? An extremely important point expressed so long ago, yet many years later Elkonin (1973b) must continue to complain that, 'purely pragmatic aims in beginning reading are still being given priority at times even today, to the detriment of the child's introduction to language study and at the same time to his mental development'.

Another well-known name in Russian reading is Redozubov (1947). His leadership came after Ushinsky's.

Yet Redozubov's approach is the more traditional. His book, *The Methodology of Russian Language Instruction in the Primary School*, covered all sections of the methodology of teaching children the Russian language. He gave reading instruction great attention and importance, but perhaps his most important achievement was his strong call that learning to read must be regarded as a developmental skill that requires instruction beyond the initial primary year (as had been the conventional view in the past).

Vygotsky's (1934) work on child psychology had a general influence on Russian studies in this field, but it is another name, Egorov, that stands out in the history of Soviet research on the psychology of learning to read.

In Egorov's (1953) book, *The Psychology of Mastering the Skill of Reading*, the trend that gives a distinctive flavour to Russian reading research is already apparent. Vygotsky's general concern with concept development in childhood is applied by Egorov to the problem of how children can develop *a conceptual framework* for understanding the tasks that they are required to undertake in reading instruction. The following excerpts from Egorov's book show his approach:

> The child's speech usually has already reached a high level of development by the time he enters school. This is a vital factor because . . . it gives children a basis for analyzing speech into words, syllables and sounds which is the beginning of literacy instruction.

> Of course, if words are pronounced the child hears these words. If a separate sound is pronounced, the child hears the sound. Likewise, he distinguishes words that have rather similar sounds. But the child is not aware of all the separate sounds within the word.

> When the child arrives in school he can already differentiate very well all the sounds of his language and he discriminates words correctly on this basis. But the child does not notice exactly which sounds occur or in what order they make up a particular word. However, he must become aware of these units of speech and their temporal order if he is to learn how to write words correctly. That is why the acquisition of writing and

reading skills requires a restructuring of phonemic hearing. This makes great demands on the child's analytic and synthetic processes. It requires the child not only to distinguish words but also to be aware of their sound composition.

From this discussion it becomes clear that the literacy learning task not only rests upon the development of the child but also stimulates his mental growth. To master the sound-to-letter structure of language the child must make an abstraction from the directly presented phenomena. He must be capable of deductions. He must master the principle of transferring observed phenomena from one situation to another, and so on.

With regard to the learning of *new concepts* such as 'word', 'syllable', 'sound', 'letter', and so on . . . , if the child is unclear about the differences between these concepts, then he is hampered in the learning to read process.

The conceptual difficulties of this initial period of reading instruction are serious. Therefore, the teacher must take special care to avoid adding to the pupils' difficulties by introducing any unnecessary complications. For example, a common error in the pre-primer period is flooding young beginners with too many new concepts, such as 'sentence', 'word', 'syllable', 'sound', 'letter', and so on.

Another particular concern of Egorov's was that the *speech motor processes* should be taken into account in reading instruction. For example, he writes:

Let us imagine that a child is faced with the task of reading the word *mama*. In the brain of the child a definite system of speech motor connections corresponds to this word of oral speech, /mamə/. The child has only to place his speech organs in a position close to the one in which they are found when they pronounce this word orally for the existing connections to be totally effected. Let us now look at how the process of reading this word takes place in a child learning to read. He recognizes the letters of this word, relates them to the corresponding sound and speech motor form, and tries somehow to combine these letters in order to obtain some totality of meaning. In these attempts, the speech motor organs of the child take a position which, although it is not identical, nevertheless is very close to the one in which the word /mamə/ is pronounced in living speech. This is close enough to effect temporary connections in the brain of the child, corresponding to this word. This is how these brain mechanisms operate that are at the basis of the inferential process that takes place when children solve the problems of combining letters and syllables into words.

If Egorov's comments on linguistic concepts in learning to read are reminiscent of more recent work by such investigators as Reid (1966) in Scotland and Clay (1972) in New Zealand, what parallel can we find in Egorov's remark that, 'we have more than once stressed that the process of reading while children are mastering literacy rests in many cases on guess work'? Egorov devotes a whole section of his Chapter 3 to 'The role of guessing the sense'. It is by no means the same theory as Goodman's (1970). Nevertheless, there is a common basis in the notion that some kind of psycholinguistic guessing game plays an important part in the psychological process of reading. Like Goodman, Egorov too saw the value of studying children's 'miscues' or 'errors' in reading. Egorov writes: 'In this discussion of guessing at meaning in reading, we should not fail to consider errors of guessing . . . .' Egorov traces these 'errors' to various sources including pupils' misunderstandings of what a reader is supposed to do in the reading task. Egorov believed that:

> guessing that occurs during reading can and must be directed and controlled by the teacher. For this purpose, the teacher should select and plan reading material carefully and follow closely the progress of the child's thoughts and problem solving in learning how to read.

Note again Egorov's consistent concern for children's thought processes as they work their way towards a clearer understanding of the task of reading.

Elkonin (1963) acknowledges Egorov's fundamental contribution to his own studies of the psychology of the learning to read process. Egorov's observation that school beginners usually are quite competent in speech and listening but lack awareness of their own linguistic activities has been elaborated into what is called nowadays the 'glass theory'. For instance, Elkonin (1971) cites Luria as having stated:

> While actively utilizing grammatical language and while defining with words the corresponding objects and actions, the child cannot make a word and verbal relationship the object of his awareness. During this period, the word may be used but not noticed by the child, and frequently it presents things seemingly like a glass, through which the child looks at the surrounding world, not making the word itself the object of awareness, and not suspecting that it has its own existence, its own aspects of construction.

Much of Elkonin's experimental work has been directed towards finding practical methods of fostering children's awareness of linguistic acts. He believes that many traditional teaching procedures should be abandoned or at least modified because they make it unnecessarily difficult for children to understand concepts of the features of language that help them in reasoning about writing and speech. For example, Elkonin (1963) states that:

> children of six to seven years already know the names of many letters, sometimes the whole alphabet, but they cannot read, and if they try to do so simply put together the names of letters. This is one of the worst habits with which many children enter school to begin learning to read and it is necessary to teach them afresh.

Why? Elkonin (1973b) in a more recent article explains that:

... children who learn their ABCs at home by various methods such as cut-out alphabets and letter blocks, acquire little, if any, understanding of the differences in the sound packages of words. Instead, their attention is drawn to differences in the letters. This may lead to negative transfer in the further study of language.

(Elkonin's words remind us of Samuels' (1971) independent finding on the uselessness of teaching letter-names to young beginners in the United States.)

Elkonin's theoretical position that *nothing must confuse the child's understanding of the features of speech* that are coded in the writing system leads him to propose that the study of speech should be carried out *before the introduction of written letters*. Elkonin's (1973b) view on this matter can be summarized succinctly by two quotations:

(1) The phoneme is not a simple sound governing particular acoustic and articulatory properties. It is a sound that belongs to a definite system of phonematic contrasts. The essential distinction that must be made in this regard is between the perceived phonemes of a language and their embodiment in the natural flow of speech. It was this conclusion in particular that led us to recognize the necessity for replacing conventional phonic analysis, which has the objective of teaching the sounds of letters, by phonematic analysis which aims at giving children an understanding of the phonematic system of language.

Therefore:

(2) Letter representations impede the realization of this aim because, firstly, the characteristics of the phoneme it represents are not written into the letter. There is nothing in the letter form to show whether it is a vowel or a consonant, hard or soft, voiced or unvoiced.

This seemingly simple observation becomes profound because letters are so commonplace to adult teachers and parents that we have ceased to think about why they possess their particular shapes. Vowels and consonants are well-defined categories of speech but an analysis of the strokes of printed letters would not produce those two categories. Consider, for example, that N is a consonant in English but И is a vowel in Russian.

In my book, *Reasoning and Reading* (Downing 1979), I have described Elkonin's methods for developing children's 'understanding of the phonematic system of language'. In that book, I have collected also other methods that I have observed being used in various countries by teachers who have intuitively concluded that children need this kind of understanding and awareness if they are to arrive at a comprehensive mastery of the spectrum of language skills.

## Summing up
The aim of this paper was to explain how the Soviet Reading Research Project came into being at the University of Victoria and to share with colleagues the excitement that we are experiencing as we uncover the development of reading research in another language that hitherto has been for the most part neglected. We see some of the research in other countries being confirmed by Russian work. That is satisfying. But, perhaps, what is more intriguing are the different trains of thought that have been followed by Soviet educators and psychologists in our field of reading research.

## References
CLAY, M. (1972) *Reading: The Patterning of Complex Behaviour* Auckland: Heinemann
DOWNING, J. (1973) *Comparative Reading* New York: Macmillan
DOWNING, J. (1979) *Reading and Reasoning* Chambers
DOWNING, J. (in press) *Reading Research in the Soviet Union* Chambers
EGOROV, T. G. (1953) *The Psychology of Mastering the Skill of Reading* (in Russian) Moscow: Academy of Educational Sciences, R.S.F.S.R.
ELKONIN, D. B. (1963) 'The psychology of mastering the elements of reading' in B. and J. Simon (Eds) *Educational Psychology in the U.S.S.R.* Routledge and Kegan Paul
ELKONIN, D. B. (1971) 'Development of speech' in A. V. Zaporozhets and D. B. Elkonin (Eds) *The Psychology of Preschool Children* Cambridge, Massachusetts: M.I.T. Press
ELKONIN, D. B. (1973a) 'U.S.S.R.' in J. Downing (Ed) *Comparative Reading* New York: Macmillan
ELKONIN, D. B. (1973b) Further remarks on the psychological bases of the initial teaching of reading (in Russian) *Sovetskaia Pedagogika* 14–23
GOODMAN, K. S. (1970) 'Reading: a psycholinguistic guessing game' in

H. Singer and R. B. Ruddell (Eds) *Theoretical Models and Processes of Reading* Newark, Delaware: International Reading Association

GORETSKY, V. G., KIRIUSHKIN, V. A. and SHANKO, A. F. (1972) The quest must continue *Sovetskaia Pedagogika* 2, 39–47

REDOZUBOV, S. P. (1947) *The Methodology of Russian Language Instruction in the Primary School* Moscow: Uchpedgiz

REID, J. F. (1966) Learning to think about reading *Educational Research* 9, 56–62

SAMUELS, S. J. (1971) Letter-name versus letter-sound knowledge in learning to read *Reading Teacher* 24, 604–8

USHINSKY, K. D. (1949) *Collected Works* Vol. 6. Moscow: Academy of Educational Sciences

VYGOTSKY, L. S. (1934) *Thought and Language* (in Russian) Moscow-Leningrad, Soc.-econom. izd., and (in English) (1962) Cambridge, Massachusetts: M.I.T. Press

# 22 Beginning reading in Japan

## Takahiko Sakamoto

### Reading of Hiragana

Hiragana, which is one of the three writing systems used in Japan, is a set of phonetic symbols. Each symbol in the Hiragana system is monosyllabic without any meaning by itself. With few exceptions, each symbol has only one phonetic pronunciation. Since the relationship between written symbols and spoken syllables is so very regular, the learning of Hiragana is not difficult. The number of basic symbols in Hiragana is forty-six. With the forty-six symbols, plus other marks that give additional phonetic values, we can make up a total of seventy-one Hiragana letters, with which we can write any word or any sentence in the language.

Japanese children enter elementary school at age six, at which time the Ministry of Education requires that they start to learn the Hiragana letters. In fact, however, many children begin to learn Hiragana before school age without receiving any formal instructions, naturally absorbing Hiragana in their daily life through books, magazines, toys, TV programmes and other means, with the help of their families.

According to a nation-wide research survey on reading and writing ability in pre-school children (The National Language Research Institute of Japan 1972):

1  Many pre-school children in Japan begin to learn Hiragana at the age of four.
2  When the test was given to four year old children who were still seventeen months away from entering elementary school, those who could not read any of the seventy-one Hiragana letters at all were only 9 per cent

of all the surveyed children, while 53 per cent of them could read more than twenty-one letters and 34 per cent more than sixty.

3   When the test was given to five year old children who were due to enter elementary school in five months, only 1 per cent of all the investigated children could not read any of the Hiragana letters, while 82 per cent of them could read more than twenty-one and 64 per cent of them could read more than sixty.

4   In the city areas, 88 per cent of pre-school children could read more then sixty Hiragana letters one month before entering elementary school.

5   Girls read better than boys.

6   There was one child with an exceptionally high reading ability who could read not only all the Hiragana letters but also 566 Kanji characters before entering school.

From these findings, we can see that Japanese children start learning Hiragana at about four years of age and that their reading abilities are considerably developed before entering elementary school.

This survey also reported that the level of children's reading abilities in 1967 was higher than that of 1953. In 1953, when the children were tested in the first month of their elementary school life, they read 26.2 basic Hiragana symbols on average, out of the basic forty-six. In 1967, however, five year old children, who were tested five months before entering school, read 36.8, and even the four year old children who were tested seventeen months before entering school read an average of 24.4 Hiragana out of the forty-six symbols. That is, the four year olds in 1967 could read approximately as many Hiragana as the first graders in 1953 could.

It is believed that parents' concern about the reading of their children is one of the most important factors in pre-school children's reading. Recently, mothers' concern has increased greatly owing to the wider recognition of the importance of mental development during pre-school age.

Parents, however, do not actually teach children to read letters. According to the report of the nation-wide survey previously mentioned, to the question 'How did your child learn to read?' those who reported that they themselves taught them were less than 20 per cent of all the surveyed parents, 2094 in number. What the majority of the parents reported they usually did was to give the children picture books, give them Hiragana blocks (which were bought by about 70 per cent of the parents), read books to them, and answer their children's questions about letters, all of which were more important than teaching them letters in a lesson-like situation.

Although letters or characters are formally taught in less than 20 per cent of all Japanese kindergartens, a great amount of written Hiragana can be seen in most kinder-gartens, and children's questions about letters are answered by practically all teachers. We might say that the usual steps in teaching pre-school children to read Hiragana at home and at kindergartens are first to give children numerous chances to see Hirgana at an early stage to arouse their interest in letters, and then to answer the children's questions about letters.

Japanese children are thought to be ready to learn to read Hiragana letters when they can divide the spoken language into constituent ON. ON is the smallest unit of the Japanese language and means sound. Briefly speaking, an ON is a vowel or a combination of a consonant and a vowel. Each ON sound is written using one Hiragana letter. My name, Sakamoto, for example, has four sounds, so it is written in four Hiragana letters (SA-KA-MO-TO). When a child can divide a spoken word into its sounds, he or she is considered to be ready to start to learn to read.

### Reading of Kanji

Kanji characters are ideographs that originally came from China. They are, therefore, often called Chinese characters from a literal translation of the term into English. Kanji, however, are no longer strictly Chinese, and today are very typically Japanese. They are read differently and the signifi-cance of some characters in Japan is entirely different from that of the Chinese. Because they are ideographs, each Kanji has its own meaning, and they are therefore quite numerous. Presently, however, they are officially limited to 1850 characters for daily use. The learning of Kanji is more difficult than the learning of Hiragana, not only because Kanji are more numerous, but also because, unlike

Hiragana, each Kanji usually has several alternative readings that range from monosyllabic to quadrisyllabic sounds.

The Ministry of Education presently requires that 996 Kanji characters be learned during the six years of elementary school and 854 during the three years of junior high school, so that children complete the learning of all 1850 Kanji for daily use in the nine years of their compulsory education. Thus, children come to be able to read standard Japanese sentences in which there is a combination of Kanji and Hiragana, where 25 to 35 per cent of the total number of characters is written in Kanji and the rest in Hiragana.

It has long been believed that children do not begin to learn Kanji unless they have completed the learning of Hiragana and that Kanji is, therefore, difficult for preschool children. There is some evidence, however, which contradicts this belief. Sakamoto (1972) reported that of the 317 five year old kindergarten pupils surveyed only 14 per cent could not read any of the tested thirty-two Kanji characters five months before entering elementary school. The rest of the children (86 per cent) could read at least one Kanji. An average child could read six Kanji and over 17 per cent of all the children could read no less than one-half of the tested thirty-two Kanji. It is certain that these children learned this amount of Kanji without any formal instructions, since Kanji had never been taught at the kindergarten where the survey was conducted.

Mr I. Ishii, an experienced elementary school teacher of Kanji, began the experimental teaching of Kanji at a number of kindergartens in 1968. According to his research, the most suitable age for children to start learning Kanji is three years old. He says an average child can learn more than 500 Kanji and a brighter one can learn about 1000 Kanji before school age, if the child is taught properly at age three. One of the main principles of his programme, the so-called Ishii programme, is to arouse children's curiosity or interest in Kanji. He suggests that kindergarten teachers should not hesitate to present Kanji to children even when they cannot read at all. Another principle of the Ishii programme is repetition. Children must study a certain Kanji over and over again. Although the Ishii programme is rather intensive and hard to follow perfectly, it has been accepted by

263

more than 200 kindergartens since 1968.

The results of all subsequent experimental studies have, without exception, agreed with Mr Ishii, at least in that the children who were taught at kindergartens could read much more Kanji than those who were not taught at all. Sakamoto (1972) also reported that the experimental group of five year old children, who had been taught about 150 Kanji over the course of the previous year at kindergarten, could read an average of fifty Kanji characters ten months before entering elementary school, while the control group children of the same age, who were not taught any Kanji at all, could read an average of only five characters.

Although they admit the efficacy of teaching Kanji at this stage, many researchers as well as educators who are interested in pre-school reading are not necessarily positive in their assessment of the Ishii programme. They worry whether too much emphasis on this sort of intellectual activity at the pre-school stage might not distort the sound development of the child as a whole. Further investigation and consideration are needed in regard to the problem of teaching Kanji to pre-school children.

### Publications for pre-school children
Shuppan Nenkan (The Publication Yearbook, Shuppan Nenkan Henshu Bu, 1976), published in Tokyo, reported that more than 300 new titles of books and forty different magazines for pre-school children were published in Japan in 1975. These books are usually called picture books because they contain mainly pictures with only a limited quantity of words or letters. Recently, however, picture books which emphasize letters or stories have been published and have been selling well. The majority of picture books published now in Japan are what we call 'story picture books' with rather long stories. Some of them are original Japanese works while others are Japanese versions of foreign classics. Many of the foreign classics are not only translated into Japanese but also rewritten for pre-school children. It would be better, perhaps, to call them Japanese pre-school versions of foreign classics. There are quite a few of them: *Heidi*, *The Little Princess*, *Little Lord Fauntleroy*, *Gulliver's Travels* and the like. Although some people are against this kind of pre-school version, claiming that it

spoils the beauty of the original work, these versions are widely accepted by parents because of what they think is the importance of letting young children experience joy through books. Besides story picture books, there are what we call in Japanese 'animal picture books', 'vehicle picture books', 'daily life picture books', 'knowledge picture books', 'monster picture books', and TV picture books'. Pre-school children are also very fond of magazines written expressly for them, and the most popular title sells more than a million copies a year.

All these books and magazines are printed in Hiragana only, which enable them to be read by many pre-school children.

## Recent trends of research on beginning reading

No research on pre-school children's ability to read has been done in the last ten years because this topic is no longer appealing to Japanese researchers. Instead, researchers have started to investigate: (1) what parents do and should do about their children's reading; (2) how children react to books, and (3) what makes picture books interesting. Here are some examples of recent research reports.

Sugiyama and Saito (1973) reported that 36 per cent of the surveyed pre-school children's parents in Niigata prefecture, usually mothers, began to read books to their children when the children were one year of age, 31 per cent of them began when the children were two years old, and 23 per cent of them at the age of three. Those who had not read to their children until four years of age were only 7 per cent of all the parents. This report also concluded that the earlier the parents began to read to their children, the more fluently the children could read by themselves when they were five years of age. To the extent that the mother's concern for the reading of her child is insufficient, the child's reading development is delayed.

Izumoji et al (1975) reported that 92 per cent of the pre-school children they surveyed were read picture books at home. Mothers were most often cited as those who read picture books to their children, followed by both parents and elder siblings. Fathers alone rarely read to them. Mothers answered that they gave picture books to their children because they wanted to let children know the joy of reading and to foster their interest in reading. Twenty per cent of the mothers gave the first picture book to their children when the child was less than one year old, 50 per cent when the child was one year old, 21 per cent when two years old, 6 per cent when three years old, and 2 per cent when the child was four years old. Picture books were bought at the rate of about one to two titles a month, or about ten titles a year. They were selected by mothers, by children, by both parents and children, and by fathers, in that order. They were selected most often through browsing at book stores, followed by purchases based on book reviews in newspapers and magazines. Other sources were rarely used. The majority of mothers (74 per cent) thought that picture books were expensive, and only 12 per cent answered that they were reasonable. Fifty-nine per cent of the mothers wanted less expensive picture books, even though their appearance might not be as good. On the other hand, 31 per cent wanted sturdy, long-lasting books even though they might be a little more expensive.

Sawada *et al* (1974) reported on analysis of the elements of picture books which interest children. It was made through: (1) a content analysis of eight picture books, and (2) recording responses of sixty pre-school children during and after the telling of the stories in the picture books. Positive reactions such as 'expressions of surprise' or 'comments about the plot' occurred during the story-telling when there were: (1) unexpected happenings in the story (unrealistic or imaginary contents); (2) settings similar to those in the children's experiences; (3) repetition of phrases, and (4) awe-inspiring scenes. Negative reactions during the telling of the story such as 'not looking at the books' or 'not concentrating' were observed when the elements just mentioned were not present. Immediately following the story-telling session, the children showed superior recall of, and asked more questions about, stories whose contents elicited positive reactions during the telling. When the children ranked the books one week later, it was these same stories in almost every case which qualified as 'most interesting'.

In the study by Takagi *et al* (1975), an experimental group of eleven three year old children was told a Japanese story, 'Sorairo no tane', which was new to them, a total of three times with a three- or four-day interval between each telling. The verbal and behavioural responses of the children during the recitation of the story were observed and classified. Tests of their memory of the story were given individually three months after the third telling. A control group of nine three year olds was told the same story once, and their recall was tested three months later. During the first story-telling to the experimental group, negative reactions such as 'not concentrating' and 'extraneous talking during the story' were observed very frequently while such positive reactions as 'verbal responses to the contents of the story' were rare. During the second story-telling session, the children showed more positive and fewer negative reactions than during the first session. There were no differences between the frequencies of positive and negative reactions for the second and third sessions. Positive verbal responses were most frequently observed in the second session, while they were rare in the first session. The experimental group obtained higher scores on the memory test than did the control group.

The Consumer Goods Research Institute conducted a research on the so-called 'first book'. According to a report in the Yomiuri Newspaper (1977), four monthly magazines and 1,030 different titles of such books for children under three were available in Japan. They sold very well and the report said that 43 per cent of babies under three months old had at least one book. Also, 43 per cent of three to six month olds, 72 per cent of six to twelve month olds, 90 per cent of twelve to eighteen month olds, and 95 per cent of eighteen to twenty-four month olds had one or more of these first books. The Institute reported that the following examples are representative of the children's reactions, by group, to this type of book:

(*five months old*) They looked at pictures with bright colours, smiled at the picture of a child and a face, and made attempts to hold the book although it was impossible for them.

(*seven months old*) They tried to turn the pages.

(*eight months old*) They were clearly pleased to be read to.

(*ten months old*) They repeated the spoken words uttered by parents. For example, when a picture of food was shown to a child with the spoken word 'uma uma', a baby word for food in Japanese, the child repeated that word and touched the spoon and the plate in the picture.

(*eleven months old*) They licked and bit pictures of cats' and rabbits' faces. They were fond of a picture of a car in which a family with two children were riding. Their preference often centred on a book of automobiles.

(*fourteen months old*) These young children often selected a book of automobiles and asked their mother to speak about it.

(*nineteen months old*) At this age, the children acted out the action of a picture of a scene from daily life. For example, a child would pretend to telephone when he or she looked at a picture of someone telephoning.

(*twenty-four months old*) The new two year old liked to read or look at a book alone, and when he or she found something familiar, the child went to the mother to report the discovery.

(*twenty-six months old*) At this age, the child could memorize the text of the book. When the mother attempted to begin to read the text to the child, the child could give the text before the mother could read it.

The Institute concluded that these first books should be given to children and be accompanied by appropriate reading and speaking by the parents.

**Final comments**
There is no big or critical problem in beginning reading in Japan because of:

1    the use of Hiragana which is easy to learn;
2    parents', or more strictly speaking mothers', concern about their children's reading, and

3   the quantity and quality of publications for pre-school children.

The mothers' role in children's beginning reading is considered more important in Japan than any other factor. Mothers sometimes are too interested in their children's letter learning and force them to learn Hiragana. They have a deep concern about their children's beginning reading, but they do not know the proper ways to promote it. A mother who can select suitable books for her children, who reads these books to them again and again, who speaks to them about these books, who does not force them to learn letters, who answers all their questions about letters with a smile, and who herself likes to read is the ideal profile of a mother whose children can easily start to learn reading naturally.

## References

IZUMOJI, T., TAKENOYA, M. and MITSUI, K. (1975) Mothers' concern about picture books *The Science of Reading* 19, 1–12 (in Japanese)

NATIONAL LANGUAGE RESEARCH INSTITUTE OF JAPAN, THE (1972) *Reading and Writing Ability in Pre-School Children* Tokyo Shoseki (in Japanese)

SAKAMOTO, T. (1972) The psychology of Japanese learning *Jido Shinri* 26, 1315–80 (in Japanese)

SAWADA, M., KOBAYASHI, Y., TASHIRO, Y. and TAKAGI, K. (1974) An analysis of children's interests in picture-books *The Science of Reading* 17, 81–93 (in Japanese)

SHUPPAN NENKAN (1976) Henshu Bu *Shuppan Nenkan* Shuppan News Sha (in Japanese)

SUGIYAMA, Y. and SAITO, T. (1973) Variables of parent reading in relation to the social traits of kindergarten pupils *The Science of Reading* 16, 121–30 (in Japanese)

TAKAGI, K., KOBAYASHI, Y., TASHIRO, Y. and SAWADA, M. (1975) Responses of three-year-old children to story-telling of a Japanese picture book *The Science of Reading* 18, 105–13 (in Japanese)

YOMIURI NEWSPAPER BOOKS FOR BABIES *Yomiuri Shimbun* 18 April, 1977 (in Japanese)

# 23 The language background of Jamaican children

## Etta Ricketts

Today I propose to speak about the language background of the Jamaican child, and to trace the history of the Jamaican Creole or dialect from early times to the present. I shall also try to show the changes that have taken place over the years and discuss some of the current inadequacies of the language. I shall endeavour to state some of these inadequacies as they relate to the reading situation and, finally, give you an idea of the environmental background from which most Jamaican children come to you.

### The problem
The problem is that pupils' performance in English in Jamaica is now substandard, and the failures in English language examinations have reached alarming proportions even at the college level.

Secondly, the teaching of English from grade three upwards tends to follow the traditional approach in many schools where children are required to define and identify parts of speech. The teaching of English accents *form* instead of *content*, and grammar and spelling instead of the expression of ideas. Hence, English becomes a bore to the child and at the same time spells frustration for the teacher.

Thirdly, the use of dialect predominating over English usage, coupled with the paucity of ideas of the children due to the restricted environment in the rural areas, has been responsible for a lack of freshness found in children's writing. Even in the cities where the environment is more facilitative, the 'dialect' prevents children from expressing themselves well in English.

Fourthly, although there are regular syntactic types, the Creole may be very irregular depending on the individual.

Bailey (1966) states that any given speaker is likely to shift back and forth from Creole to English or something closely approximating English within a given utterance without ever being conscious of the shift.

Lastly, since Jamaican independence, the use of the dialect has gained momentum to the extent that the children's desire to learn standard English has taken second place.

## Historical background of Jamaican language

Since the 1950s the language situation in Jamaica, as in all Caribbean Islands, has been the object of study by several linguists and historians including Jamaican scholars now living abroad. Although English is the official language of the country, Jamaican Creole or dialect is understood by all Jamaicans and spoken in some form by most of them, including the educated.

But the paucity of literature on the development of language over the years has made it difficult for researchers to identify the origin of the Jamaican 'dialect' with any degree of certainty (Bailey 1966). However, there is evidence pointing to the prior existence of an established trade language or languages based on the European language spoken by the group which set up factories in ports on the African coast. The oldest of these languages must have been a Portuguese-based pidgin, which was either supplanted by, or formed the basis of English-Dutch and French-based pidgins, all of which were introduced into the Western World by the slaves. The Spanish occupation of the island of Jamaica, as well as the occupation by the native Arawak Indians, left only a few linguistic traces of their existence in the form of place names and plant names and animal names.

The present complicated language situation began with the coming of the English in 1655. This spelt disaster for the Spaniards who were either evicted or taken prisoners, and thus, the foundation for an English-based society was formed. At this time, some of the African slaves imported by the Spaniards fled to the hills and formed the first Maroon settlements.

Cassidy and LePage (1967) reported that 50 per cent of the troops of the conquering army consisted of men drawn from various regiments in England, and the rest were recruited from Barbados and the Leeward Islands. It is thought that the dominant linguistic element among the troops came from the Scots. Because Barbados and the Leeward Islands had an earlier settlement, it is most likely that at the time of the conquest, the patterns of Creole speech had already started to form either independently or on the common basis of a slave trade pidgin English, which in turn may have been influenced by an earlier Portuguese pidgin. Consequently, the earlier settling of the island by colonists and enslaved Africans from these islands, as well as by indentured servants from Ireland and the West of England, helped further to complicate the language of the country. The slaves coming from different tribes speaking different languages had no common means of communication, and their main social contact was with the indentured servants and poor whites who acted as book-keepers and overseers on the plantations, and not with the planters themselves. Moreover, they outnumbered the whites, and their situation grew. In 1675 there were 9,000 whites and 9,000 to 10,000 slaves. By 1700 the whites were not very much in excess of 9,000 while the negro population was then over 40,000.

By the end of the slave era, in the early nineteenth century, linguistic and historical evidence showed that the Aken and Ewe-speaking slaves were firmly established in a Creole society, speaking Creole English and despising new-comers from Africa and dominating the Maroons which their runaway slaves had joined.

Evolution
The evolution of Jamaican speech began in a West Indian environment which had its own common, distinctive, cultural flavour. What is now spoken varies from standard educated usage to dialectal folk usage. The dialectal folk usage is customarily referred to as the 'dialect' and is full of variations owing both to development and to geographical location. De Camp, who spent many years in the rural areas studying the language of the people, saw the Jamaican Creole speech as a variation of English. He described it as existing on a continuum, the speech of the educated at one end and that of the uneducated at the other, and the educated being able to communicate from one end of the

continuum to the other, while the uneducated remain restricted to one end according to the extent of their education. Between the two extremes are language varieties which Craig (1976) describes as 'systems of linguistic items'. He quoted De Camp (1971) as referring to them as 'Post-Creole speech continuum'.

Bailey (1966) described Jamaican Creole as having a syntax which represents the mixing of two related syntactic types – English and some kind of Proto-Creole with the lexicon predominantly English. She also spoke of cross interference resulting from the two vernaculars, one being a prestige language and the other being socially unacceptable.

Research done in the 1970s has shown that the educational situation that exists may be said to be bidialectal rather than bilingual. Craig (1976) states that:

A bidialectal situation can be considered to exist where the natural language of children differs from the standard language aimed at by the schools, but at the same time is sufficiently related to this standard language for there to be some amount of overlap at the level of vocabulary and grammar. The amount of overlap varies with different situations.

But the problem of language in Jamaica is not unique. This bidialectal situation extends to all the officially English-speaking territories of the West Indies. Craig (1976) sees the language of Trinidad and St Vincent as systems of linguistic items, intermediate between Creole and Standard. Stewart (1962) suggested that the Creoles of Jamaica, Guyana, Belize and the non-standard speech of the officially English-speaking West Indian territories may best be treated as regional varieties or dialects of English.

Craig (1976) states that differences are found in the French-based Haiti, and the Dutch West Indies where the educational situations that exist in the context of Creole language, are regarded not as bidialectal, but as clearly bilingual. He sees this difference as one of *degree* rather than *kind*. He explains that the sociolinguistic history has caused countries like Jamaica and Guyana – both officially English-speaking – to have larger proportions of their population speaking a language intermediate between Creole and Standard English than Haiti has. Yet Jamaica and Guyana still have a considerable proportion of speakers whose English-based Creole is just as incomprehensible to the Englishman as Haiti's French-based Creole is to the Frenchman.

The influence of the early missionaries should not be forgotten. The tendency to ignore the fact that education in Jamaica and the other islands was started by the church still exists. The church, however, still has a strong foothold in the educational life of the island. The ony source of English heard by the rural population was that which the church provided through the missionaries, mainly from Scotland, England and Ireland. They taught the early slaves to read and study the Bible, and so contact with the common man provided a linguistic pattern for them to emulate.

### The present situation

Today, the Jamaican dialect, still the language of a vast majority, is being acclaimed mainly by a young middle class to be the language of Jamaicans. Up to the late 1950s, the use of the English language was important for social mobility. As Bailey explained, it was the indicator of the level of one's intelligence. The admission of one's ability to speak the dialect was frowned upon and could have brought adverse repercussions on the speaker. In this environment, ambitious students and pupils accepted English and learned it, and their attitude towards the language was different from what it is today, even though many of them did not achieve language competence and language performance. Even at the college level there were problems, not due to the use of the dialect in writing, but to the paucity of ideas and the lack of expression created by the use of the dialect in their homes during the formative years. Their first contact with English, apart from church activities, was on admission to the elementary school at the age of seven.

Since Jamaica's independence from Great Britain in 1962, the unshackling of British customs and ideas has resulted in negative attitudes towards the English language. Books written by Bailey, Cassidy and LePage and others have helped to bring about a national consciousness regarding the Creole and a hope that the grammar and spelling will one day be standardized.

But this, along with the efforts of politicians to use appropriate language to an uneducated audience, have helped to give to the Creole a prestige it never previously enjoyed. Its frequent use by politicians, supported by the news media in various programmes, has resulted in deterioration in the use of English both in its spoken and written forms. Its perpetual use has also resulted in the inability of the children who speak it to respond immediately and naturally to standard English, and so they are cut off from a world of books.

Yet its use has served to bridge the social gap between the privileged and the underprivileged, and cemented a feeling of oneness between all Jamaicans.

## Coping with the problem

During the last fourteen years, many experiments in language teaching have been done in schools by Craig, Wilson and others. Workshops in language teaching have also been organized by the Ministry of Education in its programmes to upgrade the competence of trained as well as pre-trained teachers. The training colleges are greatly involved in this.

There has been constant assessment and evaluation of these programmes. As a result syllabuses and books have been written and numerous articles on the language situation have appeared in the local journals.

## Reading and the Creole speaker

Most of our reading problems in Jamaica stem from the impact of the Creole on English, and the Creole speaker's reading problems are intensified by his constant use of Creole outside the classroom. Craig (1975) identified these problems as:

1  to learn the relationship between written or printed shapes and the meanings they represent, and
2  to perceive or vocalize the latter meanings in terms of English sounds, English word forms and English syntax.

Children with an English-speaking background experience

the first problem, that is, to learn the relationship between printed symbols and their meanings, while the Creole-speaking child must learn that as well as perceive or vocalize those meanings in terms of English sounds, English word forms and English syntax.

Craig, in his research, identifies a number of these problems. Examples are stated below:

Initial consonant *b* in *b*oy is replaced by *bw* as in *bw*ai.
Initial consonant digraph *th* in *th*is and *th*at is replaced by *d* as in *d*is and *d*at.
*a* replaces word ending *er* as in teech*a*.
Medial consonant *t*, as in bo*tt*le, becomes bo*kk*le.
Medial vowel *o* as in h*o*t, becomes *a* as in h*a*t.
Initial consonant blend *st* as in *st*and, becomes *t* as in *t*an.
Ending *ing* as in sing*ing*, becomes sing*in*.

The Creole speaker tends to pronounce the sight words as he speaks them, but is not usually allowed by the teacher to use those sounds while reading.

Similarly he is confused with word forms and the grammatical relationships between the words he must read. Because of this, his reading tends to be mechanical and meaningless. He finds himself in a state of 'cognitive confusion', as Downing (1973) puts it. Also, because of the difficulty of the reading material he must read at a certain grade level, he spends many reading hours per week, learning vocabulary, as a prelude to reading.

In this context, the English-speaking child is facilitated by his ability to speak English. He can anticipate the end of a sentence when he begins to read. He is familiar with English inflections and grammatical markers which appear in written material he must read. These are absent in Creole.

The Creole reader's listening comprehension could be good if his teacher reads slowly and clearly with good intonation and voice inflection. But when he is required to read he is faced with the job of decoding words and getting meaning from those words which are not within his speaking vocabulary.

Reading materials are written in English, so language facility helps the English-speaking reader but not the

Creole-speaking reader. This is illustrated in the following examples:

1. The Creole lacks inflection and grammatical markers which are a part of the structure of English, and so the Creole speaker reading English words is not able to anticipate meaning and word forms. He spends much of the time trying to decode words.

2. The Creole reader is unable to identify cross-references and interrelationships between themes and topics in the material he reads, because of the lack of inflection, grammatical markers and the inflected pronoun system (who/whom/whose, he/him/his, she/her/hers, they/them/theirs, and so on not found in Creole).

3. The Creole speaker may have vocabulary problems because of differences in the use of words – for example, *back-back* may be used for *reverse*, and *one-one* for *few*.

4. Some forms of English sentence structure can be a barrier to comprehension on the part of the Creole-speaking reader. This is so because the Creole has what Craig (1975) calls a 'zero-copula' sentence – a sentence in which the verb is omitted: for example, *the shirt dirty* (the shirt is soiled). Again the terms *there is* and *there are* do not exist in Creole.

5. The change of the verb from *is* to the particle *a* as well as a change in position which is not found in English, makes a meaning difficult – for example, 'A dat mi sey' (That is what I say).

It can thus be seen that the Creole-speaking child is at a great disadvantage while trying to read.

Three possible ways of dealing with the problem are suggested by Craig (1975):

1. Produce reading materials in the Creole, for use with beginning readers. This will prove an unpopular approach to many teachers.

2. Control the language in the reading material so that only English word forms and grammar which appear in Creole speech are used – for example, 'Look Tom, look now, come and sing with us.' In this type of writing

the present and past continuous tense would not be used.

3    Teach concurrently the basic structures of English and reading, so that the Creole speaker becomes familiar with the English sentence patterns while he reads them.

This latter is one of the many approaches to reading being used. It is all a matter of attitudes, understanding and willingness to experiment, as well as a definite commitment to a very challenging problem.

Today, the British schools receive children with this very interesting background – children who have been born in an era of struggle to find their identity. They come to you with a rich background of experience with nature – of the hills and mountains, of the farms and sugar estates, of rivulets and streams, of fishing and bathing in sparkling rivers and streams. Some are from a rustic life where myriads of fireflies gleam, and fluorescent lights leap from the waves of the sea and where one wakes to the whistling of the cricket and the singing of the birds, as well as to the glorious sunrise. Some boys awake with the sun to help Dad tend the cattle and the beasts of burden, the goats and maybe the sheep, the pigs and the rabbits. Some must fetch water for the home and glean firewood from the woodlands as a prelude to the school day.

Communication at home and among peer groups is free and very expressive, but there are restraints in the classroom situation. Teacher is revered and respected. With these very exciting experiences they come, and it will take love and concern, and good understanding of their problems to build confidence and good rapport between teacher and pupil.

## References

BAILEY, B. (1966) *Jamaican Creole Syntax – A Transformational Approach* Cambridge University Press

CASSIDY, F. G. and LePAGE, R. (1967) *Dictionary of West Indian English* Cambridge University Press

CRAIG, D. R. (1975) Reading and the Creole speaker *Torch Special Issue* 1, December, Ministry of Education

CRAIG, D. R. (1976) Bidialectal Education: Creole and Standard in the West Indies *International Journal of the Sociology of Language* 8

DOWNING, J. (1973) 'The child's concept of language' in *Proceedings of the Annual Study Conference of the United Kingdom Reading Association* July

DE CAMP, D. (1971) 'Toward a generative analysis of a post Creole speech continuum'. Hymes cited by D. Craig in Bidialectal Education: Creole and Standard in the West Indies *International Journal of the Sociology of Language* 8

GREEN, J. F. (1975) 'The language situation in the English-speaking Caribbean' in The Teaching of Language *Torch Special Issue* 1, December, Ministry of Education

STEWART, W. A. (1962) 'Creole languages in the Carribean' in F. A. Rice (Ed) *Study of the Role of Second Languages in Asia, Africa and Latin America* Washington, D.C.: Center for Applied Linguistics of the Modern Languages Association of America

# The contributors

Sheila Augstein, M.Sc., Ph.D.
Deputy Director, Centre for the Study of Human Learning
Brunel University

Gwen Bray
Former Adviser in Nursery and Primary Education
to the Leeds Authority

John Chapman, Dip.Ed., M.Sc., Ph.D.
Sub-Dean, Faculty of Educational Studies
The Open University

David Crystal, B.A., Ph.D.
Professor of Linguistic Science
University of Reading

John Downing, B.A., Ph.D., F.B.P.s.S., F.R.S.A.
Professor of Psychological Foundations of Education
University of Victoria
Canada

James Ewing, B.Sc., M.Ed.
Principal Lecturer in Educational Psychology
Dundee College of Education

Keith Gardner, M.Ed.
Senior Lecturer in Education
School of Education
University of Nottingham

Elizabeth Goodacre B.Sc.(Econ.), Ph.D.
Reader in Education
Faculty of Education and Performing Arts
Middlesex Polytechnic

Tom Gorman, M.A., Ph.D.
Principal Research Officer
Language Monitoring Project
National Foundation for Educational Research

Mary Hoffman, M.A.
Consultant to Open University Reading Development Diploma
Children's Writer and Journalist

William Latham B.Sc., A.P.B.s.S.
Co-ordinator, Language Development Centre
Sheffield City Polytechnic

John Merritt, B.A., A.B.P.s.S.
Professor of Educational Studies
The Open University

Cliff Moon, Dip.Ed., M.Ed.
Deputy Head
Yatton Junior School, Avon

Sue Moore, B.A.
Course Co-ordinator
Diploma in Reading Development
The Open University

Joyce Morris, B.A., Ph.D.
Language Arts Consultant
London

Owen Parry, B.Sc.
Research Assistant, Language Development Centre
Sheffield City Polytechnic

Douglas Pidgeon, B.Sc., Ph.D.
Head Reading Research Unit
Department of Educational Psychology and Child Development
London University Institute of Education

Peter Pumfrey, M.Ed., Dip.Ed.Psych.
Senior Lecturer in Education
University of Manchester

Bridie Raban, B.A., M.Ed.
Co-Director, SSRS Research Project
University of Bristol

Etta Ricketts
Church Teachers' College
Mandeville, Jamaica, West Indies

Angela Ridsdale
State College of Victoria
Australia

Takahiko Sakamoto
Director, Department of Reading
Noma Institute of Educational Research
Japan

Derek Thackray, B.Sc., M.A., Ph.D.
Head of Education Department
St Paul's College of Education
Rugby

Laurie F. Thomas, Ph.D., F.B.P.s.P.
Director, Centre for the Study of Human Learning
Brunel University

Fiona White, B.A., P.G.C.E.
Research Assistant
The Open University

Alma Williams, M.B.E., B.A.
Consumer Educational Consultant to Consumers'
Association
Chairman of Education Committee of
International Organisation of Consumers' Unions

Sara Zimet, B.Sc., M.A., Ed.D.
Associate Professor of Psychiatry
University of Colorado Medical Center
Denver, Colorado, USA